MARKET SEG· MEN· TA· TION

Using Niche Marketing to Exploit New Markets

Art WEINSTEIN

MARKET SEG• MEN• TA• TION

Using Niche Marketing to Exploit New Markets

Art WEINSTEIN

PROBUS PUBLISHING COMPANY
CHICAGO, ILLINOIS

This publication is designed to provide accurate and authoritative information in regard to the subject matter covered. It is sold with the understanding that the publisher is not engaged in rendering legal, accounting or other professional service. If legal advice or other expert assistance is required, the services of a competent professional person should be sought.

FROM A DECLARATION OF PRINCIPLES JOINTLY ADOPTED BY A COMMITTEE OF THE AMERICAN BAR ASSOCIATION AND A COMMITTEE OF PUBLISHERS.

Library of Congress Cataloging-in-Publication Data Available

ISBN 1-55738-048-1

Printed in the United States of America

2   3   4   5   6   7   8   9   0

With love to Sandra, my number one fan

TABLE OF CONTENTS

PART 5. SEGMENTATION RESOURCES

ACKNOWLEDGEMENTS

Many individuals have provided valuable input and insight toward the preparation of this book. First, I would like to thank Probus Publishing for support and guidance. A special mention of appreciation goes to Marvin Nesbit and Bruce Seaton of Florida International University (F.I.U.), Miami, for their advice and extremely helpful comments on the initial drafts.

Also, an expression of gratitude to Jim Paris of Urban Decision Systems and Art Boudin of Applied Research Techniques, Inc. for their critiques of the chapters on Physical and Behavioral Attribute Segmentation, respectively. Steve Morris, business librarian at F.I.U. and Ed Oswald, former business librarian for the Miami-Dade Public Library, assisted in on-line searches, case research, and appendix material. Joan Perrell, of the American Marketing Association, and Lois Steinberg of SERS must be acknowledged for facilitating the publication of important examples used in the book.

Additionally, I want to thank Dr. Howard J. Hoffman (Hoffman Dental Studio), Jorge Lopez and David Dyer (Burdines), Mike Marquez of PERSONAL BLOOD STORAGE (formerly of AMI Parkway) and Bill Schroter (Publix). Last, but not least, I want to thank my business clients for making this exhilarating book possible. And of course, thank you for reading it!

Art Weinstein

PREFACE

This book is designed to provide business practitioners with an informative, state-of-the-art guide to segmenting markets. While most marketers acknowledge the value of market segmentation—in fact, a recent survey of 303 marketing executives ranked segmentation as the third most important marketing pressure point (of eighteen functional areas tested) for 1986—few companies use this marketing tool to its full potential. In spite of the many advances made in market segmentation methodology, a majority of firms, both large and small, base their marketing strategies and tactics primarily on cursory or intuitive analyses of their potential markets. However, used effectively, market segmentation techniques are a valuable means for increasing sales and improving overall marketing performance. Recognizing your need for a practical approach to segmentation, a systematic framework upon which market segmentation can be introduced or improved in your company is provided.

The book is organized into five major parts for clarity and to facilitate rapid comprehension of the material presented. These sections are:

Part I: Segmentation Planning provides a blueprint for conducting a successful segmentation study. An overview of market segmentation; segmentation's role in the marketing plan; how to use primary, secondary, and syndicated research data; and the ten critical elements of designing the segmentation analysis are discussed.

Part II: How To Segment Markets details the major segmentation bases, highlights the procedures and mechanics of segmenting markets, notes special considerations for the industrial marketer, and explains an eight-point formula for segmenting markets.

Part III: Translating Segmentation Findings Into Strategy discusses target market selection, positioning, strategy formulation, and procedural and managerial guidelines for enhancing segmentation's value in your company.

Part IV: Segmentation Strategy Cases presents several recent in-depth case histories showing how market segmentation strategy has been used successfully by a diverse group of companies in very competitive markets.

Part V: Segmentation Resources serve as "hands-on" references for further segmentation information needs. These appendices include sources of secondary information, low-cost consumer and industrial demographics, research firms specializing in market segmentation, and a listing of suggested readings.

I feel that this book is of great value to marketing professionals, business executives and managers, and independent entrepreneurs. It can also be used as a reference for advanced marketing students who have progressed beyond marketing theory and need to learn more about how to make target market decisions.

The primary focus of this book is toward the unique challenges of consumer markets (services and retail). However, Chapter 6 addresses some of the special problems of the industrial marketer. Realizing your need for practical information, a theoretical and quantitative approach has been avoided. Instead, this book is a "how-to" guide to the effective use of market segmentation procedures, techniques, and strategies.

PART ONE

Segmentation Planning

CHAPTER ONE

Market Segmentation: An Overview

He who pays the piper can call the tune.
John Ray, 1670

The American Marketing Association has dubbed the 1980s the "Decade of Marketing." This is not surprising. Everyone is jumping on the marketing bandwagon, from Fortune 500 corporations to mom-and-pop small businesses. So called "non-marketers" such as healthcare organizations, professional service firms (accounting, legal, etc.), and financial institutions are discovering the benefits of a strong marketing program.

Having a good product or service is no longer sufficient. Companies must satisfy the needs of discriminating customers who can choose from a multitude of alternatives in the marketplace. John Naisbitt, author of *Megatrends*, stated, "In today's Baskin-Robbins society, everything comes in at least thirty-one flavors." He adds, "Do you remember when bathtubs were white, telephones black, and checks green?" In our changing and highly competitive environment, firms must display "marketing muscle" to survive and prosper.

SEGMENTATION: THE KEY TO MARKETING SUCCESS

At the forefront of this newfound marketing orientation is the need for a customer-driven focus. This has led to a renaissance in the area of market segmentation. First recognized by Wendell R. Smith in 1956, market segmentation has evolved from an academic concept into a viable "real-world" planning strategy. Figure 1–1 summarizes the success of Coca-Cola, a company that has excelled at market segmentation in the soft drink market.

Figure 1-1:

Coke Is It?

The Coca-Cola Company is a master at market segmentation. First there was Tab. Here was a product targeted to a loyal female following. These consumers responded by guzzling gallons of the soft drink annually to help stay in shape. This tremendously successful product was eclipsed by an even more popular diet cola, Diet Coke. Diet Coke emerged to fill a void in the market for a quality adult diet cola for men as well as women. Its internationally known name, superior taste, and large, targeted promotional campaigns catapulted the product to a position of prominence within two years of its introduction.

Other recent successful Coke spin-offs such as Cherry Coke and the New Coke/Classic Coke products (and controversy) have created crowded supermarket shelves for retailers and provided new profit centers for the Atlanta-based company.

Segmentation is the process of partitioning markets into segments of potential customers with similar characteristics who are likely to exhibit similar purchase behavior. It has emerged as a primary marketing planning tool and the foundation for effective overall strategy formulation in a variety of companies throughout the U.S. The objective of segmentation research is to analyze markets, find a niche, and develop and capitalize on this superior competitive position. This can be accomplished by selecting one or more groups of consumers/users as targets for marketing activity and developing a unique marketing program to reach these prime prospects (market segments). In a practical sense, market segmentation efforts need to be managed to be effective. It is impossible to pursue every market opportunity so you must make strategic choices in the market. Figure 1-2 illustrates what the Coke family of products might resemble if segmentation decisions were taken to extremes.

A backyard philosopher once said, "I wouldn't want to have everything, and besides, where would I put it all?" This is analogous to what most marketers know. Consider the following:

1. Everyone is not a prospect for every product or service offered (not everyone eats at McDonald's, drives a General Motors car, or owns an IBM personal computer).
2. A firm's product or service mix must be controlled for maximum efficiency.

Figure 1–2

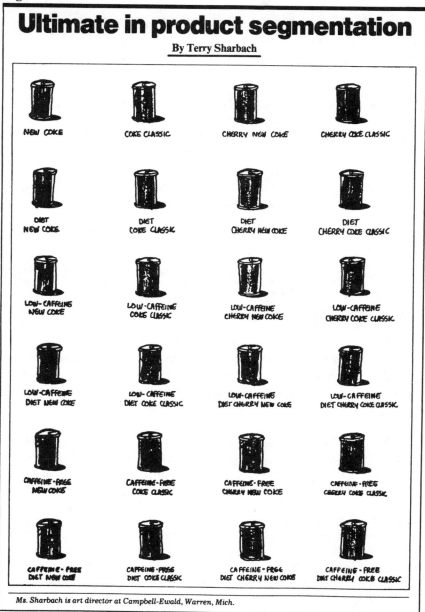

Ultimate in product segmentation

By Terry Sharbach

NEW COKE | COKE CLASSIC | CHERRY NEW COKE | CHERRY COKE CLASSIC

DIET NEW COKE | DIET COKE CLASSIC | DIET CHERRY NEW COKE | DIET CHERRY COKE CLASSIC

LOW-CAFFEINE NEW COKE | LOW-CAFFEINE COKE CLASSIC | LOW-CAFFEINE CHERRY NEW COKE | LOW-CAFFEINE CHERRY COKE CLASSIC

LOW-CAFFEINE DIET NEW COKE | LOW-CAFFEINE DIET COKE CLASSIC | LOW-CAFFEINE DIET CHERRY NEW COKE | LOW-CAFFEINE DIET CHERRY COKE CLASSIC

CAFFEINE-FREE NEW COKE | CAFFEINE-FREE COKE CLASSIC | CAFFEINE-FREE CHERRY NEW COKE | CAFFEINE-FREE CHERRY COKE CLASSIC

CAFFEINE-FREE DIET NEW COKE | CAFFEINE-FREE DIET COKE CLASSIC | CAFFEINE-FREE DIET CHERRY NEW COKE | CAFFEINE-FREE DIET CHERRY COKE CLASSIC

Ms. Sharbach is art director at Campbell-Ewald, Warren, Mich.

Reprinted with permission from the September 23, 1985 issue of *Advertising Age*, copyright, Crain Communications, Inc., 1985.

Recently, there have been increased costs in all facets of business including personnel, equipment, and materials. Production must be precisely matched to customers' needs and wants to use resources most effectively.

3. Since the product/service mix and customer pool are limited, it is most efficient to match your products to customer needs and wants.

SEGMENTATION IN ACTION

Most marketing professionals recognize that market segmentation is both a science and an art. One can learn about market segmentation analysis through the guidelines and techniques discussed in this book and other valuable references (see Appendix C: Selected Readings). Also, it is a marketing discipline that can be acquired and enhanced by experience, observation, and strategic thinking.

There are many alternative methods for segmenting markets. Many of these approaches are derived from the consumer behavior field. Consumer decision making is an objective yet emotional process whereby various factors influence the purchase decision. Motivations and needs, perceptions, demographics, product awareness levels, and purchasing habits are components of an individual's total lifestyle (see Figure 1-3). These dimensions (and others to be discussed later) can all be used in segmenting markets. Which segmentation method is best? That depends on circumstances and the particular business situation the firm is facing.

Let's assume that a major oil company wants to segment the gasoline market. There are several possible ways this could be done. A geographic sales analysis of their dealers might be conducted. Demographic and socioeconomic measures (age, sex, income, etc.) could be studied. Product consumption (regular vs. unleaded vs. premium vs. diesel grades) could be evaluated. Additionally, credit card utilization, loyalty, and price sensitivity by customers are some of the other dimensions or bases that can be used in segmenting this market. As you can see, the options are many, and further research to determine the best approach or approaches would be necessary.

The following mini-examples illustrate some of the most common segmentation dimensions in action.

a) Geographic—the neighborhood retailer
It is expected that many small retailers can obtain approximately 75% of their sales within a one- to three-mile radius of their store. Appendix 4-2, Defining Your Trade Area, addresses this issue in detail.

Figure 1–3:

The Consumer Decision-Making Process
(Total Lifestyle Composition)

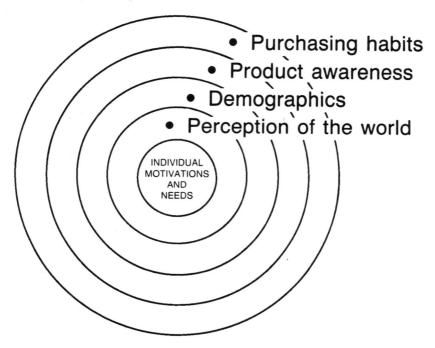

- Purchasing habits
- Product awareness
- Demographics
- Perception of the world

INDIVIDUAL
MOTIVATIONS
AND
NEEDS

This information is from articles written and designed by Sorkin-Enenstein Research Service, Inc. and may not be reproduced or disseminated without the express permission of Sorkin-Enenstein Research Service, Inc.

b) Demographics—the dancewear shop
Of prime importance to this store is the number of females aged fourteen to thirty-nine since they are the most likely to purchase leotards, leg warmers, and related exercise clothing and accessories.

c) Socioeconomic—department stores
Two major variables of concern to department stores are consumer income levels and social class. It is no secret that different department stores target and attract a different class of customer.

d) Psychographics—banking
Financial institutions are changing rapidly due to deregulation and increased competition from within and outside of the industry. Many progressive banks are attempting to differentiate their services by better understanding their customers' needs, personality traits, and lifestyles. Psychographic research can

assist banks in learning about their customers' attitudes and perceptions of the institution.

e) Product Usage—the liquor industry

Markets can be segmented according to the consumption levels of various user groups (e.g., the heavy users). The liquor industry provides an excellent example of this volume dimension. Product usage analysis, as shown in Table 1-1 below, gives credence to the often cited but seldom evidenced 80/20 rule. This maxim states that approximately 80% of a firm's sales come from only 20% of its customers or products. Note the closeness of this 20-80 relationship in various sectors of the liquor market.

Table 1-1:

Product Usage Analysis, The Liquor Industry

Product	% Heavy Users	% Consumption
Beer and Ale	17.8%	62.8%
Bourbon	27.2%	80.9%
Brandy & Cognac	12.3%	60.1%
Vodka	12.9%	64.2%
Wines	20.5%	73.6%

Source: Axiom Market Research, Target Group Index.

f) Benefits—the toothpaste market

The dentifrice product class is a good illustration of benefit segmentation in the consumer goods industry. Toothpaste manufacturers have successfully differentiated their products and expanded their markets by promoting specific benefits to targeted markets on a need basis. The many benefits offered to different segments include cavity prevention, fresh breath, white teeth, and stain deterrence. These needs are filled (pardon the pun) by Crest, Close-Up, Ultra-Brite, and Topol, respectively.

The six aforementioned segmentation dimensions are some of the more common tools available, but are by no means all of the alternatives. These methods and related segmentation bases will be explored in detail later in the book. Another approach which may be appropriate in some cases is creative segmentation. Creative segmentation utilizes an atypical variable that is effective in explaining purchase behavior. A Chicago automobile dealership provides an excellent example of creative segmentation. Its service department representatives observed all radio dials of cars brought in for service over a specified period. It then used this information to determine customers' radio listening preferences and proceeded to buy advertising spots on the more popular stations. Sometimes the novel approach may be needed to add a fresh perspective on a business situation.

SEGMENTATION OPTIONS

A company has two basic strategic choices: to segment the market or treat the entire market as potential customers for its goods or services. This latter option, known as aggregation, means that the firm uses an undifferentiated marketing strategy. There are few companies that can minimize their costs and maximize their returns with an aggregation strategy. One can argue that utilities can employ this strategy, since you must have their service in an essentially monopolistic environment. But even that's not true anymore. In today's free market, you do not have to use the electricity provided by your local power company if you do not choose to (some options include solar panels, windmills, and other alternative energy sources). Additionally, the recent AT&T breakup has opened the floodgates for new competition in the once uncontested tele-communications industry.

Despite the fact that aggregation is for virtually no one, many companies handle their marketing as if everyone is a likely customer, rather than targeting those who are the **most likely** customers for their product. Recognizing the great diversity in the marketplace, it is clearly desirable to segment markets to improve marketing performance. By segmentation we mean development of differentiated marketing strategies for the different needs of the marketplace. Segmentation options include differentiation, concentration, and atomization.

Differentiation

If a firm identifies and actively markets its products or services to different segments of the market based on different needs, a differentiation strategy is being used. The computer retailer that separately targets the home user, business professional, and small business is employing a differentiation approach to marketing microcomputers, peripherals, software, and supplies.

A distinction needs to be made between market and product differentiation. Market differentiation (a segmentation strategy) is customer-oriented and is dependent upon market demand, while product differentiation (not a segmentation strategy) is supply-side-oriented. Product differentiation is desirable for commodity-type products such as bar soap. Since soap is viewed by consumers as basically the same and it is used for a single purpose (cleanliness), creating product variations are important. Product differences such as branding, size, color, scent, and packaging assist the marketer in distinguishing the product from the competition. On the other hand, market differentiation is a broader functional area. It includes product differences, as well as unique promotional, price, and distribution strategies targeted to two or more specific market segments.

Concentration

The concentration strategy means the firm decides to serve one of several potential segments of the market. Using the above example, under a concentration segmentation approach the computer retailer may be interested in marketing its products and services only to small businesses, ignoring potential opportunities in the home user or business professional segments. Concentrated marketing is less expensive than differentiated marketing, and may be the appropriate choice for a new business with limited resources.

Atomization

The least used segmentation option, atomization breaks down the market to the finest detail — often to the individual customer level. This strategy might be appropriate for a manufacturer of highly costly and specialized equipment. If you were selling $50,000 industrial cranes for example, you would be faced with a small market for this product. A customized marketing program to your few, but key, prospects would have to be designed.

THE BENEFITS OF SEGMENTATION

The overall objective of using a market segmentation strategy is to improve your company's competitive position and better serve the needs of your customers. Some specific objectives may include increased sales (in units and dollars), improved market share, and enhanced image/reputation. This is not to say that it's impossible to accomplish these goals using mass marketing tactics. However, by focusing in on areas that your firm can best serve, it is more likely to prosper. Aggregation is the shotgun approach to marketing, while segmentation is the high-powered rifle.

There are four major benefits of market segmentation analysis and strategy. These are:

1. **Designing responsive products to meet the needs of the marketplace.**
   Through researching customer preferences—an essential component of segmentation analysis—the company moves toward accomplishing the marketing concept (customer satisfaction at a profit). The firm places the customer first and designs and refines its product and service mix to satisfy the needs of the market.

2. **Determining effective and cost efficient promotional strategies.**
   As a planning tool, segmentation identification and analysis is extremely valuable in developing the firm's communication mix. Appropriate advertising campaigns can be designed and targeted to the right media vehicles. This marketing investment can be supplemented by public relations initiatives and sales promotion methods. In addition to mass promotional thrusts, the personal sales process can be greatly improved by providing sales representatives with background customer research, recommended sales appeals, and ongoing support.

3. **Evaluating market competition, in particular the company's market position.**
   A segmentation study explores the firm's market position—how the company is perceived by its customers and potential customers relative to the competition. The 1980s have been characterized by intense competition and volatile markets in many industries. Segmentation research can provide a competitive intelligence mechanism to assess how well your company compares to industry standards. Additionally, this analysis is useful for detecting trends in changing markets.

4. **Providing insight on present marketing strategies.**
   It is important to periodically reevaluate your present marketing strategies to try to capitalize on new opportunities and circumvent potential threats. Market segmentation research is useful in exploring new markets (perhaps secondary smaller or fringe markets which might have otherwise been neglected by concentrating on primary markets). Furthermore, effective segmentation provides a systematic approach for controlled market coverage, as opposed to the hit-or-miss effectiveness of mass marketing strategies.

In summary, segmentation analysis provides that necessary research base upon which all other marketing strategies can be successfully formulated and implemented. Is your company using market segmentation techniques as effectively as possible? Figure 1–4 provides a checklist of fifteen key issues to explore further, so you can answer this question.

Figure 1-4:

Segmentation Checklist

How Well is Your Company Using Market Segmentation Techniques?

1) Does your company segment the market? If not, why not?
2) What strategy is used—differentiation, concentration, or atomization?
3) What segment(s) of the market are you trying to serve?
4) How successful are you at meeting this objective?
5) What is your typical customer profile?
6) Are target market definitions based on research?
7) What dimensions (methods) are used to segment markets?
8) When was your last segmentation analysis conducted?
9) How frequently are updates obtained?
10) What is your budget for segmentation analysis?
11) Are product decisions based on segmentation research?
12) Are promotional decisions based on segmentation research?
13) Are pricing and distribution decisions based on segmentation?
14) Is segmentation analysis used in assessing competition, trends, and changes in the marketplace?
15) Is segmentation analysis used to evaluate your present marketing efforts (for example, markets to pursue)?

LIMITATIONS OF SEGMENTATION

The picture isn't totally rosy however, and the marketer must be cognizant of some potential shortcomings of segmentation analysis. These include:

1. **Segmentation findings only provide a composite profile of a group.** Although research can provide meaningful marketing information, some forms of segmentation analysis reflect only expected segment decision making, and do not necessarily indicate individual purchase behavior. Two men may both be thirty-five years old, college educated, and earn $40,000 annually. By using demographic analysis only, the marketer may erroneously stereotype these consumers as similar prospects. In reality, they may have different interests, attitudes, and perspectives on life. Further investigation into their lifestyles is possible through psychographic research. This can

help the marketer by presenting a more complete picture of a market situation.

2. **The great diversity of consumer lifestyles in the 80s has made segmentation more difficult in many markets.**

In the past, a so-called "typical" family consisted of a husband, wife, two children, and a dog. Segmenting markets given this scenario was relatively easy. This is not true anymore. The rise of women in the labor force, increases in divorces and single person households, and today's changing lifestyles (e.g., convenience-seeking, health and fitness conscious, etc.) have created a plethora of opportunities and problems for marketers.

3. **Segmentation research is not a remedy for other marketing or organizational deficiencies.**

The best segmentation information is worthless unless it is supported by consistent product, promotional, pricing, and distribution strategies that are regularly evaluated and revised as situations dictate. In addition, market segmentation strategies are not a panacea for other potential organizational limitations.

4. **Segmentation's effectiveness is limited by management's ability to implement strategic implications.**

A marketing orientation requires a strong commitment by the firm. This includes support in the areas of personnel, resources to hire marketing consultants, time investment of management, and the willingness to act on prescribed recommendations. This does not occur overnight. Findings from a segmentation analysis need to progress from the "report on the executive's shelf" stage to the "working document" stage.

SEGMENTATION: SOME MISUNDERSTANDINGS RESOLVED

There are three major misconceptions about market segmentation held by many business professionals. These will be explored and hopefully resolved in this section.

Myth #1: Market segmentation is a partitioning process.

The overall effect of segmentation is to divide markets into two or more manageable sub-markets. However, in reality, segmentation is a gathering process, since potential customers are assembled together by commonalities in specific characteristics to form segments.

Myth #2: Segmentation is only a marketing process or technique.

This is another half truth. Although segmentation is a marketing process, its real impact comes from its role as a marketing strategy. As will be discussed in Chapter 2, market segmentation is the primary strategic element in a company's marketing plan. It is the foundation upon which all other marketing actions can be based.

Myth #3: Everyone is part of a segment in a given market.

Although this might be an ideal situation for the marketer, in actuality all people do not fit neatly into a market segment. It is likely that a small percentage of the population will be unclassifiable based on the specified segment formation criteria (to be discussed in Chapter 3). These aberrant individuals have one or more inconsistencies in key segmentation decision characteristics, and as such, are not good prospects for concentrated marketing activity.

SEGMENTATION SUMMARY SHEET: THE OVERVIEW

The decade of marketing:

- Large and small firms have embraced marketing
- So-called "non-marketers" (e.g., healthcare, professional services, banking) have discovered the power of marketing
- Customers have more product choices than ever before
- Market segmentation has evolved into an important "real-world" planning tool

Market segmentation:

- A process of partitioning markets into segments of similar potential customers likely to exhibit similar purchase behavior
- The foundation for overall marketing strategy
- Goal—to analyze markets, find a niche, and develop and capitalize on a superior competitive position
- Match goods and services to customer needs and wants

Segmentation in action:

- Market segmentation is an art and a science
- Dimensions or bases are methods for segmenting markets
- Some common dimensions briefly reviewed — geographic, demographic, socioeconomic, psychographic, product usage, and benefits (creative segmentation is also a possibility)

Segmentation options:

- Aggregation (mass marketing) vs. segmentation
- Segmentation options — differentiation, concentration, or atomization
- Differentiation—serve two or more segments of the market based on differing needs
- Concentration—serve a unique segment of the market
- Atomization—develop custom marketing programs for each key prospect

The benefits of segmentation:

- Designing responsive products
- Determining effective/efficient promotional strategies
- Evaluating competition and market position
- Providing insight on present marketing strategies

The limitations of segmentation:

- Findings only provide a composite profile of the market
- Changing lifestyles of the 80s have made segmentation more difficult in many markets
- Segmentation is not a remedy for other organizational problems
- Segmentation's effectiveness is limited by management's ability to implement strategic implications

Three segmentation myths refuted

CHAPTER TWO

Segmentation's Role
In The Marketing Plan

Method goes far to prevent trouble in business; for it makes the task easy, hinders confusion, saves abundance of time, and instructs those who have business depending, what to do and what to hope.

William Penn, 1694

For segmentation strategy to work effectively, it must be an integrated part of a company's marketing plan. The marketing plan is a systematic approach to coordinating all marketing activities—a blueprint for action. This custom document, developed specifically for a particular firm's needs, should be part of an overall business plan and long-range strategy. A well developed marketing plan is a dynamic tool capable of anticipating change and reflecting the future.

The marketing plan should be prepared for a specified time frame. Typically, the working or operational marketing plan is developed annually, with frequent periodic updates and revisions when circumstances dictate. For example, if a major competitor enters or leaves the market, industry regulations change, or a new product or technology comes on the scene, the marketing plan should be modified to reflect the latest situation. Often a master (longer-term) marketing plan will also be advisable for a business.

Figure 2–1 illustrates one of General Electric's marketing plans. This company uses a variety of different plans for their various divisions. As you will note from the detail in this diagram, marketing planning is taken very seriously at G.E. Your firm can also benefit greatly by carefully planning all marketing activities.

BENEFITS OF A MARKETING PLAN

According to the Bank of America, California, failing to plan and inattention to marketing are two of the four major business pitfalls (the

Figure 2-1:

A General Electric Marketing Plan

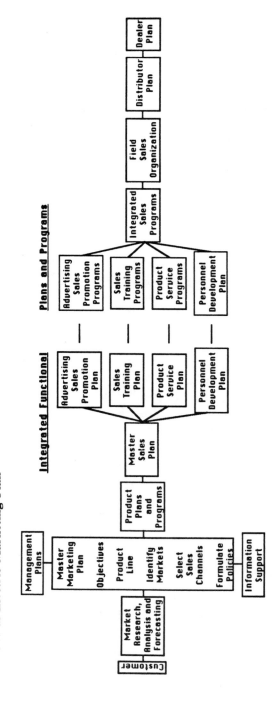

Courtesy of General Electric Company.

others are insufficient leadership and unsound financial management). The formal, written marketing plan helps to remedy this potential lack of a marketing planning focus. The advantages to the firm in having a marketing plan include:

- It helps to produce desired results by giving your business direction and organization.
- It is an excellent planning and control tool. Results can easily be compared to the forecast.
- A marketing plan is a useful management aid. A wealth of marketing information is at your fingertips.

ELEMENTS OF THE MARKETING PLAN

Proper segmentation requires sound marketing planning. The marketing plan is that framework upon which effective marketing decisions can be built. The five required components of a good marketing plan are depicted in Figure 2–2. Let's explore these major elements of the marketing plan.

Market and Situation Analysis

Fact finding is the purpose of the market and situation analysis which is also commonly called environmental analysis. A company has two environments to research — it's own (the internal environment), and the industry in which it competes (the external environment).

The Internal Environment. Every firm should periodically place itself under the "microscope." One of the best ways of assessing your current marketing situation is to conduct a marketing audit. This is not an easy task, however. As Hal W. Goetsch, former director of marketing for the American Marketing Association points out, marketing audits can present problems for a company when it attempts to administer them internally. He states, "Even when a conscientious effort is made to see the situation objectively, the focus can be blurred by tradition, unquestioned procedures, personalities, manipulated programs, corporate politics, indifference, or laziness. Too often the picture is faulty because facts are missing, guesses are not reliable, or important elements of the marketing environment have been ignored or overlooked."

To resolve this problem, the audit can be administered by outside mar-

Figure 2–2:
The Five Steps To Successful Marketing Planning

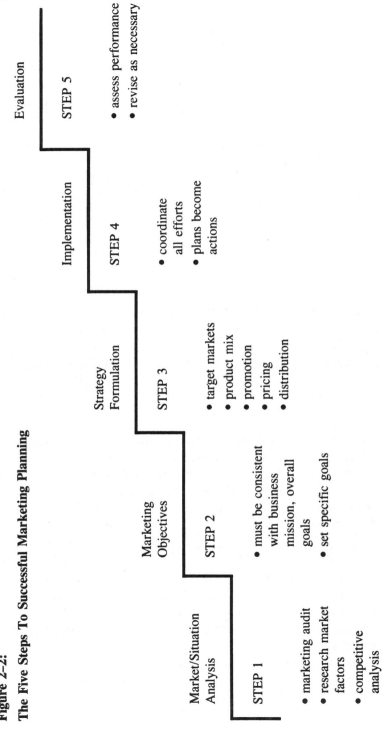

Market/Situation Analysis	Marketing Objectives	Strategy Formulation	Implementation	Evaluation
STEP 1	STEP 2	STEP 3	STEP 4	STEP 5
• marketing audit • research market factors • competitive analysis • assess uncontrollables	• must be consistent with business mission, overall goals • set specific goals	• target markets • product mix • promotion • pricing • distribution	• coordinate all efforts • plans become actions	• assess performance • revise as necessary

keting consultants to minimize bias and maximize objectivity. An effective marketing audit will gather information about your current marketing efforts, but more importantly analyze the "marketing health" of your firm (similar to the ways a medical check-up assesses one's physical well being). Strengths and weaknesses of the company are identified, with the objective being to capitalize on the former, while rectifying the latter. An example of Goetsch's basic marketing audit questions for a business is provided in Figure 2-3. The audit must be adapted however, to meet the information gathering needs of a particular firm or industry. For example, the author, in cooperation with two associates, has developed and administered custom audits to several dentists in the South Florida area.

The External Environment. This is actually a compilation of several "sub-environments." These include market factors, the competitive situation, and other marketing uncontrollables.

Market factors include such considerations as identification and description of consumer needs and wants, research on market size/potential, possible business affiliates, etc. A competitive analysis is required to determine direct and indirect competition, as well as for developing sound counterpositioning strategies. Marketing uncontrollables complete the market analysis by examining such areas as the economic environment, regulatory rulings/agencies, technological forces, media impact, and social and lifestyle considerations. The result of a comprehensive environmental analysis will be a concise profile for a given market situation. An abbreviated market profile for the microcomputer industry is provided in Figure 2-4. Also, Appendix 2-1 at the end of this chapter offers further insight on the preparation of a market analysis.

Marketing Objectives

Objectives are the marketing results sought by management. As the foundation for marketing strategy, goal setting is useful in:

- Providing direction for the marketing plan (determining what you want to accomplish)
- Motivating the staff (identifying what you should be accomplishing)
- Providing a timetable for implementing the marketing plan (noting if you are on schedule)
- Measuring marketing performance (evaluating whether or not you are meeting your goals).

Figure 2–3:

Marketing audit questions

By Hal W. Goetsch

MARKETING COMMITMENT:
Corporate culture
1. Does the chief executive believe in marketing planning and is formal planning ingrained with all top managers?
2. Are plans prepared with the participation of functional managers, or dictated by the president?
3. Do you have a coordinated marketing program or an isolated sales department?
4. Are you using the computer as a marketing tool and do your managers understand its capabilities?
5. Do you implement a marketing plan, measure performance, and adjust for deviation?
6. Are all marketing functions under the direction of one executive who reports to the chief executive officer?

PRODUCTS/SERVICES:
The reason for existence
1. Is the product/service free from deadwood? Do you have a well-defined, continuous program to weed out unprofitable products and add new ones?
2. What is the life cycle stage?
3. How will user demands or trends affect you?
4. Are you a leader in new product innovation?
5. Do you have a systematic liaison with the research/development group?
6. Are inexpensive methods used to estimate new product potentials before considerable amounts are spent on R&D and market introduction?
7. Are new products introduced with forecasts and budgets?
8. Have you investigated possible advantages resulting from new materials or technology?
9. Do you have different quality levels for different markets?
10. Are packages/brochures effective salesmen for the products/services they present?
11. Do you present products/services in the most appealing colors (formats) for markets being served?
12. Are there features or benefits to exploit?
13. Has the safety of the product/service been brought to a satisfactory level?
14. Is the level of customer service adequate?

15. How are quality and reliability viewed by customers?

CUSTOMER: User profiles
1. Who is the current and potential customer?
2. Are customers younger or older, on average, than those of competitors?
3. Are there geographic aspects of use: regional, rural, urban?
4. Why do people buy the product/service; what motivates their preferences?
5. Who makes buying decisions; when, where?
6. What is the frequency and quantity of use?

MARKETS: Where products/services are sold
1. How is the market shaped; where is the center of gravity?
2. Have you identified and measured major segments?
3. Are you overlooking small but profitable segments of the market in trying to satisfy the tastes of the majority?
4. Are the markets for the products/services expanding or declining?
5. Should different segments be developed; gaps in penetration?
6. Do segments require marketing differentiation?

SALES HISTORY: Previous results
1. How do sales break down within the product/service?
2. Do you know where sales are coming from; segments and customer classification?
3. Are there abnormal cycles or seasonalities and, if so, how do you plan for them?
4. Do sales match previous forecasts?
5. Which territories/markets do not yield potential?
6. Are growth and profit trends reflected?

COMPETITORS: Their influence
1. Who are the principal competitors, how are they positioned, and where do they seem to be headed?
2. What are their market shares?
3. What features of competitors' products/services stand out?
4. What are their strengths and weaknesses?
5. Is the market easily entered or dominated?

PRICING: Profitability planning

1. What are the objectives of current pricing policy: acquiring, defending, or expanding?
2. Are price limitations inherent in the marketplace?
3. Are price policies set to produce volume or profit?
4. How does pricing compare with competition in similar levels of quality?
5. Do you understand how your prices are set?
6. Is the price list understandable and current?
7. Does cost information show profitability of each item?
8. What is the history of price deals, discounts, and promotions?
9. Are middlemen making money from the line?
10. Can the product/service support advertising or promotion programs?
11. Will size or manufacturing process require more volume?
12. Are there cost problems to overcome?
13. Are profitability and marketing cost known by the customer?

MARKETING CHANNELS:
Selling paths

1. Does the system offer the best access to all target markets?
2. Do product/service characteristics require special channels?
3. Have you analyzed each market with a view toward setting up the most profitable type of presentation: direct vs. reps, master distributors or dealers, etc.?
4. What are the trends in distribution methods?
5. Do you provide cost-effective marketing support, selling aids, and sales tools?

SALES ADMINISTRATION:
Selling efficiency

1. Have you analyzed communications and designed paperwork or computer programs to provide meaningful management information?
2. Are customers getting coverage in proportion to their potential?
3. Are sales costs properly planned and controlled?
4. Does the compensation plan provide optimum incentive and security at reasonable cost?
5. Is performance measured against potential?
6. Are selling expenses proportionate to results and potentials within markets or territories?

7. Are there deficiencies in recruitment, selection, training, motivation, supervision, performance, promotion, or compensation?
8. Do you provide effective selling aids and sales tools?

DELIVERY & INVENTORY:
Physical performance

1. Are adequate inventories kept in the right mix?
2. Is inventory turnover acceptable?
3. Do orders receive efficient, timely processing?
4. Are shipping schedules and promises kept?
5. Is the product/service delivered in good condition?
6. Are forecasts for production planning acceptable?
7. How does performance compare with competition?
8. Are warehouses and distribution points properly located?

ADVERTISING: Media program

1. Are media objectives and strategies linked to the marketing plan?
2. What are the objectives of the ad program?
3. How is media effectiveness measured?
4. Is advertising integrated with promotion and sales activity?
5. Is the ad agency's effectiveness periodically evaluated?
6. Do you dictate copy theme and content to the agency?
7. Are you spending realistically, in relation to budget?
8. Do you use trade publications effectively?
9. How do you choose the ad agency?

PROMOTION: Sales inducement

1. Does the promotion support a marketing objective?
2. Was it carefully budgeted?
3. Is it integrated with advertising and selling activity?
4. How is it measured for results?
5. What was the reason for its success or failure?
6. Are slogans, trademarks, logos, and brands being used effectively?
7. Is point-of-sale material cost-effective?
8. Do you have satisfactory displays of products/services?
9. Are you effectively using couponing, tie-ins, incentives, sampling, stuffers, combination offers?
10. How do you evaluate trade shows for effectiveness?

PUBLIC RELATIONS: Prestige building

1. Do you have a clear idea of the type of company you want people to think you are?
2. Do you have a consistent communications program?
3. What kind of ideas and impressions have you created about your company?
4. Do you really know what your image is on a factual basis, or are you relying on customers' letters, salesmen's reports, and publicity in the press?
5. Does your company name, brand, and logo add to or conflict with the image you want?
6. Are you getting a share of favorable, unpaid publicity in editorials of the media?

FIGURE 2-4:
MARKET PROFILE 1983
The Microcomputer Industry

An Overview

Recent technological improvements in both hardware (equipment) and software (programs) have led to a virtual overnight computer revolution in the United States. Millions of Americans, school children as well as corporate presidents, are benefiting from the computer age. Several industry analysts expect computers to be as prevalent as the television set in American households. This is largely attributable to the mass marketing strategies that major computer manufacturers are implementing as prices have fallen dramatically during the past few years.

Computers come in all sizes and price ranges, and are designed to perform specific tasks. A recognized classification divides the industry: microcomputers, minicomputers, mainframes, and supercomputers.

Micros are the fastest growing segment in the computer industry, with a projected annual growth rate of 46% in unit sales and 43.5% increase in dollar sales through 1986.[1] Microcomputers are also commonly referred to as desktops or personal computers. It should be emphasized that personal computers are not just for home use. The technology found in personal computers is quite advanced, and the majority of personal computers are now being used in business applications. According to Dataquest, Inc. of San Jose, California, personal computer sales should grow to approximately $6.7 billion for 1983, up from $4.7 billion in 1982[2]. In 1983, new sales for desktop computers are expected to approach the two million unit mark by year end.[3]

Market Segments

Desktop computers appeal to four major groups of buyers: 1) the businessperson/professional, 2) the home user/hobbyist, 3) the scientist/engineer, and 4) the educational market. The business/professional market is by far the largest. In 1982, approximately 55% of the personal computers sold were purchased strictly for business applications. The home/hobby market provided over 30% of unit sales, while the scientific and educational segments accounted for the balance, about 15%.[4]

The Marketplace

"There are currently some 150 desktop vendors worldwide, ninety of whom are U.S. manufacturers."[5] Dozens of firms have recently entered this potentially lucrative market, including several major Japanese firms. The dominant forces in the personal computer field at this time include IBM, Apple, and the Tandy Corporation (Radio Shack).

Future Industry Trends

The microcomputer industry has been characterized by continual improvements in performance at significantly reduced prices. Desktops are becoming easier to operate, and the latest generation of products are extremely "user-friendly," permitting easy interaction between human and machine. New software applications and modifications in existing programs have made the personal computer a necessary tool for the 1980s.

Many of the small computer manufacturers are not expected to survive the industry shakeout likely to occur over the next few years.

[1] *Standard and Poor's Industry Survey* (Basic Analysis, Office Equipment, Computers and Peripherals, p.015).

[2] "The Squeeze Begins in Personal Computers," *Business Week*, May 30, 1983, p.91.

[3] "Computer Firms Ask, 'What Recession?', " *Miami Herald*, January 1983, p. 6F.

[4] Ibid, p.6F.

[5] *Standard and Poor's*, op.cit., p. 016.

Author's Note: The above synopsis was extracted from a market analysis developed for a client of mine in the computer industry.

Goals are objectives made specific, measurable, and time-oriented. Furthermore, goals should be realistic, objective, clear, and concise. Some typical marketing goals include sales (in units, dollars, and/or percentage change increases), market share, prospect visits, inquiries, and awareness/recognition for your company or product. Examples of some specific goal statements organized into major marketing functional areas are listed in Figure 2–5. These are provided as guidelines only, and should be adapted and expanded where necessary to meet the needs of your firm's marketing plan.

Strategy Formulation

Once the environment has been carefully researched and analyzed, and objectives set, it is then possible to formulate appropriate marketing strategies for the business. Strategies need to be developed for two major areas—target markets and marketing mix elements (product, promotion, pricing, and distribution).

Target Market Selection—Strategic Element #1

Ideally target market identification, evaluation, and selection should be undertaken prior to determining specific strategies in the other marketing areas. If you know who your likely customers are, you are in a much better position to provide desired products and services to this market segment. Similarly, promotion, pricing, and distribution strategies can be tailored to segment needs. As strategic element number one, segmentation techniques act as a bridge to effectively link customers' needs and desires to a company's offerings. Figure 2–6 summarizes the segment profiles for the XYZ Company, a private-sector provider of financial-aid services for college students.

Marketing Strategy and the 4 Ps—The Other Players

Product, promotion, price, and place (distribution) strategies—the 4 Ps— are the "meat" of a company's marketing plan. For maximum effectiveness they should be broadly based on segmentation findings, as well as other strategic variables (e.g., company resources, management's values and policies, potential risk and return, etc.). Strategies are the way in which marketing operations will be conducted prior to actual implementation. Unlike the external environment, the firm has complete control over the marketing methods it can employ to meet its objectives.

Figure 2–5:

Segmentation Checklist

Typical Marketing Goal Statements

1) Sales Productivity/Volume Goals

Increase the number of customers _____ % by December 31, 19___.

Increase penetration into a specific market with existing products by _____ % by December 31, 19__ .

Increase sales volume of product X by _____ % in selected regions, districts, and territories by specific dates.

Attain sales performance goals on calls per man, orders per call, calls per day, etc. by given amounts by specific dates.

2) Profitability Goals

Increase overall return on investment by _____ % for the next fiscal year.

Increase profit rate for key regions, districts, and territories by _____ %, by a specific date.

3) Market Share Goals

Increase by _____ %, market share in "X" market by December 31, 19__ .

Attain market share sub-goals for regions, districts, and territories by June 30, 19__ .

4) Distribution Goals

Establish _____ new distributors in specific geographic regions by December 31, 19__ .

5) Advertising/Promotion Goals

Increase awareness of company products among key purchase influences in specific new markets by _____ % by December 31, 19__ .

Develop high quality inquiries at $_____ /inquiry for company products.

6) Product Development Goals

Introduce _____ new products to fill out product-line offering by specific dates.

7) Pricing Goals

Prices should be competitive (within 5% of primary competitors) and yield a minimum unit contribution to profit of _____ %.

8) Other Objectives

Other objectives must also be set for manpower development and training, margins, budget adherence, customer relations, and your service program.

Adapted with permission of the Chilton Book Company, Radnor, PA. This material was first published in the *Marketing Problem Solver*, 2nd edition, p. 78.

Figure 2–6:

The XYZ Company

Background

The XYZ Company is a computerized financial-aid research company, designed to assist college students in locating funds for higher education. Corporations, foundations, philanthropic organizations, and professional associations provide millions of dollars annually to students throughout the country through scholarships, grants, and loans. XYZ, a South Florida-based company, wants to provide "dollars for scholars."

Objective

XYZ is interested in determining the potential for this service in the state of Florida.

The Approach

1) Expected customer profile: These services are most likely to appeal to the following type of person.

    a) young—sixteen to twenty-nine (there are undergraduate and graduate services)
    b) lower-middle to middle income household
    c) an educated consumer or from an educated household
    d) enrolled or likely to enroll in a private college
    e) liberal thinking, non-traditionalist or product innovator

2) Market segments by education level

    a) college student (undergraduate)
    b) college student (graduate)
    c) high school senior

3) Florida potential: college market

Type of college	Total students	Targeted students
State Universities	132,947 (9)	132,947 (9)
Jr./Community Colleges	206,859 (28)	178,148 (16)
Private Institutions	78,955 (44)	45,888 (7)
Totals	418,761 (81)	356,983 (32)

By targeting thirty-two of the eighty-one colleges and universities in Florida (39.5%), it is possible to reach 356,983 students (85.3%). A similar volume approach toward high schools within the individual counties in the state can also be used. The above data is from the *1982 Florida Statistical Abstract*.

4) Target markets: Further segmentation research is needed.

Author's Note: The above example is from an actual segmentation project conducted for a small business client. The company name has obviously been disguised.

Strategies should not be developed in isolation from each other. Rather, you should strive for consistency and compatibility among all of the strategic elements. Tactics, the short-term strategies (often viewed as lasting less than a year), are the nuts and bolts portion of the plan. Tactics consist of such marketing initiatives as advertising budgets, media schedules, sales force organization, and pricing lists, to name a few.

The development of strategies and tactics from market segmentation research is discussed further in Chapter 8. Additionally, several in-depth strategy profiles are featured in Part IV of the book, Segmentation Strategy Cases. Figure 2–7, The Marketing Planning Cycle, illustrates the inter-

Figure 2–7:

The Marketing Planning Cycle

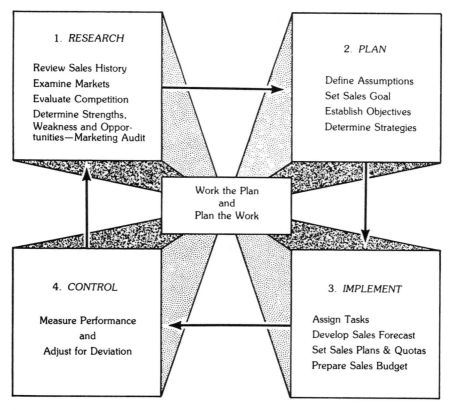

Reprinted with permission. H.W. Goetsch, *How to Prepare and Use Marketing Plans for Profit,* Marketing for Profit, Inc., 1979, p. 12.

relationship between research, goal setting, strategic planning, and implementation and control.

Effective marketing strategy combines sound marketing decision making with a sprinkling of business creativity. Miller Brewing Company's Lite beer is a classic example of successful marketing strategy. This Philip Morris subsidiary pioneered a new segment in the beer market (light beer) by targeting sports-loving, middle-aged men, many of whom were watching their weight, but enjoyed the pleasures of drinking beer. Miller's innovative advertising campaigns—in particular, their television commercials—featuring sports personalities, humor, variety (dozens of different spots were run), and controversy (great taste vs. less filling), led to a position of market dominance. Lite offered America a good tasting, low calorie beer alternative, and the product's sales skyrocketed almost overnight. Miller also benefited from the health-conscious young adult market and the brand's popularity with women. The Seven-Up Company, another Philip Morris division, also exhibited stellar marketing creativity by carving a niche in the marketplace as the "Uncola."

Implementation and Evaluation

At this point, the overall marketing plan is laid out. Will it work? To gauge the success of your marketing program, the plan must be executed and evaluated.

Implementation. In this phase, strategies are translated into action. Tactics, the company's short-term marketing plans, are featured. Specific timetables, budgets, and assignment responsibilities are carried forth. Communication within the company is critical in this stage, as employees at different levels are called on to get the "marketing machinery" rolling. At this point, the marketing plan progresses from a report to a working document.

Evaluation. Just as the implementation phase is the "how it will be done" part of the plan, evaluation determines "how well you are actually doing." Control measures are maintained to check whether specific objectives are being met, variances in performance that have occurred, whether efforts are on schedule, and what changes may be prescribed.

One type of marketing tool that can be used for implementation and evaluation purposes is an advertising budget/media planning model, as shown in Figure 2–8. This summary form (adaptable to most business situations) was used to track advertising efforts (in dollars) for a small

Figure 2–8:
Quarterly Advertising Budget/Media Plan

MEDIA ACCOUNT	BUDGET	ACTUAL	VARIANCE	Month 1					Month 2					Month 3				
				1	2	3	4	5	1	2	3	4	5	1	2	3	4	5
PRINT (incl. newspapers, publications)																		
Daily A	6000	5880	120			588	588		1176	1176	588	588	588	588				
Daily B	3000	2925	75			307	307		686	307	686	0	325	307				
Community C	1000	0	1000															
	10,000	8805	1195															
BROADCAST (incl. radio, TV)																		
Radio Station A	3200	3312	(112)			552	552		552	552	552	552						
Radio Station B	2000	1560	440						390	390	390	390						
Radio Station C	2800	3744	(944)			624	624		624	624	624	624						
	8000	8616	(616)															
OTHER (incl. directory, direct, outdoor, etc.)																		
Production Costs	1000	1200	(200)			1200												
Ad Specialties/Sales Promotion	1000	1500	(500)			1500												
	2000	2700	(700)															
TOTALS	20,000	20,121	(121)															

Miami-based specialty coffee distributor. This model was one of the starting points in developing an eight-week, $20,000, multi-media advertising campaign.

The key to a marketing plan is its practicality. Marketing planning is not a one-shot process, but a recurring business activity. As such, it requires regular reviews and monitoring by management. Revisions and updates should be expected—the goal is a workable plan that will improve your marketing performance.

SEGMENTATION SUMMARY SHEET: THE MARKETING PLAN

The marketing plan:

- A systematic approach to conducting/coordinating all marketing activities
- Dynamic tool capable of anticipating change/reflecting the future
- Typically prepared annually with updates

Benefits of a marketing plan:

- Helps to produce desired results (provides direction and organization)
- Excellent planning and control tool
- Useful management aid (wealth of information at your fingertips)

Elements of the marketing plan:

1) Market and Situation Analysis
   - marketing audit
   - external environmental analysis

2) Marketing Objectives
   - provides direction
   - motivates the staff
   - provides a timetable for marketing activities
   - provides a mechanism to measure performance

3) Strategy Formulation
   - target markets (strategic element #1)
   - the 4 Ps (product, promotion, price, place)

4) Implementation
   - strategies become actions

5) Evaluation
   - control measures (are objectives being met? variances? on schedule? required changes?)

Marketing planning:

- Must be customized to a company's situation

- Practicality is key
- Not a one-time process
- Revisions and updates assist in developing a workable plan

APPENDIX 2-1:

Compiling A Market/Industry Overview?
Follow This Outline

by Peter Beck, Information Specialist
Find/SVP, New York

The problem: produce an "overview" of an industry, market, or service sector—something that can be compiled and comprehended quickly, yet covers all the essential aspects of the subject; something that can stand on its own and serve as the framework for further, more focused research. A researcher with good knowledge of secondary sources can plunge right in and start collecting information; no special preparation is necessary. However, without a model or outline as a guide, it will be difficult to decide whether or not certain details ought to be included, and to be certain that there are no significant gaps. The task is not impracticable, but a haphazard methodology makes the research comparatively less rapid and less efficient.

Most overviews are put together in this fashion, without an underlying structure to focus and guide the research. While such a method is adequate, it leaves too much to chance. Moreover, when the same researcher is asked to provide similar information for a completely different market or industry, he will have to return to square one, "reinventing the wheel" each time an overview is required. But there is a better way.

In learning to meet the demands of our clients, we have derived an outline for conducting overviews. It may seem disarmingly simple but, as in most problem-solving tasks, simplicity is a virtue. While the same results might be obtained using a less-directed, more random approach, more time would be required and thoroughness could not be guaranteed. Further, if you ever found yourself in a position of having to complete five very different overviews in the same day, you would be grateful for such an outline. Without it, your task would be nearly impossible; with it, you could succeed and, perhaps more importantly, be certain that your results were thorough and useful.

The first step is to determine the size of the market. Ideally, market size will be represented both in dollars and units, but finding one or the other will suffice for a quick overview. Next, identify the "major players," the top three or four companies (manufacturers, suppliers, etc.) in the industry. And as a complement—frequently this is difficult, but nonetheless essential — determine the leading companies' market share. (Knowing that Campbell's is the leader in the soup category takes on a different cast when you realize its market share is 80%!)

In all likelihood, older versions of the sources already employed can be accessed in order to supply information for the next step in the outline: historical trends. Growth of the market, shifts in composition or rank of the leaders, new technologies, legislation, lawsuits, mergers and acquisitions—details of this type should be noted for a period of at least two to three years and as far back as five years when the emergence of influential factors would be missed otherwise.

To be complete, an overview must contain information on the market situation for the past, present, and future. Therefore, you will need to supply projections, but nothing too elaborate or involved; while everyone would like to see year-by-year projections out to the year 2000 and beyond, three to five years is adequate at this juncture.

The overview now contains information on how large the market is, who's in it, how it got to where it is, and where it's going. These are the absolute essentials and no overview can be complete if it omits any of them. The rest of the overview involves looking for information that is often not readily available, and the particulars of the market being studied may necessitate substituting other factors for those given here.

User demographics and psychographics can help round out the picture and explain some of the market behavior seen in the past or anticipated in the future. The projections should also be augmented by a look at what's new. Products, promotions, techniques, strategies, etc.—a sketch of the new and emerging developments that may have an impact on a market.

For a well-documented market, this outline is useful because it helps focus and direct the research. For a small, new, or poorly documented market, the outline is essential. It enables you to be certain that the inevitable "gaps" remain unfilled only because information is unavailable, and never as a result of slipshod research. Knowing, with certainty, what is not available (and why) often can be just as useful as the information that actually is available.

Following this outline, sifting and sorting through the available information, a researcher will be able to gain significant insight into the market in question. The time invested can be minimal. Yet, this insight will enable the researcher to draw informed conclusions and make appropriate recommendations; for example, abandoning or pursuing further research. In this way, the outline extends its usefulness. Thus, in addition to serving as a functional model for gathering information, it provides a perspective from which to study and evaluate the material gathered.

This material first appeared in an article in Marketing News. Reprinted with permission of the American Marketing Association.

CHAPTER THREE

Planning The Segmentation Analysis

It was not the possibility of planning as such which has been questioned . . . but the possibility of successful planning.

F.A. Hayek, 1935

The most important factor in determining whether a segmentation study will provide the desired results is the planning and research framework upon which the information will be gathered, analyzed, and evaluated. This research design is the blueprint for action which lays out a systematic approach to data collection and analysis. It is the ''game plan'' for the marketer to stay on track with specified objectives to minimize costs by reducing unforeseen expenses.

There is no one best research plan for segmentation studies, as a lot depends on market and situational factors. Since there is no standard package, virtually every segmentation analysis will have to be customized. However, there are some necessary components of research design that must be specified prior to beginning the study. The ten required elements of a good segmentation plan are:

1) Establish research objectives
2) Specify target population measurement units
3) State relevant definitions
4) Recognize segmentation viability/segment formation criteria
5) Select segmentation bases
6) Choose appropriate data collection methods
7) Employ sampling procedures
8) Analyze the data
9) Consider budgetary constraints
10) Know how the information will be used

Let's examine these ten areas in detail.

1) RESEARCH OBJECTIVES

The first step in conducting a segmentation analysis is to establish appropriate objectives for the study. The goal is to be able to answer the question "What are you trying to accomplish in the research project?" Closely linked to the research objectives are two other central issues: the background of the company and its situation (setting the scene), and the purpose of the research (management's desires). Figure 3-1 provides a framework for tackling these areas.

Objectives provide you with a checklist of information needs useful for strategy development. Some typical research objective questions appropriate for a segmentation study are listed in Figure 3-2.

The above is a sample of twenty key research objective questions that should be asked prior to conducting a segmentation analysis. However, it is by no means exhaustive. Depending on the firm's research needs, some or all of the above list may be used as a starting point. Undoubtedly, additional questions will be needed as well. The next step is to formulate the question into a workable statement. For example, the question on heavy users might be translated into the following research objective:

- To determine what percentage of the market consumes six or more cups of yogurt per month.

Obviously, a second research objective would then be needed to identify this segment.

2) TARGET POPULATION MEASUREMENT UNITS

Market segments are groups of individuals or organizations with similar characteristics. In analyzing markets, the marketer must specify a unit of measure to quantify the size and scope of the target consumers or users in designated segments. In consumer marketing, some common descriptors include customers, shoppers, prospects, and patients. In industrial applications, purchasing agents, decision makers, managers, influencers, and clients are some typically targeted individuals. Once the basic descriptor has been identified, additional modifiers (segmentation bases and variables) can be utilized to better understand and explain the market segments.

Sometimes the targeted prospect is not the obvious prospect. For example, research has shown that women purchase 70% of men's underwear. Recognizing this statistic, Jockey's strategy to use Jim Palmer as its "pitchman"

Figure 3-1:

Research Objectives

Project Background Checklist

1. Briefly, what is the company's history? What is the company's "personality"—go-go, conservative, or what?
2. What are its major product lines? What's the relative importance of each product line?
3. What is the product's sales history? Is it growing, stable, or declining?
4. What are the competitive products? What are the market shares? What new products have entered the market?
5. In one sentence: What is the problem? Then expand on that one sentence: Who? What? When? Where? Why? How?
6. Is this a big problem or a little problem?
7. What previous research has been done on this subject? What did it show?

Project Purpose Checklist

1. What decision will be made or what action will be taken as a result of the research?
2. What are the implications of this action? Is it a "big deal" or a "little deal"?
3. What are the alternatives available?
4. What are the risks in the decision or action?
5. What are the potential payoffs of the decision?
6. When will the decision be made? Are there externally enforced deadlines on the decision?

Project Objectives Checklist

1. What *specific* information should the project provide?
2. If more than one type of information will be developed from the study, what is most important? What are the priorities for the information?
3. What results are expected? Is there agreement among those involved with the project? If not, why not?
4. Have decision rules been established for evaluating the results? If so, what are they? If not, why not?

Discussing these questions should provide enough understanding to help you begin designing the study.

Reprinted, by permission of the publisher, from *Practical Marketing Research,* by Jeffrey L. Pope, p. 48. © 1981 Jeffrey L. Pope. Published by AMACOM, a division of American Management Associations, New York. All rights reserved.

Figure 3-2:

Segmentation Checklist

Research Objective Questions

1) What are some of the possible market segments for your product or service?
2) How do these segments compare with your present customer profile(s)?
3) How large are these potential target markets?
4) What is the expected profitability of serving these sub-markets?
5) How are these segments defined? (names, sizes, key variables)
6) What is unique about the specific groups?
7) Where are the potential customers located?
8) How much should be allocated to the various markets, now? In the future?
9) What segments are competitors pursuing?
10) What unique niche (competitive advantage) does your company have compared to others in the market?
11) What past segmentation studies have been employed?
12) How useful were past segmentation findings/strategies?
13) Who are the heavy users for your product or service?
14) What features or benefits are sought by customers?
15) What alternative marketing strategies and tactics are available?
16) Does your product or service meet segment needs? (any changes required?)
17) What promotional appeals can best be used toward the target markets?
18) How price sensitive are the markets?
19) What role do distribution channels play in the market?
20) How will customer purchase behavior be monitored to measure marketing effectiveness?

was a sound one. Would women react as favorably to Yogi Berra? Additionally, in some markets there is a dual decision-maker. Breakfast cereals generally must appeal to both the child and the parent.

3) RELEVANT DEFINITIONS

In addition to the customer, other major definitions are important in planning the segmentation analysis. The market trade or service area is a critical one. The population of prospects for a company must have a definite geographical limitation or boundary. It is virtually impossible for the firm to effectively serve the needs of the entire market. Factors which affect the market definition include: the nature of the business (retailers will attract most of their customers from within a given geographic radius or so-many minute drive of their shop), the goods or services offered (the uniqueness and availability of products), competition, and physical boundaries (i.e., expressways, access roads, topography, etc.).

Other definitions to be specified in a segmentation study might include, but are not limited to, the demographic and socioeconomic classifications to evaluate, criteria for determining benefits or lifestyles, and consumptive measures (e.g., what constitutes a heavy vs. light user in a given product class).

4) SEGMENTATION VIABILITY/SEGMENT FORMATION CRITERIA

For a market segmentation analysis to be effective, there are some essential market/industry factors and segment formation criteria that must be met.

Market Characteristics

Not every market is segmentable. Other markets which can be segmented may not be feasible to pursue from a marketing perspective. There are four key issues that must be assessed. Positive responses to these questions indicate that market segmentation is worth pursuing. These pivotal criteria can be called the 4 Rs of the market decision, and are listed in Figure 3–3.

R1. Rating the market. By rating a market or industry, the marketer attempts to valuate, both objectively and subjectively, its potential relative to other market opportunities. The goal is to quantify the size of the aggregate market and possible sub-markets prior to segmentation. For segmentation to be viable, the market must be identifiable and measurable.

One of my clients, a dentist, was interested in specializing in cosmetic

---

Figure 3–3:
The 4 Rs

Can the market be **rated** relative to other markets?
Is the market **realistic** in size?
Can customers be easily **reached**?
Will customers **respond** to marketing initiatives?

---

dentistry (e.g., bonding, implants, and related aesthetic services) and wanted to know the relative size of this potential market in his service area. Research indicated that only 10% of the potential dental patients in his area were prime candidates for cosmetic dentistry. On the other hand, two other segments, emphasizing preventive and preventive/remedial dentistry, accounted for more than 44% of the market potential. (See Chapter 7 for a detailed account of this segmentation analysis.)

R2. Realistic in size. The market considered must be large enough to support more than one type of marketing approach. The segments identified must be of sufficient magnitude so that distinct marketing programs can be developed for the target markets. For example, if a retail rare coin dealer was interested in selling Civil War currency to collectors, given the limited number of potential customers for the product, segmentation into two or more sub-markets would not be prudent.

R3. Reach. Are potential segments readily accessible? For segmentation to work effectively, groups have to be reached easily to minimize marketing investment and maximize performance.The widespread availability of trade journals such as *Adweek* or *Progressive Grocer* and directories such as *The Electronics Buyer's Guide* or *The Aviation Buyer's Directory* provide excellent opportunities to reach desired market segments. Additionally, thousands of highly targeted mailing lists can be purchased or rented. Once a profile of your customers has been established, comparisons to media kits, *Standard Rate and Data Service* (SRDS) media summaries, and other media references can be made for effective advertising planning.

In a project conducted for a minority-owned Goodyear automotive franchisee, a low-cost promotional plan was designed based on a demographic market analysis. It was recommended that the target market could be reached by using discount coupons, special offers, and premiums; supporting school sporting events and neighborhood activities; and employing media vehicles targeted to the predominately black population (radio stations and community newspapers).

R4. Responsiveness.   Will the identified prospects respond to your marketing initiatives? The identification of a reasonable number of potential customers that can be reached is of little value if they are nonresponsive to your marketing efforts. Thorough market research will assist in determining whether there is a genuine need for your product or service before expensive promotional dollars are expended.

A small retail office supply business illustrates this point. Research conducted indicated that the owner's merchandise mix, store hours, and promotional strategy were inappropriate for his suburban location. By gearing products to the home-user segment rather than the corporate segment, extending store hours to meet the needs of the two-income working professional, and revising advertising and selling tactics, revenues were increased significantly within a three-month period.

Segment Formation

Assuming "yes" can be answered to all of the 4 Rs, market segmentation analysis is probably worth undertaking. The next issue to consider is how to form good market segments. The following general criteria can be used as a guideline. Specific segment formation standards must also be developed, and adapted to your business situation.

Homogeneity within the segment.   This is the test for similarities among group members. Individuals within the segment should fit some sort of "typical profile." Given the similarities in specific characteristics, it is likely that members will exhibit similarities in purchase behavior.

Heterogeneity between segments.   This is the test for differences among the various market segments. Segments should be distinctive from one another and have their own "personality." It should be clear which group an individual belongs to based on key attributes. Different segments generally have different needs/buying motives which can be targeted by the marketer.

Sizable population.   Most segmentation studies identify two or more segments for the company to consider pursuing. Over-segmenting a market (dividing the market into a multitude of mini-markets) is extremely costly and generally an ineffective marketing strategy. In some instances, combining two or more small markets is advisable. It is then possible to form a segment of sufficient size to efficiently market products or services to a targeted population. Are there 100 prospects or 100,000 for your good or service?

Meaningful segment data. For segmentation formation to be effective, the "acid test" is the value of this marketing information. Good market segmentation research provides the marketer with operational data that is practical, usable, and can readily be translated into strategy.

5) BASES FOR SEGMENTATION

Markets can be segmented in a variety of ways. There is no one clear, best method. It depends on a company's given marketing situation and the type of information needed by management. A segmentation base is a dimension for segmenting a market, and in most cases, several bases will be considered simultaneously to provide the best possible customer profile. One dichotomy for classifying segmentation dimensions is physical versus behavioral attributes.

Physical attributes commonly used in segmenting markets include geography, demography, and socioeconomic factors. Behavioral attributes often used as market segmentation bases include psychographics, product usage, benefits, perceptions and preferences, situations/occasions, media exposure, and the marketing mix factors. Physical attribute segmentation will be discussed in detail in Chapter 4, while behavioral attribute segmentation will be featured in Chapter 5. A brief overview of the major physical and behavioral dimensions follows.

I. The Physical Attributes

Geographics. One of the simplest ways to divide markets is by geographic areas. These segmentation bases can include market scope (global, national, statewide, or local), population density (urban vs. suburban), climate-related factors (sunbelt vs. frostbelt), standardized market area measures (as defined by national marketing research firms), or U.S. Census Bureau classifications.

The key with geographic variables is to determine the market area, based on the needs of the marketer. For example, a Miami-based language training institute specializing in business and conversational Spanish might want to consider expansion to California, Texas, or New York City—areas that also have large Hispanic populations.

Demographics. Simply stated, demographics are statistics dealing with characteristics of a given population. It includes such basic consumer information as the number of individuals or households, age distribution, sex, marital status, family or household size, and ethnic and religious background.

Socioeconomics. Almost always used in conjunction with demographics, socioeconomic variables, as the name implies, deal with social class and economic measures of a population. Typical socioenomic factors analyzed in a segmentation study include education levels, occupation, and household income. Various home ownership measures (such as, ownership vs. rental; type of dwelling—single family, townhouse, condominium, or apartment; home value; length of residence in an area; etc.) often are explored to better understand consumer markets. The combination of demographic and socioeconomic factors are commonly lumped together and called ''demographics'' by researchers.

Through the use of demographics, markets can be assessed by both the number of potential customers and their income levels to approximate purchasing power. A local child-care center was considering relocation. Through analyzing census tracts to find areas where a significant number of upscale working mothers with children less than six years old resided, it was possible to select a new site for the business.

The above segmentation bases are primarily consumer-oriented. For industrial marketing (selling products or services to businesses), geographic segmentation is a major physical dimension used in analysis. Designated sales territories and/or market areas can be readily identified and evaluated for marketing potential and segmentation viability. Other important physical dimensions which can be employed in segmentation analysis include Standard Industrial Classification (SIC) codes, location, size of prospective customer, and personal demographics of key business decision-makers. Segmenting industrial markets is the scope of Chapter 6.

II. Behavioral Attribute Segmentation

Psychographics. Also often referred to as lifestyle analysis, psychographics tries to classify consumers by their attitudes, feelings, and personality, as opposed to just demographic statistical data. Psychographic analysis recognizes that individuals who have similar interests, enjoy similar activities, and have a similar outlook on life should be grouped together for marketing purposes—while others demographically alike, but "mentally different," will be less likely to respond similarly to marketing initiatives.

Used in conjunction with demographics, however, this approach can be a powerful tool in painting a realistic profile of designated market segments. In a recent retail market study, psychographics was one of three major segmenting dimensions used to generate unique customer profiles distinguishing department store shoppers from those who prefer discount stores.

Product Usage. This base analyzes consumption of a good or service and classifies users into different market segments. A typical classification for a market might be heavy users vs. average users vs. light users vs. non-users. Appropriate marketing strategies revealed from an examination of purchasing habits may show that your firm should:

- Target heavy users, since they account for the lion's share of industry sales (note: this group will also be of prime interest to the competition, however).
- Attempt to increase consumption in one of the other segments.
- Use a hybrid strategy. Go after both heavy users and one or more of the other segments with a differentiated marketing approach.

If peanut butter were the product category you were competing in, you would observe that the heavy user segment would consist largely of families with children under age eighteen. Any of the three strategies proposed above may be appropriate in the right situation. The exact strategy selected will depend on several factors, including further research to be conducted, your present marketing situation, and management's objectives.

Benefits. This is one of the most accurate means for pinpointing what consumers are seeking, although often one of the more difficult segmentation bases to measure. The marketer must try to determine precisely what the prospect wants or needs, as the individuals will buy products from the company that can best provide these benefits.

Take the airline industry as an example. People fly different airlines for a variety of reasons. These include: economy, good service, catering to the business traveler, flying to the "right" destinations, the airline's reputation, etc. Benefits sought by one segment may differ considerably from benefits desired by another customer group.

Product usage and benefit segmentation apply to industrial applications as well as consumer markets. Psychographics which explore human emotions, are typically thought of as consumer-oriented. However, the industrial marketer must realize that people are behind all business decisions, and the astute planner considers personal factors in the decision process as well.

Other Behavioral Dimensions. Perceptions and preferences, situations/occasions, media exposure, and marketing mix element segmentation provide other important approaches to defining and understanding markets (see Chapter 5).

6) DATA COLLECTION

The first five elements discussed are the planning guidelines for the segmentation study. The next step is to determine the best method for gathering the information desired. Prior to data gathering however, one needs to be cognizant of the alternative research methods available. The first step is to assess the value of secondary data—information collected for a purpose other than the current research project—in meeting research objectives.

Trade associations and sources such as *The U.S. Industrial Outlook* or *Standard and Poor's Industry Surveys* can be very helpful in determining the size of the market, major competitors in the industry, and other basic information. Secondary information was used as one determinant of the feasibility of establishing a battery (automobile, truck, industrial) assembling plant in South Florida. Data supplied by the Independent Battery Manufacturers Association and the Battery Council International included such valuable references as statistics annuals, convention proceedings, and *The Battery Man* (a trade journal).

Then, primary data—information collected for a given purpose/project—will have to be assembled. If you were seeking information on consumers' perceptions about your product, a primary research approach would be required. Secondary data would not help in answering such a specific question.

The basic data collection options include face-to-face and telephone interviews, direct mail, focus groups, and observation methods. The data collection form is the research instrument used to collect the marketing information needed (e.g., questionnaires, surveys, observation forms, etc.). They need to be customized to fit the situation at hand. In many segmentation studies, a combination of primary, secondary, and syndicated data (to be discussed shortly) will be used, with multiple data collection methods and forms used for information gathering.

Research: The Key to Segmentation

A good segmentation study is built on objective, workable marketing information. The American Marketing Association defines marketing research as, "the systematic gathering, recording, and analyzing of data about problems relating to the marketing of goods and services." In other words, marketing research is that business activity which can assist the marketer in making sound business decisions. Just as gasoline powers an automobile, marketing information is the energy source that guides the segmentation study. The higher grade the fuel (information), the better the performance of the vehicle (the segmentation study).

The results of segmentation analysis may indictate that your company should make some planning changes or undertake a new marketing approach for particular market segments. This corporate refocus may require strategic or tactical adjustments in the various aspects of the marketing mix. Mistakes in the controllable offerings in any of these areas can span the gamut from costly to disastrous. Marketing research helps to minimize risks (confirm some expectations and dispel others), and is the solid foundation upon which effective segmentation decisions can be based.

Additionally, research improves the odds of an anticipated occurrence actually happening. Put yourself in the shoes of a high-rolling racetrack bettor for a moment. Imagine the value it would be to you knowing that three of the eight horses running in a big race definitely would not win. Although this wouldn't guarantee that your horse would win, your chances have surely increased substantially given this scenario. The same is true of segmentation research. You may not have all the facts about the marketplace, but the knowledge that you now possess about the "field" can greatly enhance your market position.

Primary vs. Secondary Data

The researcher has basically two sources to tap in assembling marketing information, primary and secondary data. In a sense, primary data is a misnomer, since secondary data should generally be sought first. Secondary data should be incorporated into the segmentation project wherever feasible, as it offers tremendous cost and time savings over primary research. Although data manipulation may be required, and publication lags and inappropriate measurement or classification units may be encountered, secondary research is a logical starting point for a segmentation study. Table 3–1 summarizes the major sources of secondary information. The reader is urged to carefully review Appendix A: Sources of Marketing Information, for further details on these references.

Although secondary sources are important for solving "pieces of the puzzle," primary data is required to provide the balance of the marketing information that management needs. For most segmentation studies, primary research will be the major source of information. Behavioral segmentation dimensions such as psychographics, product usage, and benefits are all customized projects demanding specific research for a given situation. Even demographics, which is available from secondary sources, requires updated market measures, projections, and detailed analysis to maximize its value.

Data can be viewed as raw facts, statistics, numbers, or other characters. The goal of the marketing research process is to translate data into meaningful marketing information. Information represents knowledge or intelligence that assists management in making business decisions. To obtain the necessary primary information for strategic planning and control, a systematic research process should be followed. A general framework for such a marketing research project is detailed in Figure 3–4.

The research approach a firm uses will depend greatly on the stage of segmentation analysis that the firm is in. For example, if a company has never formally analyzed the marketplace to derive potential target segments, exploratory research is recommended. The purpose of this research is to obtain as much market information that may be relevant to the situation as possible. Since precise information needs are indeterminable at this stage, secondary sources will play a prominent role in the research. As the market information is sifted through and a better understanding of basic relationships becomes evident, primary research projects can be undertaken.

At the other extreme is the well-versed company which has defined and described the market in terms of segment profiles (perhaps through demographics, psychographics, product usage criteria, or a combination of bases). A need for a higher level segmentation analysis is called for. A causality design can be introduced, whereby purchase behavior is linked

Table 3-1:

Secondary Sources of Marketing Information

Category	References
Trade Journals	Ulrich's International Periodicals Directory, Standard Rate and Data Service—Business Publications Rates and Data, Bacon's Publicity Checker, Writer's Market, and IMS/Ayer Directory of Publications
Trade Journals (Special Issues)	Harfax Guide to Industry Special Issues, Special Issues Index, Ulrich's Irregular Serials and Annual
Business Indexes	Predicasts F&S Index, Business Periodicals Index, Wall Street Journal Index, New York Times Index
Directories	Encyclopedia of Associations, National Trade and Professional Associations of the U.S., Findex Directory of Marketing Research Reports, Thomas Register, MacRAE's Blue Book, State Industrial Directories, Standard and Poor's Directories, Dun and Bradstreet Directories, Directory of Directories
Statistical Sources	U.S. Industrial Outlook, Standard and Poor's Industry Surveys, Predicasts Forecasts, Department of Commerce publications, County Economic Data
Computerized Data Bases	Predicasts' series, ABI Inform, Trade and Industry, etc.
Other	Note demographic sources discussed in Appendix A

While the table above lists specific sources for marketing information, in many cases additional leg work is required. For example, trade journal references can be consulted to determine the alternative periodicals in an industry. These publications then have to be obtained. Similarly, business indexes are helpful for locating citations or abstracts, but specific articles then must be researched in collecting the desired information.

Figure 3–4:

The Marketing Research Process

1) Specify problem(s)/objectives of the study.

2) Determine what is presently known and what information is needed. Formulate possible hypotheses and consider the impact of alternative courses of action.

3) Design a survey instrument (personal or telephone interview, mail or self-administered questionnaire, focus group, observation forms, Delphi technique, etc.).

4) Design the appropriate sample for the survey.

5) Collect the data (the fieldwork).

6) Analyze the data.

7) Prepare a report of the findings. This does not have to be a formal report, but rather a written document that provides direction in using the information gathered.

to isolated variables. Benefit segmentation or perceptual research often try to establish this cause and effect relationship. Although this latter approach may seem to be ideal, it has some drawbacks. The research is much more complex, since it uses sophisticated multivariate analytical techniques, it is more costly, and identified segments may be more difficult to reach than through traditional descriptive segment profiles.

Segmentation research can take many forms. It can vary from an initial full-blown or baseline study to an investigation into one or more aspects of a market. Some compromises may often be necessary, recognizing the company's research needs and budgetary constraints. Ongoing or periodic studies should also be planned, given the dynamic nature of markets.

Although at times it can be costly, research should be a high priority in a firm's marketing budget. The alternative to research is trial and error. Can your company afford the cost of failure through guess work? The cost of "missing the boat" is often much greater than the cost of solid information. Marketing research can be thought of as a high-yielding cash value insurance policy. It can protect the company from marketing mistakes, but also return great dividends through identifying potential new opportunities. Despite the inherent value of research, there is still a place for "gut feel" in the business environment. Intuition through years of experience can provide a stimulus for the creative implementation of basic findings. This "judgment call" may at times be the difference between what works and what doesn't.

Syndicated Services: The Hybrid Approach

Secondary sources generally will solve part of the problem, and primary research is complex and costly. Is there an alternative or middle ground? Perhaps. Syndicated or standardized information services sometimes can be of great value in meeting a firm's research needs.This hybrid approach is a cross between primary and secondary sources, at fees considerably below custom research projects. Essentially, syndicated research is cooperative information. Two or more companies are purchasing related information from a common research supplier. One of the best known marketing research firms offering syndicated services is the A.C. Nielsen Company. Nielsen, the largest marketing research company in the world based on revenues, and now part of the Dun and Bradstreet Corporation, provides standardized services through several of its divisions, including The Food and Drug Index and The National Television Index (Nielsen TV Ratings).

There are some research firms specializing in syndicated segmentation services as well. Examples of some of the companies offering such services are listed in Table 3-2.

Although these and other companies (e.g., CACI's ACORN service and Dun and Bradstreet's Market Identifiers) provide valuable information which can greatly enhance segmentation findings, when used in isolation the information provided is generally insufficient for adequate segmentation analysis. Additional primary and secondary data is needed to present the total picture. An additional shortcoming of the syndicated services (in particular, the lifestyle services) is the fact that they are market-driven, as opposed to product-driven (recognize consumer characteristics only, and don't consider key attributes about specific product categories or individual product items). This will be addressed further in Chapter 5, in the psychographics and lifestyle section. For additional information on the services provided by the syndicated services and other marketing research firms specializing in market segmentation, see Appendix B: Companies Providing Market Segmentation Services and the examples in Chapters 4 and 5.

Table 3–2:		
Syndicated Segmentation Services		
Company	Service Name	Description
Donnelley Marketing Information Services	ClusterPlus	Forty-seven Lifestyle clusters
Claritas	PRIZM	Forty Neighborhood lifestyle clusters through geo-demographic targeting
Yankelovich Clancy Shulman	Monitor	Fifty-two Social trends relevant to consumer marketing
SRI International	VALS	Nine Values and Lifestyle segments of Americans
Simmons Market Research Bureau	Study of Media and Markets	Surveys media habits, product consumption, demographics and lifestyles relating to 750 product classes, 3,500 brands & seven media

An Assessment: Primary, Secondary, or Syndicated Sources

The bottom line is that a company should use whatever source of information that can best meet its needs at a cost it can afford. Typically, this will mean a combination of primary and secondary sources. This research can either be conducted in-house through the marketing research department or contracted to a commercial marketing research firm or marketing consultant. Syndicated services should also be considered, subject to the scope of the information needs.

Additionally, universities can be of great value in designing and/or implementing segmentation studies. Many universities have research bureaus or specialized business centers that can provide advice and technical assistance for such projects. And of course, marketing faculty can be an excellent source for obtaining consultants specializing in segmentation analysis.

7) SAMPLING PROCEDURES

Sampling is a most efficient and effective means of collecting information from a given population. By using a sampling approach, data can be projected to provide a realistic profile of a market at a minimal cost. The objective of sampling is to minimize research errors, provide data reliability, and produce representative findings. Major considerations involved in designing the research sample include the sampling frame, alternative sampling techniques, and the sample size.

The sampling frame is the master listing of population elements to be evaluated. It is presumed that the sampling frame is similar to the total population under study. In a marketing research study for a major automobile dealership, a sampling frame of 1,900 recent car buyers from the past five years was used. Obviously, this was not the total unit sales of a specific automobile nameplate for this period, but rather one dealer's roster. The sampling frame is that subsample upon which a sample can be drawn.

The next decision is the selection of a sampling process. There are two broad categories to choose from: nonprobability or probability samples. Nonprobabilistic samples are the simplest and least expensive to use. These include convenience, judgment, and quota samples. The second group consists of probabilistic samples which are more objective, difficult to administer, and costly than the former group. Random, stratified, cluster, and systematic samples are some of the most frequently used probability-based samples. Figure 3–5 provides a brief description of these sampling processes.

The size of the ideal sample is difficult to specify, and depends on several factors. Among these include the type of sampling techniques selected, the data analysis approach used, the population characteristics, and the time, budget, and marketing researchers available for the study.

8) DATA ANALYSIS

Once the data has been gathered, it must be analyzed to provide meaningful information to the marketer. However, data analysis begins before the

Figure 3–5:

Types of Samples

I. Nonprobabilistic Samples

Convenience samples. Participation based on being near the study.

Judgment samples. Expert opinions used or supposed representativeness built into the study.

Quota samples. Key characteristics of the sample match those of the population.

II. Probabilistic Samples

Random samples. Every population element has an equal chance of participating in the study.

Stratified samples. The population is grouped into two or more subsets, and all subsets are then randomly sampled.

Cluster samples. The population is again grouped into subsets, but whole subsets are sampled separately.

Systematic samples. This is one of the easiest and best approaches to probability sampling. After a random start, every nth element (e.g., every 5th, 20th, or appropriate number) is systematically selected for inclusion in the sample.

data is collected. To maximize the value of the findings, the researcher should have a clear understanding of what information is being sought. Blank data tables can be developed to provide a research model for the segmentation analysis.

For primary research, data analysis consists of three major procedures; coding, tabulating, and statistical analysis. Coding simplifies further analysis by classifying responses into predetermined categories. Tabulating, a basic data analysis procedure, provides the researcher with a mechanism to assess general relationships for key marketing variables. One of the most important data analysis techniques available, cross-tabulation, extends the value of tabulation by studying inter-relationships among groups of marketing variables. Statistical computations can span the gamut from simple analysis (e.g., computing means, variances, or percentages) to advanced analyses (the multivariate techniques). Appendix 3–1 provides a non-technical summary of the major multivariate techniques used in segmentation analysis. In data analysis, practicality is of the essence. A complex segmentation model is not advisable if a simpler design adequately provides the required information.

For secondary research, data analysis often means updating and verifying information, manipulating figures, and adapting the data to appropriate units of measure for the given study.

9) COST FACTORS

In designing the research plan for the segmentation analysis, management's primary concern is minimizing costs. A decision has to be made on whether the research will be conducted in-house (Is there the requisite skills and time available for the project?) or through an outside agency (for example, a marketing research/consulting firm). A project conducted in-house is generally less expensive, since labor and related project expenses can be better controlled. A cost/benefit tradeoff often exists in this situation. Management must ascertain the opportunities and risks in the marketplace, as well as the impact of a potentially wrong decision. In many cases, a hybrid approach may be desirable. The company may have the resources to assist in the segmentation analysis, but experienced advisors can be consulted to design the research plan, supervise the data collection process, and/or analyze the research data.

The expected value of the information must also be considered. A $50,000 research project should not be authorized if it is likely that the study will provide only $25,000 worth of answers. In many cases, the value of the information is difficult to assess. However, if a precedent exists, it is possible to select those projects which appear promising. In summary, near-perfect information is preferable to perfect information in most business situations, when cost factors are recognized.

10) KNOW HOW THE INFORMATION WILL BE USED

This element relates directly to the first one, research objectives. Carefully prepared objectives provide you with clues to many of the answers to questions asked by management. In the course of the analysis, it is likely that the researcher will discover other interesting findings. The key however, is the usefulness of the information. Interesting facts or statistics are not important unless they can be used for marketing planning, strategy, or evaluative purposes.

Another consideration is the "real" purpose of the information. Research is sometimes authorized in order to justify a preconceived opinion, attitude, or position held on a subject by management. In such an instance, unless the findings agree with the established notion, the results of the research project will be downplayed or ignored. Marketing information serves a definite purpose in the business world. It reduces uncertainty and provides a knowledge base upon which marketing decisions can be made. The bottom line is that the information must be practical, workable, and utilized.

The ten points discussed in this chapter are the key planning and research guidelines for successfully conducting a market segmentation analysis. However, segmentation projects require more than just following a series of steps. Since every project is unique, sound planning and research procedures are critical. Other factors also can play a significant role in the analysis, and must be scrutinized. These include the personnel employed, management's values, past marketing efforts, competitive actions, and perceived opportunities and threats.

SEGMENTATION SUMMARY SHEET: PLANNING THE ANALYSIS

The ten required elements of a good segmentation plan

1) Establish research objectives
   - purpose of the project
   - determining what you want to accomplish

2) Specify target population measurement units
   - customer descriptions

3) State relevant definitions
   - market trade or service area

4) a. Recognize segmentation viability (the 4 Rs)

   Can the market be *rated?*
   Is the market *realistic* in size?
   Can customers be easily *reached?*
   Will customers *respond* to marketing initiatives?

   b. Segment formation
      - homogeneity within the segment
      - heterogeneity between segments
      - sizable population
      - meaningful segment data

5) Select segmentation bases
   - physical (geography, demography, socioeconomic)
   - behavioral (psychographics, product usage, benefits, etc.)

6) Data collection
   - secondary, primary, and syndicated data
   - the seven step research process
   - use a combination approach (various sources of information)

7) Employ sampling procedures
   - nonprobabilistic vs. probabilistic samples

8) Analyze the data
   - coding, tabulating, statistical analysis
   - do not use a complex model if it is not needed
9) Consider budgetary constraints
   - in-house vs. outside vendors
   - recognize cost/benefit tradeoffs (anticipate expected value of research)
10) Know how the information will be used
   - planning objectives are critical
   - information must be practical, workable, and utilized

APPENDIX 3-1:

Multivariate Statistical Techniques

The following synopsis provides a non-technical overview of analytical techniques frequently employed in sophisticated segmentation studies. These techniques will be briefly reviewed, emphasizing the practical approach to market segmentation. This is not to say that these techniques are not practical—they can be—when used in the right situation by experienced researchers. However, they will generally only be used once a basic understanding of a market exists. In this capacity, they can be very helpful for enhancing and complementing prior segmentation findings. The objective of this appendix is not to explain how to use multivariate analysis (that is a book in itself), but rather to acquaint the marketing planner with potential applications for these procedures. The interested reader is advised to consult advanced marketing research or statistics texts for further information on multivariate statistical techniques.

These are the major multivariate options.

Factor Analysis. In summary, factor analysis is a marketing research technique that analyzes a series of variables and reduces them to a smaller number of key factors to better explain a given marketing situation. Factor analysis is useful in psychographic and benefit research segmentation. There are two major types of factor analyses used in market segmentation studies.

R-factor analysis reduces the amount of data by finding similarities in responses to particular variables. Q-factor analysis (the more important customer segmenting means) finds groupings of people who respond similarly to selected questions.

Cluster Analysis. Under this procedure, a group of variables (e.g., demographic, socioeconomic, and psychographic bases) are analyzed, and through clustering techniques, segments can be formed which have similarities in the overall statistical measure, and are therefore likely to exhibit similar purchasing behavior.

Multidimensional Scaling. Also referred to as perceptual mapping, this analytical technique graphically represents product attributes based on consumers' perceptions and preferences for brands, product or service categories, and/or ideal products. The objective of multidimensional scaling is to identify market segments of consumers with similar needs or attitudes toward products. Since more than two attributes cannot be visually depicted in two-dimensional space, variables are computer-reduced to portray appropriate market measures. This technique is frequently used in benefit and perceptual segmentation studies.

Conjoint Measurement. Also called multiple trade-off analysis, this analytical method measures the impact of varying product attribute mixes on the purchase decision. This statistical approach ranks consumer perceptions and preferences toward products. These are then evaluated and grouped for segment homogeneity.

Automatic Interaction Detector (A.I.D.). The marketing "decision tree" is the focus of this analytical tool, whereby a systematic series of dichotomous options are evaluated for relevance to the variable in question. If product usage was the central research issue, the first branch (set of alternatives) might be users versus non-users. Next, the various characteristics of users would be hypothesized and evaluated. Further analysis into heavy, medium, or light users could then be used to determine appropriate segment profiles.

Other Multivariate Techniques. Multiple regression analysis, discriminant analysis, and canonical analysis are also sometimes used in market segmentation analysis.

a) Multiple regression—a mathematical equation is derived measuring a single variable (e.g., product consumption) based on two or more independent variables (e.g., age and household income).

b) Discriminant analysis—useful for comparing differences between segments, discriminant analysis usually is performed through a computer-generated equation. This technique is effective in profiling users vs. non-users, heavy vs. light users, loyal vs. non-loyal customers, or product X vs. product Y buyers, to show a few applications.

c) Canonical analysis—In Myer's and Tauber's book, *Market Structure Analysis,* they state that this multivariate technique "can relate two or more sets of variables, measured across a group of respondents, in both a clustering and predictive way. Other techniques do one or the other, but not both."

PART TWO

How To Segment Markets

CHAPTER FOUR

Physical Attribute Segmentation

Nowadays people can be divided into three classes—the Haves, the Have-Nots, and the Have-Not-Paid-For-What-They-Haves.

Earl Wilson, 1964

How important to the marketer are issues such as:

- Where do potential customers live?
- How old are they?
- What are their income levels?
- What are their occupations and educational backgrounds?
- Are they homeowners or renters?

These critical questions and a host of others can be answered by analyzing the physical attributes of a population. Demographic, socioeconomic, and geographic segmentation bases and variables provide important marketing information about individuals within specific markets.

Segmenting markets by these physical dimensions is a logical starting point for several reasons:

1) The data is relatively easy to obtain.

2) It is less expensive than other forms of segmentation research.

3) It provides a quick snapshot of a market (an understanding of market structure and potential customer segments).

4) Populations can be sampled and accurately projected to represent characteristics of the entire market.

5) The information gathered can be of great value for decision making in many markets.

GEOGRAPHICS

Physical attribute segmentation begins with geographic factors. Where people live, work, and play has a great impact on their purchasing behavior. As Table 4-1 illustrates, regional differences can greatly affect product consumption. Geographic analysis is also one of the simplest methods for dividing markets into possible target segments. Therefore, this approach is the first step to consider when segmenting markets.

Geographic Bases

There is no single, best method for geographically segmenting the market. Factors to consider include the market you're competing in, available company resources (assets, capital, and personnel), competitors' strate-

---

Table 4-1:

Who's Number 1?

The Top U.S. Markets (per capita) for Selected Products

City	Product Class
Atlanta	Antacids and Aspirin
Dallas/Fort Worth	Popcorn
Denver	Vitamins
Grand Rapids	Rat Poison
Indianapolis	Shoe Polish
Miami	Prune Juice
New York	Laundry Soap
New Orleans	Ketchup
Oklahoma	Motor Oil Additives
Philadelphia	Iced Tea
Pittsburgh	Coffee
Portland (Oregon)	Dry Cat Food
Salt Lake City	Candy Bars and Marshmallows
Savannah	MSG and Meat Tenderizers
Seattle	Toothbrushes

Source: SAMI (Selling Areas-Marketing Inc.), FORTUNE Magazine, "© 1985 Time Inc. All rights reserved."

gies, flexibility in the manipulation of the marketing mix variables, and the firm's operating philosophy. Major geographic segmentation dimensions can be grouped into two categories, market scope factors and geographic market measures. Specific geographic bases (sub-groupings) and variables (sub-group elements) to consider are:

I. By Market Scope:

Global Scope. Domestic market only, selected international markets (e.g., Canada or Great Britian), international regional markets (e.g., Latin America or the Far East), or worldwide.

National Scope. Entire U.S. market, regional (Southeast or Pacific Northwest), selected states, or selected metropolitan areas.

Statewide Scope. One state only (author's note: This segmentation strategy has worked very successfully for Publix Super Markets and Burdines Department Stores. See case histories in Part IV for further information.), regional (Southern California), selected counties, or selected cities.

Local Scope. County, municipality, township, zip code and/or a neighborhood focus.

II. By Geographic Market Measures:

Population Density. Urban, suburban, or rural. Levels of population density. Barbecue grills for example, sell well in suburban areas, not cities.

Climate-Related Factors. Sunbelt vs. frostbelt, or other classifications. The product's usage can determine natural geographic markets. For example, suntan lotion can be sold year round in Florida, while ice scrapers require frigid, northern weather conditions.

Standardized Market Area Measures. Arbitron's Areas of Dominant Influence (ADIs), A.C. Nielsen's A,B,C, and D market measures, or Designated Market Areas (DMAs).

Census Classifications. Consolidated Metropolitan Statistical Areas (CMSAs), Primary Metropolitan Statistical Areas (PMSAs), Metropolitan Statistical Areas (MSAs), census tracts, and census blocks are some of the more important geographic breakdowns the marketer needs to be familiar with. See Figure 4–1 for a further discussion of Census Classifications and Standardized Market Measures.

The above classifications provide a basic framework of the most common dimensions upon which geographic market decisions can be based. The

Figure 4–1:

Geographic Market Measures

Analyzing the Acronyms

The Census Classifications

An area qualifies for recognition as a metropolitan statistical area (MSA) in one of two ways: if there is a city of at least 50,000 population, or a Census Bureau-defined urbanized area of at least 50,000 with a total metropolitan population of at least 100,000 (75,000 in New England). In addition to the county containing the main city, an MSA also includes additional counties having strong economic and social ties to the central county, determined chiefly by the extent of the Census urbanized area and census data on commuting to work. An MSA may contain more than one city of 50,000 population and may cross state lines. The previous term ''Standard Metropolitan Statistical Area'' (SMSA) was shortened to MSA.

If an area has more than one million population and meets certain other specified requirements, it is termed a ''Consolidated Metropolitan Statistical Area'' (CMSA). This consists of major components called ''Primary Metropolitan Statistical Areas'' (PMSAs). Many of these PMSAs were formerly recognized as SMSAs.

As of October 12, 1984, there were twenty CMSAs, seventy-one PMSAs, and 257 MSAs defined. Further information on the official standards may be obtained from the Secretary, Federal Committee on Metropolitan Statistical Areas, Population Division, Bureau of the Census, Washington, D.C. 20233. The Editor and Publisher Market Guide and the U.S. Statistical Abstract (see Appendix A) also contain a listing of all of the U.S. CMSAs, PMSAs, and MSAs. Census tracts and blocks, while not acronyms (so far), are very important measures of localized areas. Census tracts are small geographic units with populations of approximately 4–12,000 people, while census blocks provide the finest detail available, data on individual streets. Aggregating tract and block data can provide the neighborhood business (the retailer, bank, or shopping center developer, for example) with precise data to make market decisions. Jim Paris of Urban Decision Systems, Inc. notes that block data is seldom used for demographic analysis, however. He states, ''Few items are available at that level, and what is available is frequently suppressed to avoid violating the privacy of an individual or household.''

Standardized Market Area Measures

The Area of Dominant Influence is a geographic market design that defines each television market exclusive of the others, based on measurable viewing patterns. Arbitron identified 211 ADIs for 1985. The A.C. Nielsen Company defines markets by county size, with A counties being the largest metropolitan areas and D counties the smallest, predominately rural areas. B and C counties fall between the A and D classifications. Nielsen also uses Designated Market Areas (DMAs) to measure television market coverage. DMAs and ADIs are similar in purpose (defining markets), but differ somewhat in market composition.

Source: Much of the data used in the Census Classification section was extracted from the Supplementary Report, *Metropolitan Statistical Areas,* Office of Management and Budget, Bureau of Census. Some of the data on Standardized Market Area Measures is from the *Broadcasting Cablecasting Yearbook 1985.*

categories are not mutually exclusive, however. Within some classifications, more than one variable should be examined, and several forms of geographic bases should be explored and analyzed to maximize the value of the marketing information.

DEMOGRAPHICS AND SOCIOECONOMICS

Demography is the statistical study of human populations and their vital characteristics. Socioeconomic factors, which are closely linked to demographics, are used to analyze a population in terms of economic and social classes. The broad definition of demographics as used in market analysis typically includes both demographic and socioeconomic variables. For illustrative purposes, we will examine these two areas separately (see Table 4–2). Later in this chapter, these segmentation bases will be combined with geographic bases, as geodemographic analysis is explored.

Demographic Bases

Many of the common demographic dimensions are interrelated, or similar, from an analytical perspective. Recognizing this, it is possible to group these variables into four major categories. Since demographic

Table 4–2:

Demographics vs. Socioeconomics

Demographics	Socioeconomics
Population	Education
Number of Households/Families	Occupation
Household Size/Family Size	Income
Age Distribution	Home Ownership Factors:
Family Life Cycle	• homeowner vs. renter
Marital Status	• type of dwelling
Sex	• mobility/stability
Race*	Social Class
Nationality*	
Religion*	

*Author's Note: While race, nationality, and religion are inherent attributes like age and marital status, some demographers feel that in actual practice they are used as if they were related to economics and social class (socioeconomic variables).

analysis has been the traditional approach to market segmentation, and these dimensions are understood by most managers, comments about these bases will be kept brief. It should be noted, however, that prior to conducting demographic or socioeconomic analysis, a geographic market area (as discussed in the first part of this chapter) must be specified.

Group 1: Market Size Factors

This group consists of population, the number of households or families, and household or family size. The key variable that must be gathered in a demographic study is the total population of the market in question. Although total population is not a segmenting variable (since rarely is it feasible to go after the whole market), it acts as a comparative yardstick upon which other dimensions can be evaluated. For example, by knowing the total population in a market, it is possible to state that 16% of the individuals within that market are under eighteen years old.

The number of households or families in an area provides a similar measure. However, instead of determining how many individuals are within a given market, the number of "buying centers" are identified. A doctor looking to expand his practice would find this statistic helpful. If one family member utilized his services, it is likely that the others would follow suit when they needed medical attention.

The third variable within this group, household or family size, is a derivation of the other two. By dividing the number of households or families into the total population, the average household or family size for an area can easily be calculated. In the metropolitan Miami area, the average household size is 2.3 people. Such information can be of great value in assessing market potential, particularly for a company offering goods or services with a widespread appeal.

Group 2: Age and Stage

The underlying premise behind the factors in group two, age distribution and family life cycle, is that individuals classified by certain age groups (e.g., 25-34) or stages in their family life cycle (unmarried; married—no children, young children, or teenagers; or empty nest) would exhibit certain similarities in purchasing behavior. This is evidenced in many product categories. Teenagers purchase a large share of the record albums sold in the U.S., middle-age consumers buy most of the life insurance, and senior citizens account for a disproportionate share of health care expenditures.

Group 3: Men and Women

This grouping looks at marital status and sex categories. Marital status can be an important variable for many marketers. Health club owners, home builders, and travel agents are among those who have recently recognized the significant purchasing power of single people. Due to changing lifestyles—including the high divorce rate, increases in single-parent families, and cohabitation—research into marital status for many markets is required to present a more representative profile of potential customers.

The second half of this grouping looks at the numbers of males and females in a market. While there still are many male- or female-oriented products (Right Guard versus Secret deodorant) or services (nail care) in the marketplace, many changes have occurred in purchasing behavior. A lot of this is due to the redefinition of traditional male-female roles that has taken place as women have entered the labor force in record numbers.

Group 4: Race, Nationality, and Religion

A local advertising slogan proclaims the message, "We're all different, we're all the same." This theme relates well to the variables in group four. There is a great diversity of people in America. We have different ethnic backgrounds, countries of national origin, and religious preferences. These differences can greatly affect individuals' values, beliefs, and needs—and at times, purchasing behavior. Table 4-3, for example, shows that New York City's Hispanics have a highly concentrated purchasing influence on grocery products which can increase a brand's overall market share by 50% or more in that area. In fact, Spanish Origin population is a frequently requested and important demographic variable in many market analyses.

Yet, for some product categories, these differences will have little or no bearing on consumption patterns. There have been more interracial marriages than ever before, religion has been deemphasized by some

---

Table 4-3:

The Leverage of Hispanic "Bloc" Purchasing in N.Y.

Brand	% Non-Hispanic Users	% Hispanic Users	% Total Users
Libby's Canned Fruit	8%	40%	14%
Mazola Salad Oil	19%	67%	25%
Hawaiian Punch	22%	72%	32%
Oscar Meyer Hot Dogs	14%	42%	19%
Breyers Ice Cream	29%	57%	32%
Parkay Margarine	23%	60%	28%
Tang Drink	4%	33%	11%
Vittarroz Rice	1%	33%	5%
Green Giant Frozen Vegetables	11%	66%	15%
CoTylenol Cold Remedy	16%	28%	18%

Reprinted with permission of the American Marketing Association. Elisa Soriano and Dale Dauten, "Hispanic 'Dollar Votes' Can Impact Market Shares," Marketing News, September 13, 1985, p. 45.

people, and cultures and nationalities are assimilating into American society. These forces serve to "blend" America, and minimize differences among people.

Socioeconomic Bases

Just as demographic measures can be combined for discussion purposes into smaller groups, socioeconomic factors also can be viewed as clusters.

Group 1: The Monetary Factors

It is no secret that a person's educational background, occupation, and income are interrelated. There is a direct relationship between these three variables. Generally, the more education a person has, the greater the likelihood of a better position and increased earnings. However, people have varying propensities to buy, and income alone cannot always accurately predict purchase behavior. One certified financial planner recently told me that some of his clients get by on $25,000 a year, while others are "struggling" on $125,000 annually.

One market segment in particular has gained notoriety during the past few years, the young affluent professional sector. As numerous companies have targeted the dual-income baby-boomer generation, such new acronyms as Yuppies (young urban professionals), Yaps (young aspiring professionals), and Yummies (young upwardly mobile mommies) have become part of the marketer's jargon.

However, if you are not careful, this media publicity can backfire on you. A large number of companies have focused their efforts on the Yuppies, even though the estimated size of this market segment hovers around 5% of the population. With so many goods and services chasing this limited customer sub-market, the saturation point can often be quickly reached. Additionally, other potentially profitable market opportunities may be neglected or even missed. The Sears Financial Network (Allstate Insurance, Dean Witter Securities, and Coldwell-Banker Real Estate companies) have recognized that most financial concerns are targeting consumers in the upper 10% income bracket. They have responded by going after middle America, a lucrative market largely ignored by major competitors.

Group 2: Homeownership Factors

Among the variables comprising this group are the issues of homeowner vs. renter, the type of dwelling that households reside in, and household mobility and stability measures. Homeowners are better prospects than renters for a number of products and services. Examples include furniture, major appliances, and wall coverings (products), and lawn care, exterminating, and insurance (services). On the other hand, renters are preferable choices for rental furniture and roommate referral services.

The type of dwelling one lives in also can influence purchase behavior. The owner of a single family home has different needs (and many similar ones as well) for goods and services than the owner of a multi-family dwelling, townhouse, condominium, or the apartment resident.

Household mobility and stability factors are also interesting marketing statistics. The former measures the population turnover (influx and exodus) for an area within a designated time frame. The latter examines the length of time households reside in a given area. According to Donnelley's *Market Profile Analysis,* one major metropolitan area has an average household mobility factor of .32. This means that within the past year, thirty-two out of every 100 residences have changed over (households have either moved in or out). Stability would indicate the percentage or numbers of households that have resided in an area for a given period; for example, less than a year, one to three years, three to five years, or more than five years.

These statistics can arm the marketer with very valuable knowledge. Some of this information can be critical in marketing decision making. Here are some examples:

- A stable community may be difficult to penetrate for a new company in the area. Since the residents tend to be older, they are more likely to be set in their ways.
- In an area with a high turnover ratio it may be easier for a company to attract new customers, but developing long-term customer relationships will probably be more difficult.
- A neighborhood with many new homeowners may be an excellent segment to target for certain types of businesses. See Figure 4–2 for further evidence of this point.

Figure 4–2:

Targeting the New Homeowner

When people move into a new home, they are in a buying mood. They need all sorts of products and services—everything from appliances and wall coverings to a new dentist and dry cleaner. A study of recently moved families conducted for Dataman Information Services indicated:

- New homeowners spend eight to ten times more in their first year in a new home than established residents.
- New residents completely restructure their buying habits within the first thirty to ninety days in their new homes. They will buy more products and services within the first six months than in a normal two-year period.
- They have above-average income, and/or have advanced their income level.
- They are credit-worthy—having just qualified for a mortgage loan.
- They have no point of reference yet. They are looking for businesses to patronize and are receptive to direct mail and telephone solicitation offers.

Reprinted with permission from Dataman Information Services, an Atlanta-based direct mail firm.

Group 3: Social Class

Social class is a reflection and compilation of many of the aforementioned demographic and socioeconomic bases. While space doesn't permit a detailed discussion, a couple of key points need to be made about this variable. Traditionally, the lower-lower to upper-upper social class pyramid was the most common method of categorizing individuals by caste, although this method was somewhat simplistic. Today more advanced cluster-based geodemographic systems are frequently used by major companies throughout the United States. These include services such as Donnelley's Cluster-Plus, Claritas' PRIZM, and CACI's ACORN. These are discussed further in Appendix B: Companies Providing Market Segmentation Services. Donnelley's forty-seven unique ClusterPlus segments are described in Figure 4–3.

Figure 4–3:

ClusterPlus Descriptions

Cluster Code	Demographic Characteristics
S 01	Highest SESI, Highest Income, Prime Real Estate Areas, Highly Educated, Professionally Employed, Low Mobility, Homeowners, Children in Private Schools
S 02	Very High Income, New Homes and Condominiums, Prime Real Estate Areas, Highly Mobile, Well Educated, Professionally Employed, Homeowners, Families with Children
S 03	High Income, High Home Values, New Homes, Highly Mobile, Younger, Well Educated, Professionally Employed, Homeowners, Married Couples, High Incidence of Children, Larger Families
S 04	High Income, High Home Values, Well Educated, Professionally Employed, Married Couples, Larger Families, Highest Incidence of Teenagers, Homeowners, Homes Built in 60's
S 05	High Income, High Home Values, Well Educated, Professionally Employed, Low Mobility, Homeowners, Homes Built in 50's and 60's
S 06	Highest Incidence of Children, Large Families, New Homes, Highly Mobile, Younger, Married Couples, Above Average Income and Education, Homeowners
S 07	Apartments and Condominiums, High Rent, Above Average Income, Well Educated, Professionally Employed, Mobile, Singles, Few Children, Urban Areas

S 08	Above Average Income, Above Average Education, Older, Fewer Children, White Collar Workers
S 09	Above Average Income, Average Education, Households with Two or More Workers, Homes Built in 60's and 70's
S 10	Well Educated, Average Income, Professionally Employed, Younger, Mobile, Apartment Dwellers, Above Average Rents
S 11	Above Average Income, Average Education, Families with Children, High Incidence of Teenagers, Homeowners, Homes Built in 60's, Small Towns
S 12	Highly Mobile, Young, Working Couples, Young Children, New Homes, Above Average Income and Education, White Collar Workers
S 13	Older, Fewer Children, Above Average Income, Average Education, White Collar Workers, Homeowners, Homes Built in 50's, Very Low Mobility, Small Towns
S 14	Retirees, Condominiums and Apartments, Few Children, Above Average Income and Education, Professionally Employed, High Home Values and Rents, Urban Areas
S 15	Older, Very Low Mobility, Fewer Children, Above Average Income and Education, White Collar Workers, Old Housing, Urban Areas
S 16	Working Couples, Very Low Mobility, Above Average Income, Average Education, Home-owners, Homes Built in 50's, Urban Areas
S 17	Very Young, Below Average Income, Well Educated, Professionally Employed, Highly Mobile, Singles, Few Children, Apartment Dwellers, High Rent Areas
S 18	High Incidence of Children, Larger Families, Above Average Income, Average Education, Working Couples, Homeowners

Figure 4-3 (continued)

Cluster Code	Demographic Characteristics
S 19	High Incidence of Children, Larger Families, Above Average Income, Average Education, Younger, Married Couples, Homeowners, Homes Built in 60's and 70's, Primarily Rural Areas
S 20	Areas with High Proportion of Group Quarters Population, Sub-divisions available including College Dormitories, Homes for the Aged, Mental Hospitals and Prisons
S 21	Average Income and Education, Blue Collar Workers, Families with Children, Home-owners, Lower Home Values, Rural Areas
S 22	Below Average Income and Education, Older, Fewer Children, Single Family Homes, Primarily in the South
S 23	Below Average Income, Average Education, Low Mobility, Married Couples, Old Homes, Farm Areas, North Central Region
S 24	Highly Mobile, Young, Few Children, Low Income, Average Education, Ethnic Mix, Singles, Apartments, Urban Areas
S 25	Younger, Mobile, Fewer Children, Below Average Income, Average Education, Apartment Dwellers
S 26	Older, Mobile, Fewer Children, Below Average Income, Average Education, Mobile Homes, Retirees, Higher Vacancy Rates, Primarily Rural Areas
S 27	Average Income and Education, Single Family Homes, Lower Home Values, Homes Built in 50's and 60's
S 28	Below Average Income, Less Educated, Younger, Mobile, High Incidence of Children, Mobile Homes, Primarily Rural Areas

S 29	Older, Low Mobility, High Proportion of Foreign Languages, Average Income, Below Average Education, Old Homes and Apartments, Urban Areas, Northeast Region
S 30	Low Income, Poorly Educated, Higher Vacancy Rates, Families with One Worker, Farms, Rural Areas
S 31	Older, Fewer Children, Low Income, Less Educated, Low Mobility, Retirees, Old Single Family Homes
S 32	Old, Few Children, Low Income, Below Average Education, One-Person Households, Retirees
S 33	Below Average Income, Less Educated, Blue Collar Workers, Manufacturing Plants, Homes Built in 50's and 60's, Very Low Mobility, Low Home Values
S 34	Older, Below Average Income, Average Education, Blue Collar Workers, Low Mobility, Rural Areas
S 35	Old Housing, Low Income, Average Education, Younger, Mobile, Fewer Children, Apartment Dwellers, Small Towns
S 36	Average Income, Less Educated, Blue Collar Workers, Hispanic, Families with Children
S 37	Average Income, Below Average Education, Blue Collar Workers, Manufacturing Areas, High Unemployment, Primarily in the North Central
S 38	Old, Lowest Incidence of Children, Very Low Income, Less Educated, Apartment Dwellers, One-Person Households, Retirees, Urban Areas
S 39	Older, Very Low Mobility, Very Old Housing, Below Average Income and Education, Blue Collar Workers, Manufacturing Areas
S 40	Older, Very Low Income, Less Educated, One-Person Households, Retirees, Few Children, Old Homes and Apartments

Figure 4-3 (concluded)

Cluster Code	Demographic Characteristics
S 41	Below Average Income, Less Educated, Blue Collar Workers, Manufacturing Plants, High Unemployment, Rural Areas
S 42	Low Income, Poorly Educated, Low Mobility, Blue Collar Workers, Manufacturing Plants, Rural South
S 43	Southern Blacks, Families with Children, Single Family Homes, Low Mobility, Low Income, Less Educated, Unskilled, High Unemployment
S 44	Urban Blacks, Very Low Income, Less Educated, High Unemployment, Singles, Mobile, Apartment Dwellers, Large Metro Areas
S 45	Urban Blacks, Very Low Income, Less Educated, Unskilled, High Unemployment, Old Housing
S 46	Poorly Educated, Very Low Income, Hispanic, Families with Children, Apartment Dwellers, Unskilled, High Unemployment
S 47	Lowest SESI, Urban Blacks, Very Low Income, Less Educated, Unskilled, Very High Unemployment, High Incidence of Female Householders with Children, Old Housing

According to Donnelley, knowing in which cluster a consumer lives provides a reasonable means of understanding how that consumer will behave in the marketplace. The product potential index (penetration index average = 100) for a domestic luxury car can be compared by Cluster-Plus segments. Not surprisingly, there are significant differences in potential for this product, ranging from an index of 271 for Cluster S 01 (highly affluent professionals who are homeowners in prime suburban neighborhoods) to a low index of 19 for Cluster S 41 (low income blue collar workers living in the rural fringes of manufacturing areas).

Expanding the Analysis and the Importance of Trends

The demographic and socioeconomic groupings bring order to the basic statistical population measures by clustering factors that exhibit similarities in character. The variables discussed are not the only ones available to the marketer. The Census of Population and Housing identifies a number of additional breakdowns that could be considered, depending on the needs of the study. Appendix 4–1, the American Association of Advertising Agencies' "Recommended Audience Segments for Consumer Media Data," also provides an excellent reference for selecting appropriate demographic variables for segmentation analysis.

Trend analysis is the projection of relevant demographic and socioeconomic variables to predict future characteristics of a market. This additional step is sometimes neglected or relegated to a minor component of the analysis. However, if prudently used, trend analysis can be a powerful marketing tool for intermediate and long-term planning.

Figure 4–4 demonstrates the importance of this technique in analyzing the market potential for two alternative census tracts. Based on 1970 and 1980 population figures, Census Tract B is the more attractive alternative for the marketer (assuming of course, that all other variables are held constant for illustrative purposes). However, this situation is changed dramatically when 1985 data is reviewed and forecasts assessed. As you can see from this graph, trend analysis can be an important component of the segmentation study.

GEODEMOGRAPHICS: THE BEST OF THE MESH

To maximize the value of the physical dimensions, a composite geodemographic model should be used for segmentation analysis. The basic premise behind geodemographics is that the sum of the whole is more powerful

Figure 4–4:

Demographic Trend Analysis for Two Census Tracts

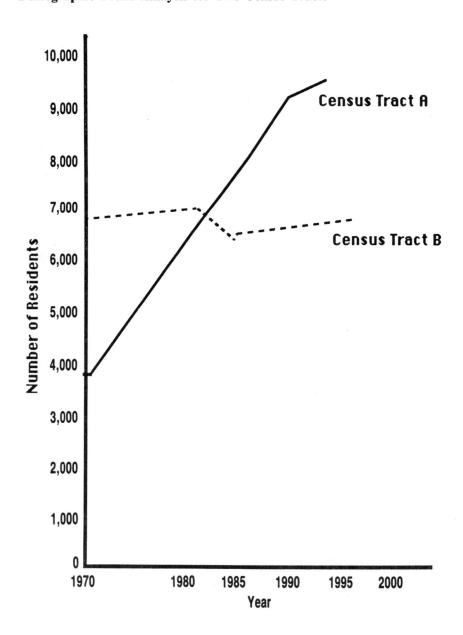

than the individual parts (geography, demographics, and socioeconomic factors). This technique consists of the following four steps:

1) *Define the trade or service area by relevant market scope and/or geographic market measures.* This has been discussed earlier. However, Appendixes 4–2 and 4–3 present further guidelines for defining trade areas for retailers and personal service firms.

2) *Specify pertinent demographic and socioeconomic bases to analyze.* Generally, one or two variables will not be sufficient for segmenting markets. An analysis of all potentially useful dimensions should be planned prior to beginning the analysis. Figure 4–5 gives an example of relevant physical variables to study for a dental practice.

3) *Determine where to obtain the geodemographic data.* This information is available from a variety of sources. These include public and academic libraries; local, county, or state planning departments or data centers; universities (business development centers and computerized information centers); other computerized services; marketing research/consulting firms; demographic research firms; and in-house primary research projects. The cost of such data can vary from free of charge (excluding the cost of time) to several thousands of dollars, depending on a company's research needs and the scope of the analysis. Appendix 4–4 provides a detailed example of some of the valuable information available from a private-sector demographics firm, Urban Decision Systems.

4) *Analyze and evaluate the marketing information.* This most critical stage depends to a great extent on the three previous ones. The major objective you are pursuing is obtaining practical information. Does it assist you in solving specific marketing problems? If the answer to this question is no, it is likely that the study was not planned out as well as it could have been. Assuming the study provided the needed information, the next step is to translate the findings into segmentation strategy.

DEMOGRAPHICS OR GEODEMOGRAPHICS?

Throughout this chapter, we have treated geographics, demographics, and socioeconomics as three separate entities. This was done to better illustrate both the differences and similarities among these physical dimensions. More commonly, however, marketers lump the three together for

Figure 4–5:

Typical Segmentation Variables for Dental Practices

Variables	Categories
Geographic	
Distance traveled to get to dental office	Radius expressed in blocks or miles
Place from which patient usually comes to office	Home, Work, Shopping Area
Demographic	
Age	0–6, 7–17, 18–25, 26–40, 41–55, 56–65, 66 and over
Sex	Male, Female
Family Size	Young, single; young, married, no children; young, married, preschool children; young, married, youngest child age 6 or more; older, married, children under age 18; older, married, no children under age 18; older, single; other
Race	Caucasian, Black, Oriental, Other
Ethnicity	Latin American, Southeast Asian, German, Scandinavian, Italian, Eastern European, Middle Eastern, Japanese, Other
Socioeconomic	
Income	Under $15,000; $15,000–$24,999; $25,000–$35,000; over $35,000
Occupation	Student, homemaker, blue collar worker, white collar worker, professional, executive, retired, unemployed
Education	Less than four years high school, high school graduate, some college, college graduate, more than four years college
Social Class	Lower-lower, upper-lower, lower-middle, middle-middle, upper-middle, lower-upper, upper-upper

Reprinted from the Dental Marketing Planner, 1983, pp. 69–70, with permission of the American Dental Association.

planning and analysis purposes and use the less technically correct term demographics, as opposed to geodemographics. Not wanting to rock the boat, at this point it is appropriate to stick with marketing convention and further references to demographics will refer to this broader definition.

LOW-COST DEMOGRAPHICS

Good demographic data does not have to be expensive. There are some excellent secondary sources of demographic information that are available at no charge through your local public or university library. These "library demographics" are both underutilized and underestimated as demographic planning tools. It is my belief that library demographics represent one of the best avenues for securing market information for companies with a limited research budget. There are dozens of quality demographic references which are readily obtainable at most public libraries. Table 4–4 shows the widespread acceptance of consumer demographic sources, based on a survey conducted of thirty public and academic libraries throughout the U.S. Appendix A: Sources of Marketing Information consists of brief abstracts of some of the more important sources of consumer and industrial demographics.

Researchers should not limit themselves to libraries in the search for secondary demographic data. There are some other good sources for low- and no-cost demographics as well. These include government agencies (federal, state, and local branches), universities, and various other local sources.

Let's look at some places you can call on to acquire demographic data.

Federal Agencies.   The Census Bureau's publications are reviewed in some detail in Appendix A. These and a host of others are available for purchase at a very reasonable cost from the Washington office or any of the regional data centers. Also, don't neglect other federal agencies. Many times demographic information may be obtained through the Department of Commerce, Small Business Administration, or other government agencies. It is interesting to note that the U.S. government is the single largest gatherer of statistical information in the world. In fact, according to a recent article, "Addicted to Statistics," appearing in *Eastern Review* magazine September 1985, it was stated that "the U.S. government alone spends $1.4 billion a year collecting statistics, and it publishes 6,000 books of them annually."

Table 4–4:

Library Demographics, Consumer Sources

Reference	% Libraries Available At
U.S. Statistical Abstract	100%
Rand McNally Commercial Atlas and Marketing Guide	100%
Sales and Marketing Management's Survey of Buying Power	91%
U.S. Census of Population and Housing	91%
State Statistical Abstract	82%
State Population Censuses	73%
Demographics from Local/County Agencies	68%
Demographics from State Agencies	59%
Donnelley's Market Profile Analysis	27%
CACI's Sourcebook of Demographics and Buying Power	18%
Editor and Publisher Market Guide*	14%
Statistical Reference Index*	14%
REZIDE: National Encyclopedia of Residential Zip Code Demography	14%
Other (nine additional consumer demographic sources were cited)	N/A

*These two sources were not on the original questionnaire. As a result, it is highly likely that these references are more widely available than the survey figures indicate.

State Agencies. While the amount of state-generated statistical information is considerably less than that available in federal publications, this still can be a good source to tap in assembling consumer demographics. A good starting point at the state level is your state data center. All fifty states have a designated data center that can assist marketers in obtaining demographic information. The October 1984 issue of *American Demographics* magazine featured an article entitled "The State of the States' State Data Centers," which can be consulted for further information on this resource.

Local Agencies. There is also a great deal of information available locally to assist in your demographic planning needs. Many cities and counties can provide demographics which are often more pertinent to your situation, since they are localized. For example, a client of mine, who was relocating his office supply store, went to the Dade County Planning Department to "try" to obtain some demographic information. A couple of hours later and only $36 poorer, he left the agency with literally an armful of reports, maps, and statistical publications. This information was vital in making future strategic marketing decisions for his business.

Universities. Colleges and universities can also be a prime source of demographic information. At Florida International University, for example, demographics are available from no less than three different places: the library, the computer center (detailed census information down to the block level is available for a fee), and the Small Business Development Center. This latter source, a co-sponsored project involving the Small Business Administration and forty-three state university systems, often can assist the new or emerging small business in basic demographic analysis. At the FIU Small Business Development Center, for example, a program called CACTUS (Computerized Analysis of Census Tracts Under Study) has been developed which examines twenty-three different demographic variables for all 237 census tracts in Dade County.

Other Sources. Additionally, you can often check with local chambers of commerce, professional associations, shopping center developers or management, and/or the local media to obtain demographic data.

PURCHASED DEMOGRAPHICS

Suppose you don't want to do it yourself. Although some technical assistance may be available from the low-cost sources, most of the data compilation and analysis is your responsibility. What are your other demographic options? You can purchase one of two types of demographic studies; canned or custom demographics. Canned, or packaged, demographics is relatively low-cost data using predetermined census areas or other geographical classifications for virtually all of the recognized demographic variables. Typically, this information is provided by research firms specializing in demographics who have compiled extensive in-house data banks. Since these companies serve many clients, savings can be passed on by utilizing similar formats for most applications. Appendix B provides a listing of services offered by these demographic specialists.

Custom demographics, the more costly alternative, is recommended when your research needs vary markedly from what is generally provided, or further analysis is called for when analyzing a market situation. Demographic consultants may repackage the canned information, analyze it, supplement it with some primary research, and prepare a report of their findings/recommendations for management's review. While you can sometimes obtain canned demographics (numbers only, no analysis) for as low as $100, custom demographics can cost several thousand dollars and up, depending on the scope of the project.

Again, it all goes back to the central issue—your research needs. Perhaps the low-cost demographic sources meet your information needs, but you may need a project consultant to assist in research design and interpretation

---

Figure 4–6:

Segmentation Checklist

Buying Demographics

1) Where does the consultant obtain the demographic data?
2) How current is the information?
3) How accurate is the information?
4) Is assistance in specifying the appropriate demographic variables available?
5) Is assistance in understanding and implementing the findings available?
6) Are projections included?
7) Are graphics provided?
8) How frequently will updates be needed?
9) How practical is the information?
10) How much will it cost?

of the findings. When using demographic consultants, you should always work closely with them to maximize the value of the marketing information. Figure 4-6 provides a list of ten important questions to ask your demographic consultant before starting any project.

One side note. If you are presently computerized (IBM, Apple, or other popular microcomputer), you may want to consider purchasing computerized demographic data bases. Many of the demographic research vendors now offer a wide variety of demographic products (software, maps, etc.) which are particularly good for regular users of this information. Typically, this software is comparable in price to other specialized business applications software (several hundred dollars and up). Again, refer to Appendix B for further details on these products.

SEGMENTATION SUMMARY SHEET: THE PHYSICAL ATTRIBUTES

Advantages of physical attribute segmentation:
- The data is relatively easy to obtain
- It is generally less costly than behavioral information
- It provides a quick snapshot of a market
- It is easily projectable
- It is very useful in marketing decision making

Geographic Bases:

Market Scope	Geographic Market Measures
Global	Population Density
National	Climate-Related Factors
Statewide	Standardized Market Area Measures
Local	Census Classifications

Demographic Bases:

Group 1—Market Size Factors

Group 2—Age and Stage

Group 3—Men and Women

Group 4—Race, Nationality, and Religion

Socioeconomic Bases:

Group 1—Monetary Factors

Group 2—Homeownership Factors

Group 3—Social Class

Expanding the study: Additional variables and trend analysis

The four steps to geodemographic analysis:

1) Define the trade area

2) Specify pertinent demographic and socioeconomic bases and variables

3) Determine where to obtain the data

4) Analyze and evaluate the marketing information

Geodemographics = demographics

Sources of low- and no-cost demographics:

- Libraries
- Government Agencies
- Universities
- Other Sources (chambers of commerce, professional associations, shopping center developers/management, local media)

Purchased demographics: Canned and Custom Demographics

APPENDIX 4–1:

Recommended Audience Segment Data
(1986 Revision)

The following guide provides the latest standard breakdowns for demographic characteristics according to the American Association of Advertising Agencies. The purpose of this guide is to provide advertising and marketing professionals with a tool for collecting and analyzing media and marketing data with comparable reporting standards.

These revised breakdowns reflect recent demographic, economic, and sociological changes in the population. In addition, consideration has also been given to data refinements which will permit the user to further differentiate between the marketing media characteristics of population segments, such as reporting the number of children under the age of eighteen. This type of data will help to distinguish differences between the living patterns of families that have children and those that do not have any children.

This appendix can be used as a handy checklist to be sure that you are considering all demographic variables in your segmentation studies.

Reprinted with permission of the American Association of Advertising Agencies.

AAAA's RECOMMENDED STANDARD SEGMENTS FOR DEMOGRAPHIC CHARACTERISTICS IN SURVEYS OF CONSUMER MEDIA AUDIENCES

DATA TO BE GATHERED AND REPORTED (IF POSSIBLE, TO BE DIRECTLY ACCESSIBLE)

DATA TO BE REPORTED FOR:

CHARACTERISTIC	MINIMUM BASIC DATA TO BE REPORTED	ADDITIONAL DATA — HIGHLY VALUED	PERSONS	HOME-MAKERS	HOUSE-HOLD HEAD	HOUSE-HOLDS
I. PERSONS CHARACTERISTICS						
A. HOUSEHOLD RELATIONSHIP	PRINCIPLE WAGE EARNER IN HH (DEFINES HH HEAD)		x	x	x	
	PRINCIPLE SHOPPER IN HH (DEFINES HOMEMAKER)					
	SPOUSE					
	CHILD					
	OTHER RELATIVE					
	PARTNER/ROOMMATE					
	OTHER NON-RELATIVE					
B. AGE	UNDER 6	2 - 5	x	x	x	
	6 - 11	6 - 8				
	12 - 15	35 - 49				
	16 - 20	25 - 49				
	18 - 20					
	16 OR OLDER					
	18 OR OLDER					
	18 - 24					
	25 - 34					
	35 - 44					
	45 - 49					
	50 - 54					
	55 - 64					
	65 - 74					
	75 OR OLDER					

CHARACTERISTIC	MINIMUM BASIC DATA TO BE REPORTED	ADDITIONAL DATA — HIGHLY VALUED	DATA TO BE REPORTED FOR:			
			PERSONS	HOME-MAKERS	HOUSE-HOLD HEAD	HOUSE-HOLDS
C. SEX	MALE					
	FEMALE		x	x	x	
D EDUCATION	LAST GRADE ATTENDED		x	x	x	
	GRADE SCHOOL OR LESS (GRADE 1-8)					
	SOME HIGH SCHOOL					
	GRADUATED HIGH SCHOOL					
	SOME COLLEGE (AT LEAST 1 YEAR)					
	GRADUATED COLLEGE	ANY POST GRADUATE WORK				
	IF CURRENTLY ATTENDING SCHOOL	— (IF PERTINENT TO STUDY) —				
		LIVE HOME				
		LIVE AWAY				
		— LIVE IN STUDENT HOUSING				
		— LIVE OFF CAMPUS				
	FULL-TIME STUDENT					
	PART-TIME STUDENT					
E MARITAL STATUS	MARRIED	SPOUSE PRESENT	x	x	x	
		SPOUSE ABSENT				
	WIDOWED					
	DIVORCED OR SEPARATED	SPOUSE WORKING				
	SINGLE (NEVER MARRIED)					
	PARENT	ENGAGED				
	PREGNANT					
	'LIVING TOGETHER'					

CHARACTERISTIC	MINIMUM BASIC DATA TO BE REPORTED	ADDITIONAL DATA — HIGHLY VALUED	DATA TO BE REPORTED FOR:			
			PERSONS	HOME-MAKERS	HOUSE-HOLD HEAD	HOUSE-HOLDS
F. RELIGION — POLITICAL		PROTESTANT [ACTIVE (Practicing) / INACTIVE (Non-Practicing)] CATHOLIC / JEWISH / OTHER / NONE / POLITICAL — CONSERVATIVE / — LIBERAL / — MODERATE	x	x	x	
G. RACE	WHITE / BLACK / OTHER		x	x	x	
H. PRINCIPLE LANGUAGE SPOKEN AT HOME	ENGLISH / SPANISH / OTHER		x	x	x	
H1. OTHER LANGUAGES SPOKEN AT HOME	ENGLISH / SPANISH / OTHER		x	x	x	

CHARACTERISTIC

I. INDIVIDUAL EMPLOYMENT INCOME

MINIMUM BASIC DATA TO BE REPORTED

UNDER $10,000

$10,00 - 14,999

$15,000 - 19,999

$20,000 - 24,999

$25,000 - 29,999

$30,000 - 39,999

$40,000 - 49,999

$50,000 - 74,999

$75,000 AND OVER

IEI BY QUINTILE

INCOME INTERVAL

QUINTILE	% ADULTS	LOW - HIGH	MEDIAN INCOME
1	20	— 10.156	6.391
2	20	10.757 19.999	13.959
3	20	20.000 29.999	24.953
4	20	30.000 43.243	34.967
5	20	43.244 —	60.150

ADDITIONAL DATA — HIGHLY VALUED

$75,000 - 99,000

$100,000 AND OVER

IEI INCOME BY QUINTILE AS DETERMINED BY THE SURVEY ZIPTILES

OTHER INCOME

DATA TO BE REPORTED FOR:

	PERSONS	HOME-MAKERS	HOUSE-HOLD HEAD	HOUSE-HOLDS
$75,000 - 99,000	x	x	x	

CHARACTERISTIC	MINIMUM BASIC DATA TO BE REPORTED	ADDITIONAL DATA — HIGHLY VALUED	DATA TO BE REPORTED FOR:			
			PERSONS	HOME-MAKERS	HOUSE-HOLD HEAD	HOUSE-HOLDS
J. OCCUPATION AS DEFINED BY BUREAUS OF THE CENSUS	ARMED FORCES					
	CIVILIAN LABOR FORCE		x	x	x	
	EMPLOYED	HOLD MORE THAN ONE JOB				
	— FULL TIME (35 or More Hours Per Week)					
	— PART TIME (Less than 35 Hours Per Week)					
	SELF EMPLOYED	IN HOME / OUT-OF HOME				
	UNEMPLOYED — LOOKING FOR WORK	PRIVATE COMPANY / GOVERNMENT				
	MAJOR OCCUPATIONAL CATEGORIES					
	— MANAGERIAL PROFESSIONAL	PREDOMINANTLY — DAY WORK / — EVENING/NIGHT WORK				
	— TECHNICAL	TECHNICAL RELATED SUPPORT OCCUPATIONS				
	— ADMIN SUPPORT (INCL CLERICAL)					
	— SALES					
	— OPERATIVE, NON-FARM LABORERS, SERVICE WORKERS, PRIVATE HOUSEHOLD WORKERS					
	— FARMERS, FARM MANAGERS, FARM LABORERS					
	— CRAFTSMEN					
	— OTHER					
	INDUSTRY OF EMPLOYMENT					
	JOB TITLE					
	NOT EMPLOYED					
	RETIRED					
	STUDENT (FULL TIME)					
	HOMEMAKER (Not Employed Outside Home)					
	DISABLED					
	TEMPORARILY UNEMPLOYED					
	OTHER					

II. HOUSEHOLDS CHARACTERISTICS

CHARACTERISTIC	MINIMUM BASIC DATA TO BE REPORTED	ADDITIONAL DATA — HIGHLY VALUED	PERSONS	HOME-MAKERS	HOUSE-HOLD HEAD	HOUSE-HOLDS
A. COUNTY SIZE	A COUNTY B COUNTY C COUNTY D COUNTY		X	X	X	X
B. GEOGRAPHIC AREA AS DEFINE BY BUREAU OF THE CENSUS	INSIDE METROPOLITAN STATISTICAL AREA — MSA CENTRAL CITY — MSA SUBURBAN — MSA OTHER OUTSIDE METROPOLITAN STATISTICAL AREA URBAN RURAL	METROPOLITAN STATISTICAL AREA POPULATIONS 4,000,000 AND OVER 1,000,000 — 3,999,999 500,000 — 999,999 250,000 — 499,999 100,000 — 249,999 50,000 — 99,999 URBAN: URBANIZED AREA — CENTRAL CITY — URBAN FRINGE — OTHER URBAN — PLACES OF 10,000 — 50,000 POPULATION — PLACES OF 2,500 — 9,999 POPULATION				
C. GEOGRAPHIC REGION	AS DEFINED BY BUREAU OF THE CENSUS — NORTHEAST — NORTH CENTRAL — SOUTH — WEST NIELSEN GEOGRAPHIC AREAS — NORTHEAST — EAST CENTRAL — WEST CENTRAL — SOUTH — PACIFIC	CENSUS GEOGRAPHIC DIVISION — NEW ENGLAND — MID ATLANTIC — EAST NORTH CENTRAL — WEST NORTH CENTRAL — SOUTH ATLANTIC — EAST SOUTH CENTRAL — WEST SOUTH CENTRAL — MOUNTAIN — PACIFIC MAJOR MARKET UNDUPLICATED TV COVERAGE AREAS	X	X	X	X
D. PRESENCE/AGE OF CHILDREN IN HOUSEHOLD	NO CHILDREN UNDER 18 YOUNGEST CHILD 6-17 YOUNGEST CHILD UNDER 6	YOUNGEST CHILD 12-17 YOUNGEST CHILD 6-11 YOUNGEST CHILD 2-5 YOUNGEST CHILD UNDER 2	X	X	X	X
E. HOUSEHOLD TYPE		FAMILY MEMBERS ONLY NON-FAMILY MEMBERS ONLY BOTH FAMILY AND NON-FAMILY MEMBERS	X	X	X	X

CHARACTERISTIC	MINIMUM BASIC DATA TO BE REPORTED	ADDITIONAL DATA — HIGHLY VALUED	DATA TO BE REPORTED FOR:			
			PERSONS	HOME-MAKERS	HOUSE-HOLD HEAD	HOUSE-HOLDS
F HOUSEHOLD SIZE	1 MEMBER 2 MEMBERS 3 MEMBERS 4 MEMBERS	NUMBER OF ADULTS (Persons 18 and Over) MALE/FEMALE HH FEMALE ONLY HH MALE ONLY HH	X	X	X	X
G NUMBER OF CHILDREN UNDER 18 IN HOUSEHOLD	NONE ONE MORE THAN ONE	NUMBER OF CHILDREN 6 - 17 NUMBER OF CHILDREN UNDER 6 NUMBER OF CHILDREN BY HOUSEHOLD SIZE	X	X		X
H HOUSEHOLD INCOME	SEE I, INDIVIDUAL EMPLOYMENT INCOME	$ 75,000 - 99,999 $100,000 AND OVER HOUSEHOLD INCOME BY QUINTILE AS DETERMINED BY SURVEY ZIPTILES	X	X	X	X
I OTHER HOUSEHOLD CHARACTERISTICS		NUMBER OF ADULTS EMPLOYED FULL TIME	X	X	X	X
J HOME OWNERSHIP	OWN HOME — PRIVATE OWNERSHIP — COOPERATIVE OWNERSHIP — CONDOMINIUM RENT HOME	RESIDENCE FIVE YEARS PRIOR TO SURVEY — LIVED IN SAME HOUSE/HOME — LIVED IN DIFFERENT HOUSE/HOME — IN SAME COUNTY — IN DIFFERENT COUNTY — IN SAME STATE — IN DIFFERENT STATE	X	X	X	X
K TYPE HOUSING UNIT	SINGLE FAMILY HOME MULTIPLE FAMILY HOME APARTMENT MOBILE HOME OR TRAILER		X	X	X	X

NOTE: THE RECOMMENDED MINIMUM AND ADDITIONAL DATA STANDARDS APPLY TO GENERALIZED SURVEYS THOSE SURVEYS DONE TO MORE SPECIFIC PURPOSES—E.G. PARTICULAR GEOGRAPHIC SECTIONS OF THE COUNTRY, AFFLUENT MARKETS, PUBLICATIONS DIRECTED TOWARDS A SPECIFIC TARGET, ETC.—MAY CHOOSE TO COLLAPSE OR EXPAND CHARACTERISTIC SEGMENTS AS APPROPRIATE TO THEIR CONTEXT

APPENDIX 4–2:

Defining Your Trade Area

The following outline presents guidelines for defining trade areas. Remember, these are guidelines only—specific retailers may use different definitions.

Trade areas are usually divided into two and sometimes three segments:

- *Primary Trade Area*—the trade area from which the store receives approximately 75% of its customers—the area immediately surrounding the store.

- *Secondary Trade Area*—the trade area from which the store receives an additional 15–25,o of its customers—an area more distant from the store than the primary trade area. Many retailers only use these first two segments, thus secondary trade area would encompass approximately 25% of store customers.

- *Tertiary Trade Area*—the remaining area from which the store may be drawing customers (generally less than 10% of its customers).

These segments apply to any type of retail and most types of service operations. However, the size of the segments will vary depending upon the type of product/service sold and the type of area in which the store is/will be located. The following chart divides retail stores into one of two categories, based primarily on the type of products sold at the store. There may, however, be some overlap.

1. *Convenience Goods*—products/services which consumers purchase on a regular/repeat basis. Consumers will not normally travel great distances for convenience goods.

Retail Examples: Grocery Stores, Convenience Stores, Auto Aftermarket, Fast Food Restaurants, Drug Stores, Liquor Stores, Hardware Stores, Ice Cream Shops, etc.

Service Examples: Banks, Savings and Loan Associations, Photo Stores, Hair Salons, etc.

2. *Shopping Goods*—these are usually products/services which are higher ticket items, purchased on an irregular basis—greater distances will normally be traveled.

Examples: Furniture Stores, Department Stores, Catalog Stores, Variety Stores, Shoe Stores, Apparel Stores, Clothing Stores, Appliance Stores,

Home Improvement Centers, Toy Stores, Full Service Restaurants, etc.
The following are guidelines for trade area sizes for these store categories, by type of area in which the store will be located:

DEFINING TRADE AREAS

CONVENIENCE GOODS	Radius	SHOPPING GOODS	Radius
Urban Area		**Urban Area**	
Primary	1 Mile	Primary	3 Miles
Secondary	2 Miles	Secondary	5 Miles
Tertiary	3 Miles	Tertiary	10 Miles
Suburban Area		**Suburban Area**	
Primary	1 Mile	Primary	10 Miles
Secondary	3 Miles	Secondary	15 Miles
Tertiary	5 Miles	Tertiary	20 Miles
Rural Area		**Rural Area**	
Primary	2 Miles	Not Applicable	
Secondary	5 Miles	"	
Tertiary	8 Miles	"	

The same type of trade area segmentation should be applied to shopping centers. Basically there are three types of shopping centers: Neighborhood—primarily convenience shopping; Community—a mix of stores offering both convenience and shopping goods; and Regional Centers—primarily shopping goods. As an example, you would most likely find a grocery store in a Neighborhood or Community Shopping Center, not in a Regional Mall. On the other hand, it is very rare to find a full-line department store in a Neighborhood Center. Thus trade area segment size for shopping centers will follow the same pattern as for stores which are their tenants.

APPENDIX 4–3:

Geometric Trade Areas

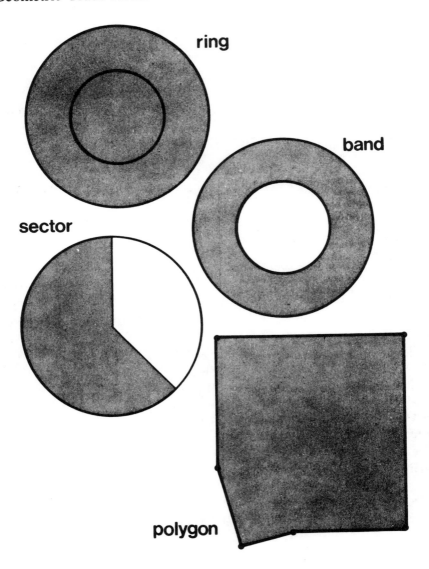

Source: Urban Decision Systems, Inc., Los Angeles, CA.

APPENDIX 4–4:

An Example of Demographic Analysis

The following demographic reports generated for Client X are for a trade area consisting of concentric radii at 1.0 and 2.5 miles from the corner of Alicia Parkway and Trubaco in Mission Viejo, California.

For illustrative purposes, we will examine only the four reports for the one mile ring—the primary trade area. These reports are entitled Area Profile, Population Profile, Income, and Demographic Trends (exhibits I through IV, respectively).

The Area Profile answers a wide range of questions, such as:

- Do the residents of this area match my customer profile?
- How upscale are they, based on income, occupation, education, and housing value?
- Are they family people and, if so, do they have children?
- How old is the housing stock in the neighborhood?
- Are they homeowners or renters?

The Population Profile is useful for site evaluation and general market research. The Income report provides detailed household and family income figures for three time periods (1980 census, the current year, and a five-year forecast). Lastly, the Demographic Trend report compares thirty-seven census indicators across the same three time periods.

The information used in this appendix appears by permission of Urban Decision Systems, Inc., Los Angeles, CA.

EXHIBIT I

```
AREA PROFILE: 1980                      URBAN DECISION SYSTEMS, INC.
MISSION VIEJO,CA:ALICIA PKWY & TRABUCO                     12/03/85
1.0 MILE RING
```

```
POPULATION          16919   RACE: Black        0.7%   HOUSEHOLD INCOME      %
In Grp Qtrs          0.0%         Other        5.4%   0-10T        356    6.7
                                                      10-20T       787   14.8
HOUSEHOLDS           5319   FAMILIES           4686   20-25T       673   12.6
1 Person             8.5%    W/children       65.1%   25-30T       801   15.1
2 Person            29.1%   Marr Couples      90.7%   30-35T       713   13.4
3-4 Person          46.9%    W/children       64.0%   35-40T       655   12.3
5+ Person           15.5%   Avg Family Size    3.38   40-50T       707   13.3
Avg Hshld Size       3.18   NONFAM HSHLDS     11.9%   50-75T       488    9.2
                                                      75T+         138    2.6
SPANISH ORIGIN       5.7%   IN ARMED FORCES    0.7%   Median          $ 30298
                                                      Average         $ 32392
AGE                    %    OCCUPATION            %
0-5          1835    10.8   Prof/Tec   1718    21.4   AGG.INCOME        171.9M
6-13         2856    16.9   Mgr/Prop   1787    22.3
14-17        1212     7.2   Clerical   1232    15.4   SCHOOL YRS COMPLETED
18-20         598     3.5   Sales      1426    17.8   Pop Age 25+         9719
21-24         698     4.1    WH/COL    6163    76.9   Median Sch Yrs      14.2
25-34        3701    21.9   Crafts      666     8.3   High Sch Only      29.0%
35-44        2929    17.3   Opertivs    303     3.8   Any College        62.8%
45-54        1323     7.8   Service     687     8.6
55-64         977     5.8   Laborer     153     1.9   18-34 IN COLLEGE   23.2%
65+           790     4.7   Farm Wrk     39     0.5
Median       29.0          BL/COL     1848    23.1   VEHICLES/HSHLD        %
                                                      0             49    0.9
SEX                    %   LABOR FORCE UNEMP PARTIC   1           1123   21.1
Male         8413    49.7      4906    1.9%  86.9%    2           2628   49.4
Female       8506    50.3      3325    3.9%  56.5%    3+          1519   28.6


HOUSING UNITS        5799   HOUSING VALUE         %   RENT                  %
Owner-Occ           77.2%   0-30T       10     0.3    0-99           0    0.0
Renter-Occ          14.6%   30-50T       3     0.1    100-199        2    0.3
Vac/Yr-Rnd           8.1%   50-80T      64     1.7    200-299       23    2.9
Vac/Season           0.2%   80-100T    428    11.1    300-399      154   19.1
Condominiums         637    100-150T  2481    64.2    400-499      262   32.6
Mobile Homes           0    150T+      877    22.7    500+         354   43.9
Stability           28.0%   Median     $ 128744       Median       $  483
Turnover            19.5%   Average    $ 132690       Average      $  468

UNITS/STRUCTURE        %    MOVED IN              %   BUILT                 %
1            5414    93.4   1970-80           97.9    1970-80            90.2
2              11     0.2   1960-69            2.1    1960-69             9.7
3-4           135     2.3   1950-59            0.0    1950-59             0.0
5+            239     4.1   <--1949            0.0    <--1949             0.1
```

```
Source: 1980 Census                                                      (AP)
-----------------------------------------------------------------------------
Urban Decision Systems/PO Box 25953/Los Angeles, CA 90025/(213) 820-8931
```

EXHIBIT II

POPULATION PROFILE: 1980
MISSION VIEJO,CA:ALICIA PKWY & TRABUCO
1.0 MILE RING

URBAN DECISION SYSTEMS, INC.
12/03/85

| POPULATION | 16919 | HOUSEHOLDS | 5319 | AVG HH SIZE | 3.18 |
| GRP QTRS/INST | 1 | FAMILIES | 4686 | AVG FAMILY SIZE | 3.38 |

AGE		%	MALE	FEMALE	HOUSEHOLD TYPE		%<18	%65+
<1	306	1.8	148	158	Families	4686	65.1	9.8
1-2	625	3.7	304	321	Married-cpl	4250	64.0	
3-4	601	3.6	289	312	Male/no wife	114	62.3	
5	303	1.8	160	143	Fem/no husb	322	80.7	
6	315	1.9	158	158	Non-family	633	3.0	15.9
7-9	1068	6.3	553	516	1-Person	451		20.7
10-13	1473	8.7	766	707				
14	304	1.8	151	154	MARITAL STATUS		% M	% F
15	310	1.8	163	147	Single	2225	55.7	44.3
16	310	1.8	150	160	Married	8629	49.9	50.1
17	288	1.7	143	145	Divorced	605	41.4	58.6
18	223	1.3	113	110	Widowed	295	12.6	87.4
19	211	1.2	104	108	Separated	169	30.9	69.1
20	164	1.0	90	' 74				
21	162	1.0	86	75	RACE		%	%<18	%65+
22-24	536	3.2	247	289	White	15875	93.8	34.7	4.9
25-29	1557	9.2	678	878	Black	124	0.7	39.5	0.8
30-34	2145	12.7	1002	1143	Am Ind	76	0.5	32.7	1.3
35-44	2929	17.3	1564	1365	Asian/PI	538	3.2	34.9	2.4
45-54	1323	7.8	711	612	Japanese	96	0.6		
55-59	555	3.3	266	289	Chinese	116	0.7		
60-61	180	1.1	83	97	Filipino	90	0.5		
62-64	242	1.4	116	126	Korean	82	0.5		
65-74	606	3.6	291	315	India	73	0.4		
75-84	155	0.9	73	82	Vietnam	61	0.4		
85+	30	0.2	6	24	Hawaiian	9	0.1		
Total	16919		8413	8506	Guam	9	0.1		
65+	790	4.7	370	421	Samoan	1	0.0		
					Other	305	1.8	41.3	1.0
Median	29.0		29.3	28.9					
					Spanish	970	5.7	43.3	1.8

SPANISH ORIGIN BY NATIONALITY		%		
Spanish	970	5.7	SPANISH ORIGIN BY RACE	%
Mexican	554	3.3	Total	970
Puerto Rican	52	0.3	White	752	77.5
Cuban	27	0.2	Black	1	0.1
Other Spanish	338	2.0	Am Ind/Asian	36	3.7
Non Spanish	15948	94.3	Other	182	18.7

Source: 1980 Census STF1   (CP)

Urban Decision Systems/PO Box 25953/Los Angeles, CA 90025/(213) 820-8931

EXHIBIT III

INCOME: 1980-85-90   URBAN DECISION SYSTEMS, INC.
MISSION VIEJO,CA:ALICIA PKWY & TRABUCO   12/03/85
1.0 MILE RING

	1980 Census		1985 Est.		1990 Est.	
POPULATION	16919		21042		24907	
In Group Quarters	1		1		5	
PER CAPITA INCOME	$ 10161		$ 14521		$ 19074	
AGGREGATE INCOME ($Mil)	171.9		305.6		475.1	
HOUSEHOLDS	5319	%	6913	%	8442	%
By Income						
Less than $ 5,000	154	2.9	117	1.7	91	1.1
$ 5,000 - $ 9,999	203	3.8	182	2.6	153	1.8
$ 10,000 - $ 14,999	319	6.0	213	3.1	181	2.1
$ 15,000 - $ 19,999	468	8.8	350	5.1	209	2.5
$ 20,000 - $ 24,999	673	12.6	386	5.6	359	4.3
$ 25,000 - $ 29,999	801	15.1	463	6.7	342	4.1
$ 30,000 - $ 34,999	713	13.4	670	9.7	412	4.9
$ 35,000 - $ 39,999	655	12.3	718	10.4	455	5.4
$ 40,000 - $ 49,999	707	13.3	1473	21.3	1246	14.8
$ 50,000 - $ 74,999	488	9.2	1775	25.7	3271	38.8
$ 75,000 +	138	2.6	566	8.2	1722	20.4
Median Household Income	$ 30298		$ 42430		$ 55904	
Average Household Income	$ 32392		$ 44197		$ 56259	
FAMILIES	4686	%	5993	%	7231	%
By Income						
Less than $ 5,000	107	2.3	82	1.4	70	1.0
$ 5,000 - $ 9,999	133	2.8	126	2.1	106	1.5
$ 10,000 - $ 14,999	234	5.0	160	2.7	126	1.7
$ 15,000 - $ 19,999	396	8.4	211	3.5	150	2.1
$ 20,000 - $ 24,999	575	12.3	307	5.1	193	2.7
$ 25,000 - $ 29,999	720	15.4	378	6.3	256	3.5
$ 30,000 - $ 34,999	653	13.9	567	9.5	320	4.4
$ 35,000 - $ 39,999	602	12.8	628	10.5	363	5.0
$ 40,000 - $ 49,999	667	14.2	1337	22.3	1038	14.4
$ 50,000 - $ 74,999	472	10.1	1661	27.7	2975	41.1
$ 75,000 +	127	2.7	537	9.0	1634	22.6
Median Family Income	$ 31362		$ 44023		$ 58352	
Average Family Income	$ 33657		$ 45944		$ 58342	

Source: 1980 Census, July 1,1985 UDS Estimates   (INF)

Urban Decision Systems/PO Box 25953/Los Angeles, CA 90025/(213) 820-8931

EXHIBIT IV

```
DEMOGRAPHIC TRENDS: 1980-85-90          URBAN DECISION SYSTEMS, INC.
MISSION VIEJO,CA:ALICIA PKWY & TRABUCO                    12/03/85
1.0 MILE RING
```

	1980 Census		1985 Est.		1990 Proj.	
POPULATION	16919		21042		24907	
In Group Quarters	1		1		5	
HOUSEHOLDS	5319	%	6913	%	8442	%
1 Person	451	8.5	723	10.5	1028	12.2
2 Person	1545	29.1	2090	30.2	2609	30.9
3-4 Person	2496	46.9	3227	46.7	3918	46.4
5+ Person	826	15.5	873	12.6	888	10.5
Avg Hshld Size	3.18		3.04		2.95	
FAMILIES	4686		5993		7231	
		%		%		%
RACE: White	15875	93.8	19666	93.5	23245	93.3
Black	124	0.7	147	0.7	175	0.7
Other	919	5.4	1229	5.8	1486	6.0
SPANISH/HISPANIC	970	5.7	1240	5.9	1458	5.9
		%		%		%
AGE: 0 - 5	1835	10.8	2522	12.0	3087	12.4
6 - 13	2856	16.9	3378	16.1	4386	17.6
14 - 17	1212	7.2	1306	6.2	1320	5.3
18 - 20	598	3.5	586	2.8	602	2.4
21 - 24	698	4.1	715	3.4	591	2.4
25 - 34	3701	21.9	4418	21.0	4695	18.8
35 - 44	2929	17.3	4321	20.5	5695	22.9
45 - 54	1323	7.8	1580	7.5	2045	8.2
55 - 64	977	5.8	1186	5.6	1229	4.9
65 +	790	4.7	1032	4.9	1258	5.1
Median Age	29.0		29.6		30.3	
MALES	8413	%	10515	%	12505	%
0 - 20	3290	39.1	3933	37.4	4730	37.8
21 - 44	3578	42.5	4678	44.5	5490	43.9
45 - 64	1175	14.0	1415	13.5	1681	13.4
65 +	370	4.4	490	4.7	604	4.8
FEMALES	8506	%	10527	%	12402	%
0 - 20	3211	37.8	3858	36.6	4665	37.6
21 - 44	3750	44.1	4776	45.4	5490	44.3
45 - 64	1124	13.2	1352	12.8	1593	12.8
65 +	421	4.9	542	5.1	654	5.3
HOUSING UNITS	5799	%				
Owner-Occupied	4475	77.2	5809		7133	
Renter-Occupied	844	14.6	1104		1310	

```
Source: 1980 Census, July 1,1985 UDS Estimates                  (DTF)
------------------------------------------------------------------------
Urban Decision Systems/PO Box 25953/Los Angeles, CA 90025/(213) 820-8931
```

CHAPTER FIVE

Behavioral Attribute Segmentation

*There are times when I look over the various parts
of my character with perplexity. I recognize that I
am made up of several persons and that the person
that at that moment has the upper hand will
inevitably give place to another. But which is
the real one? All of them or none.*

W. Somerset Maugham, 1874

In the previous chapter it was shown that what people are (e.g., their age, family structure, income, occupation, etc.) and where they live provide useful information for segmenting markets. We will now explore behavioral approaches to market segmentation. These bases recognize that what people do (e.g., their activities, interests, habits, media exposure, and buying behavior) and how they feel about life (e.g., their attitudes, beliefs, opinions, emotions, needs, wants, and values) are often better determinants of their use of certain products or services. Unlike physical dimensions, the behavioral bases assist the marketer by probing into specific product category and brand decisions by consumers. These segmentation methods help to explain why one individual may prefer Coke, and another Pepsi. However, you should not view segmentation dimension decisions as an either/or proposition. Both physical and behavioral bases can be used to explore and exploit market niches.

The major behavioral dimensions that will be discussed in detail include psychographics, product usage, and benefits. Other behavioral bases to be briefly reviewed include perceptions and preferences, situations/occasions, media exposure, and marketing mix factors. In addition, Appendix 5–1 discusses a new base, an approach to better understanding markets called image-concept segmentation.

PSYCHOGRAPHICS

One of the more powerful market segmentation approaches, psychographics has come a long way since the term was pioneered by Emanuel Demby, a marketing research practitioner, nearly twenty years ago. In his essay, "Psychographics and From Whence It Came," part of the American Marketing Association's publication *LifeStyle and Psychographics,* Demby's three-level definition of psychographics is:

1. Generally, psychographics may be viewed as the practical application of the behavioral and social sciences to marketing research.
2. More specifically, psychographics is a quantitative research procedure that is indicated when demographic, socioeconomic, and user/non-user analyses are not sufficient to explain and predict consumer behavior.
3. Most specifically, psychographics seeks to describe the human characteristics of consumers that may have bearing on their response to products, packaging, advertising, and public relations efforts. Such variables may span a spectrum from self-concept and lifestyle to attitudes, interests, and opinions, as well as perceptions of product attributes.

Psychographics vs. Lifestyle Research

Even today, there is a great controversy among both marketing practitioners and academics as to what constitutes psychographics—and whether or not it is synonomous with lifestyle research. The consensus appears to be that there is a distinction between the two concepts. Psychographics relates to consumers' personality traits (e.g., their sociability, self-reliance, assertiveness, etc.), while lifestyles, as described by William D. Wells and Douglas J. Tigert, consist primarily of individuals' attitudes, interests, and opinions, or AIOs. In practice, personality traits and lifestyles (the more useful factor) need to be considered collectively to provide meaningful marketing information. Hence, psychographics can be defined as:

PSYCHOGRAPHICS = Personality Traits + Lifestyles

Advantages of Psychographics

Psychographic research is being used more frequently in market segmentation studies for four primary reasons: 1) to identify target markets, 2) to better explain consumer behavior, 3) to improve a company's strategic marketing efforts, and 4) to minimize risks for new products/ventures.

1. *Identify Target Markets.* Although typically used more in advanced analyses than initial segmentation studies, psychographics can be very useful in identifying and explaining markets. Consumer differences extend beyond demographics, and research must probe into an individual's state of mind (their AIOs) to piece together the total "market puzzle." Furthermore, additional market characteristics and quantitative factors, such as size and scope of the market and market share, can be analyzed from a new perspective.

Let's look at the bicycle market from a psychographic standpoint. People may choose to buy a bike for a variety of non-demographic reasons. The adult exercise segment of the market can be further subdivided by primary purchase motives. There are the fitness buffs, the jogger and cyclist, the anti-jogger, the recreational rider, and the nature lover. Psychographic analysis can provide you with a more complete profile of your target markets.

2. *Consumer Behavior.* Markets are made up of a variety of people. By analyzing consumer behavior, the marketer can better understand why the buyer acts as he or she does in the marketplace. Psychographic research can assist in meeting this objective. Buyer behavior—including such factors as brand choice, store/firm loyalty, personal motivations, attitudes, perceptions, and preferences—can all be explored via this approach to segmentation. The value of such information is readily apparent.

A company may know who the heavy users of their product are, but not why these individuals act as they do. Through psychographic research, the firm can study this small core with high relative consumption patterns to determine what they like about the product and why they buy it. This information can then be used in designing future promotional appeals to this group, as well as offering similar benefits to potential new users. Is the shopper who regularly patronizes a particular supermarket going there because it is the most convenient one, because of its fine meat and produce departments, or for other reasons? This type of vital marketing information must be obtained.

3. *Strategic Marketing.* The additional marketing information available through psychographic analysis can be employed in planning successful marketing strategies for the firm. Psychographics is most useful for companies that sell:

- expensive products (automobiles, boats)
- discretionary goods or services (VCRs, health club memberships)
- somewhat indistinguishable products (soft drinks, beer, liquor)

Strategic information gathered through a psychographic analysis can permeate all marketing areas of the company. Some examples include:

- positioning new products/repositioning existing products
- improving products or services to better meet segment needs
- recognizing the importance of price factors in a given market
- promotional strategies, in particular selecting appropriate media vehicles, advertising messages, and sales appeals
- exploring new distribution methods or improving existing channels of distribution

4. *Minimizing Risk.* The cost of a new product introduction, brand line extension, or proposed venture can be substantial. Furthermore, the vast majority of such projects fail (new product success rates are estimated at less than 10%). By incorporating psychographic research into your firm's product testing and development program, project successes become more likely. Often the key ingredient is locating the subtle product or concept variations that consumers desire (their needs and wants).

Limitations of Psychographics

Although using psychographic research in segmentation studies can be very beneficial, there are also some limitations the marketer must be aware of. These include:

1. *Problems in Data Collection and Analysis.* Unlike demographics, for example, psychographics requires a much more complex approach to obtaining the marketing information sought by management. This is because psychographics relies mostly on primary research findings and there are fewer corporate marketers and outside research vendors skilled in this more sophisticated type of analysis.

Although the psychographic study is simpler to administer than in-depth interviews (previously the most popular means of obtaining lifestyle information), data collection is often a problem due to the large number of questions asked via the survey instrument. Compounding this situation is the analysis of a voluminous amount of data, which often requires the use of the more advanced multivariate statistical techniques in seeking key marketing relationships. In some cases, the results of the research may prove inconclusive. This can present problems in finding significant differences between market segments or producing too many variations among segments. In this latter case of over-segmentation, a market combination strategy might be advisable. This involves the combination of two or more small segments into a larger one that is more efficient for marketing planning purposes.

2. Cost Factors. A well designed psychographic study is on an upper rung of the pricing ladder compared to other types of marketing research. Expect to invest $15,000 and up for a complete research package. If cost is a major consideration for your company, this type of analysis is probably not the most appropriate use of marketing funds.

Conducting a Psychographic Segmentation Analysis: Some Guidelines

As in most marketing research studies, there is no one preferred format or approach to conducting the psychographic study. However, here are ten guidelines that you will find helpful in planning the research project.

1. Seek detail. Lifestyles are a complex area. The more relevant data collected (use your judgment as to what is pertinent), the better the expected value of the analyzed marketing information. Focus groups can be an effective means of pretesting the psychographic survey instrument.

2. The personal interview format is generally preferred. Due to the wealth of data that needs to be collected, telephone surveys are often inappropriate. Similarly, direct mail often cannot be used. It suffers from a low return rate, with many unusable or incomplete questionnaires. Therefore, personal interviews are usually the best choice. Through this approach, the necessary data can be collected, alternative concepts can be tested, and even visuals can be used as needed.

3. The heart of the survey instrument is the AIO statements. To develop viable individual and segment profiles based on lifestyles, a large number (typically anywhere from two dozen to several hundred) of activity, interest, and opinion statements are the primary means of gathering information. These statements must be related to the purchase decision. Some typical AIO statements from an automobile study can be seen in Figure 5-1.

4. Measure the AIO statements on a scale basis. In many psychographic studies, a Likert five-point agree/disagree scale, or some similar scale, is developed to determine the degree of agreement/disagreement for each statement (see Figure 5-2). The magnitude of the response is a critical measure of personality traits and lifestyles.

Some industry experts recommend scales of more than five points. Art Boudin, President of Applied Research Techniques, Inc., frequently uses eleven-point scales in his segmentation studies. Since measuring dispersion (deviations from the mean) is a method for determining segment for-

Figure 5-1:

Sample AIO Statements

My family knows I love them by how well I take care of them.
My choice of a car affects how I feel about myself.
I take a look at many of the new cars that are introduced.
I'm willing to pay a higher price for a car that I'm satisfied with.
Advertisements for automobiles are an insult to my intelligence.
I take pride in doing my own car maintenance and repair whenever I can.

Reprinted with permission of Applied Research Techniques, Inc., Parsippany, NJ.

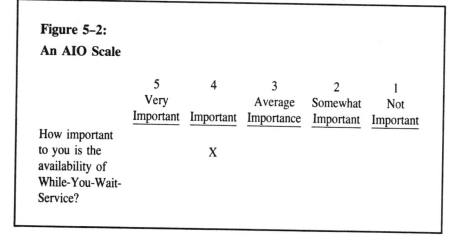

Figure 5-2:

An AIO Scale

	5 Very Important	4 Important	3 Average Importance	2 Somewhat Important	1 Not Important
How important to you is the availability of While-You-Wait-Service?	X				

mation, a good case for the more detailed scale can be made.

5. Factor analysis should be considered in data analysis. Given the sizable number of statements queried, factor analysis is required to reduce the personality and lifestyle factors down to a more manageable number (perhaps three to twelve). These are the critical factors used in defining and describing market segments.

6. Consider other analytical approaches. Although factor analysis is often the primary analytical tool used in psychographic studies, other potentially valuable techniques should also be considered. For further information review the section on data analysis and the appendix in Chapter 3.

7. *Avoid preconceived notions about the research findings.* In addition to setting research objectives, it is also helpful to develop some research hypotheses prior to conducting the research. This forces you to consider the consequences and implications of the possible findings. However, it is necessary to be open-minded about the outcome of a study. While in a majority of cases the research results will be informative and add a new perspective to present marketing planning initiatives, sometimes one must expect the unexpected. In this case, any preconceived bias must be overcome to maximize the value of potentially critical information.

8. *Do not neglect the value of secondary data.* A psychographic analysis is mostly based on well executed primary research. This does not mean that secondary data should be ignored in the data collection process. Secondary information from past studies, as well as published or syndicated sources, is a welcome accompaniment to the project and can contribute immensely to the explanation of the primary research findings.

9. *Add in other physical and behavioral dimensions to better define market segments.* We have already demonstrated the value of psychographics in market segmentation analysis. However, it should not be used in isolation. To maximize the validity of segment profiles, additional bases should be utilized. Demographics and product usage are two of the more frequently used dimensions. Other bases might be indicated depending on the particular type of analysis conducted. Figure 5-3 describes a market segment for banking services from a psychographic perspective. Note how demographic, media preference, and usage dimensions are incorporated into the profile. This target market summmary provides a starting point for strategy development.

10. *Name the segments.* Once a reasonably accurate segment portrait has been established, it is advisable to tag a descriptor to the designated segment. For a running/exercise shoe manufacturer, a name like "Weekend Athletes" clearly represents a particular segment of the market that the firm might actively pursue. One can quickly identify some key characteristics of the segments listed in Table 5-1 by their names.

Another Option: Syndicated Lifestyle Research

The marketer in need of psychographic data doesn't have to opt for a custom segmentation study. Many companies are now using syndicated

Figure 5–3:

Segment Profile for Group A for Banking Services

These are lower-middle to middle-income people with great concerns about money. Their financial objectives center around having sufficient assets to "live comfortably"—which they describe in very modest terms. They feel the pace of social change has been too fast over the past several years. And they are either unable or unwilling to keep up with it. Although they must be very careful about their money, they don't really know how to manage it or spend it properly. They seek advice from many sources before committing themselves to any financial course of action. But this reasoned approach often produces conflicting or confusing information for them. So most of their financial decisions end up being made at irrational or emotional levels.

Their parents, who were born outside of the United States, never had checking accounts, bank loans, or bank credit cards. Similarly, Group A uses only the bank's savings services, preferring to pay cash for all purchases. They enjoy coming to the bank and very likely have a favorite teller whom they try to see. In fact, a trip to the bank is something of a special occasion for them.

They pay close attention to advertising. But because they do not trust it much, they rarely act upon it. They do seem more responsive to image-oriented, rather than product-oriented, messages. Their media preferences include a great deal of indiscriminate television watching and some family magazines.

This group comprises 15% of the total market.

This information is from articles written and designed by Sorkin-Enenstein Research Service, Inc. and may not be reproduced or disseminated without the express permission of Sorkin-Enenstein Research Service, Inc.

research services as a complement to other segmentation findings. Two of the best known providers of these services are Yankelovich Clancy Shulman (YCS) and SRI International.

The Yankelovich Monitor 1985 identified fifty-two social trends relevant to consumer marketing, and six values segments. The recognition of the impact of key trends in a given market can prove to be valuable

Table 5–1:

**Psychographic Profile of the Brand X
Videocassette Recorder Purchaser**

Segment # / Name	% U.S. Male Household Head	% Brand X	Index
I. The Inconspicuous Social Isolate	8.1	31.3	386
II. The Silent Conservative	16.5	2.0	12
III. The Embittered Resigned Worker	12.8	.7	5
IV. The High-Brow Puritan	13.5	0	0
V. The Rebellious Pleasure Seeker	9.3	7.3	78
VI. The Workhard-Playhard Executive	10.7	4.0	37
VII. The Masculine Hero Emulator	18.8	43.7	229
VIII. The Sophisticated Cosmopolitan	10.4	12.0	115
TOTALS	100.0%	100.0%	100

Reprinted with permission of Applied Research Techniques, Inc., Parsippany, NJ.

for a company's strategic marketing planning. On the other hand, YCS acknowledges that the generalized typologies are more useful in understanding value systems operating today in the U.S. than specific product markets.

SRI's VALS Program (Values and Lifestyles) categorizes people based on attitudes, needs, wants, and beliefs. The VALS typology is divided into four major categories, with a total of nine lifestyle types. VALS information has been used in marketing research, advertising, product development, strategic planning, sales, and human resource development applications. Additionally, SRI has joint data bases and research services with several major national marketing research firms.

Syndicated services such as The Monitor and VALS are growing in popularity. There is some question as to their effectiveness. This form of generalized lifestyle research is market or consumer-driven, as opposed to product-driven. Individuals are analyzed as to their overall attitudes, values, and desires. Product-specific data, the more important information from a market segmentation perspective, is not obtained. Marketers can only infer how consumer segments will respond to their product offerings. Ideally, you would want to **know** this information. Since consumers react differently when exposed to alternative product stimuli, the need for situation-specific data focusing on unique markets, product classes, and product items is paramount.

Despite this major shortcoming, syndicated lifestyle research can be beneficial to a company as a supplemental means of customer analysis. Appendixes 5–2 and 5–3 list YCS's social trends and SRI's VALS typology, respectively. Also, Appendix B (the Lifestyle Analysis section) provides additional background information on these two companies.

PRODUCT USAGE

If you analyze your individual purchase behavior, you will notice that there are several goods or services that you buy on a regular basis or in large quantities from time to time. Many other products you purchase less frequently, with a vast majority of potential products seldom if ever bought. This scenario is the basis for product usage segmentation—segments are identified and targeted based on a compilation of product consumption levels within a given market.

To analyze markets based on product use patterns, it is first necessary to classify users into specific consumption categories. An often used method is non-users vs. light users vs. medium users vs. heavy users for a particular good or service. For example, in an analysis of the canned cranberry products market, light users were defined as those purchasing six or less cans per year, medium users seven to eighteen, and heavy users nineteen or more cans annually. This is represented in Table 5–2.

An additional classification scheme can compare the light half versus the heavy half consumption segments in a given market. Under this method, non-users are not considered, and the marketer determines what share of the market the two remaining segments account for. If 40% of the potential consumers for a product were non-users, we would analyze the other 60% of the market. The light half (30% of the market) might purchase 15% of the product, while the heavy half (also 30% of the market) would account for the lion's share, or 85%, of the sales. See Table 5–3.

Advantages of Product Usage Analysis

Segmenting markets based on product usage provides four major benefits. They are:

1. It is a useful dimension for understanding consumer or industrial markets based on past purchase behavior.

Table 5–2:

A Product Usage Classification for the Canned Cranberry Products Market

Segment	Annual Consumption (in cans)
Non-users	0
Light users	6 or less
Medium users	7 to 18
Heavy users	19 or more

Table 5–3:

Light vs. Heavy Half Consumption

Segment	% of Population	% of Product Consumption
Non-users	40	0
Light users (1/2)	30	15
Heavy users (1/2)	30	85
TOTAL USERS	60	100

2. It can increase consumption among heavy users in moderately competitive markets.
3. It can increase consumption among light and medium users in highly competitive markets.
4. By providing additional benefits or focusing in on neglected market segments, it is possible to attract non-users to the product.

Limitations of Product Usage Analysis

The marketer needs to be cognizant of three shortcomings associated with the product usage dimension:

1. **Product usage segments are often difficult to explain through traditional demographics only.** In many markets, additional bases should be employed in the segmentation analysis (e.g., psychographics, benefits, and/or media exposure). If the piano market were analyzed on a demographic basis, we would notice that income is the key variable affecting purchase behavior. However, there are many affluent households that do not own or want a piano. Obviously there are non-demographic variables which greatly affect consumers' purchase decisions. These factors include such issues as:

   • Does anyone in the household currently play piano?
   • Are there any children in the family that might take piano lessons?
   • What is the potential customer's music appreciation level?
   • Did they own a piano when they were growing up?
   • How do they feel about a piano as a piece of decorative furniture?

2. **There are several inherent problems associated with targeting the heavy user segment. These include:**

   a) Other companies may also recognize the value of the heavy user. Therefore, competition for customers in this segment can be great.
   b) All heavy users are not purchasers for the same reasons. Since customers have different needs, further segmentation within the heavy user category is usually advisable.
   c) Heavy users are not product-loyal. They tend to buy heavily within a product class, but often have little allegiance to individual products, services, or companies.

3. **There are some definitional problems in product usage analysis.** For instance, how do we distinguish between a heavy, medium, and light user? Also, what criteria should be used in specifying consumption segments? These and other questions must be answered by the marketing analyst.

Assessment of the Product Usage Dimension

Although product usage segmentation has at times been treated as a step-child as a segmentation base, it is still a very viable technique that can provide you with valuable information in many markets. Its use does not have the widespread acceptance of demographics, nor the explanatory value of psychographics or benefit segmentation. Additional research is needed to maximize the value of product usage analysis in the marketplace. This can be accomplished by treating product usage measures as both a primary segmentation base and as a complementary tool that can extend other segmentation findings.

Product usage analysis is also a flexible marketing research technique. Goods and services can be analyzed for consumption levels on both a unit or dollar volume basis. It is also one of the simplest segmentation methods to understand. Remember the 80/20 rule described in Chapter 1. This marketing rule-of-thumb works well in many industries and markets when both users and non-users are considered (80% of sales likely to come from 20% of the market). A corollary to this could be called the 80/50 rule. This means that approximately 80% of a firm's sales are likely to come from the 50% of the users that comprise the heavy half. Recognize that these two theorems are guideposts only and will not be appropriate in every marketing situation.

Yogurt Consumption: An Example

The Simmons Market Research Bureau (SMRB) is a leader in product usage analysis, surveying more than 750 product categories and 3,500 brands on a regular basis. See Table 5–4 and Figure 5–4 on yogurt consumption, provided courtesy of SMRB. The former (an actual example from a SMRB report) details literally hundreds of useful bits of data, tying product consumption patterns to a multitude of demographic factors in a concise, workable format. The latter charts clearly depict a "yogurt consumption profile" of the most likely consumers based on the critical demographic, socioeconomic, and geographic variables analyzed. This information shows that yogurt eaters are almost twice as likely to be women than men, and are generally young, college educated, and have above average incomes (many professionals/managers). Regionally, consumption levels in the West and Northeast are significantly higher than in the north-central and southern areas of the United States. There are few noticeable differences between heavy users and medium or light users,

Figure 5–4:
Yogurt Consumption Charts

WHO EATS YOGURT?

YOGURT CONSUMPTION
(STANDARD CROSS TABULATION)

% USING

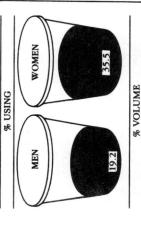

MEN 19.2 WOMEN 35.5

% VOLUME

MEN 35.6 WOMEN 64.4

INSIGHT: Women are the primary users. But which women? Who are they?

WHAT ARE THEIR GENERAL DEMOGRAPHIC CHARACTERISTICS?

YOGURT CONSUMPTION -
DEMO GROUP
(FEMALES)

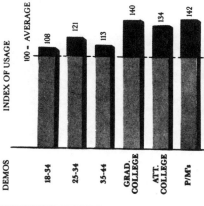

INDEX OF USAGE

100 = AVERAGE

DEMOS	
18-34	108
25-34	121
35-44	113
GRAD. COLLEGE	140
ATT. COLLEGE	134
P/M's	142
CLERICAL SALES	115

INSIGHT: College educated and professional/managerials are heavy yogurt consumers, 34% to 42% above average. (That's a good clue for the advertising copy and the media you'd use to reach them.)

WHERE DO THEY LIVE?

YOGURT CONSUMPTION - BY REGION
(FEMALES)

% USING

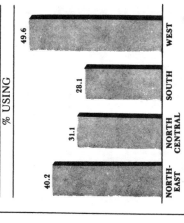

NORTH-EAST	NORTH CENTRAL	SOUTH	WEST
40.2	31.1	28.1	49.6

INSIGHT: Market potential levels vary markedly by region.

Reprinted with permission of Simmons Market Research Bureau

Table 5-4

YOGURT (NOT BOUGHT FROZEN): USAGE IN LAST 30 DAYS (ADULTS)

0420 P 10   0420 P-19

	TOTAL U.S. '000	ALL USERS A '000	B % DOWN	C ACROSS %	D INDX	HEAVY USERS SIX OR MORE A '000	B % DOWN	C ACROSS %	D INDX	MEDIUM USERS TWO-FIVE A '000	B % DOWN	C ACROSS %	D INDX	LIGHT USERS ONE OR LESS A '000	B % DOWN	C ACROSS %	D INDX
TOTAL ADULTS	167727	51672	100.0	30.8	100	14843	100.0	8.8	100	20908	100.0	12.5	100	15921	100.0	9.5	100
MALES	79263	18125	35.1	22.9	74	5543	37.3	7.0	79	6911	33.1	8.7	70	5670	35.6	7.2	75
FEMALES	88444	33547	64.9	37.9	123	9300	62.7	10.5	119	13997	66.9	15.8	127	10250	64.4	11.6	122
18 - 24	28671	9567	18.5	33.4	108	2157	14.5	7.5	85	3997	19.1	13.9	112	3413	21.4	11.9	125
25 - 34	39536	14479	28.4	37.1	121	3769	25.4	9.5	108	5925	28.3	15.0	120	4986	31.3	12.6	133
35 - 44	28978	9847	19.1	34.0	110	2947	19.9	10.2	115	4002	19.1	13.8	111	2898	18.2	10.0	105
45 - 54	22345	6667	12.9	29.8	97	2065	13.9	9.2	104	2392	10.7	10.7	86	2210	13.9	9.9	104
55 - 64	22224	5614	10.9	25.3	82	2126	14.3	9.6	108	2278	10.9	10.3	82	1210	7.6	5.4	57
65 OR OLDER	25973	5297	10.3	20.4	66	1779	12.0	6.8	77	2315	11.1	8.9	72	1203	7.6	4.6	49
18 - 34	68207	24246	46.9	35.5	115	5926	39.9	8.7	98	9921	47.5	14.5	117	8399	52.8	12.3	130
18 - 49	108058	37493	72.6	34.7	113	9821	66.2	9.1	103	15193	72.7	14.1	113	12478	78.4	11.5	122
25 - 54	90859	31194	60.4	34.3	111	8781	59.2	9.7	109	12319	58.9	13.6	109	10095	63.4	11.1	117
35 - 49	39851	13247	25.6	33.2	108	3896	26.2	9.8	110	5272	25.2	13.2	106	4079	25.6	10.2	108
50 OR OLDER	59669	14179	27.4	23.8	77	5022	33.8	8.4	95	5715	27.3	9.6	77	3442	21.6	5.8	61
GRADUATED COLLEGE	28091	11802	22.8	42.0	136	3406	22.9	12.1	137	4763	22.8	17.0	136	3634	22.8	12.9	136
ATTENDED COLLEGE	28938	11111	21.5	38.4	125	2889	19.5	10.0	113	4498	21.5	15.5	125	3723	23.4	12.9	134
GRADUATED HIGH SCHOOL	65503	19034	36.8	29.1	94	5539	36.0	8.2	92	7624	36.5	11.6	93	6070	38.1	9.3	98
DID NOT GRADUATE HIGH SCHOOL	45195	9725	18.8	21.5	70	3209	21.6	7.1	80	4022	19.2	8.9	71	2494	15.7	5.5	58
EMPLOYED MALES	54429	13724	26.6	24.3	79	4277	28.8	7.6	86	5016	24.0	8.9	71	4431	27.8	7.9	83
EMPLOYED FEMALES	43971	19282	37.3	43.9	142	5313	35.8	12.1	137	7748	37.1	17.6	141	6222	39.1	14.2	149
EMPLOYED FULL-TIME	87773	28014	54.2	31.9	104	8098	54.6	9.2	104	10758	51.5	12.3	98	9158	57.5	10.4	110
EMPLOYED PART-TIME	12627	4992	9.7	39.5	128	1492	10.1	11.8	134	2006	9.6	15.9	127	1494	9.4	11.8	125
NOT EMPLOYED	67327	18666	36.1	27.7	90	5254	35.4	7.8	88	8144	39.0	12.1	97	5268	33.1	7.8	82
PROFESSIONAL/MANAGER	25845	10560	20.4	40.9	133	3097	20.9	12.0	135	4140	19.8	16.0	129	3323	20.9	12.9	135
TECH/CLERICAL/SALES	30895	11293	21.9	36.6	119	3137	21.1	10.2	115	4267	20.4	13.8	111	3889	24.4	12.6	133
PRECISION/CRAFT	12629	3048	5.9	24.3	79	1089	7.3	8.6	97	1045	5.1	8.4	68	914	5.7	7.2	76
OTHER EMPLOYED	31031	8085	15.6	26.1	85	2264	15.3	7.3	83	3291	15.7	10.6	85	2527	15.9	8.1	86
SINGLE	35557	12395	24.0	34.9	113	3059	20.6	8.6	97	5121	24.5	14.4	116	4215	26.5	11.9	125
MARRIED	103585	30890	59.8	29.3	97	9091	61.2	8.8	99	12299	58.8	11.2	95	9501	59.7	9.2	97
DIVORCED/SEPARATED/WIDOWED	28585	8387	16.2	29.3	95	2693	18.1	9.4	106	3489	16.7	12.2	98	2205	13.8	7.7	81
PARENTS	59295	19697	38.1	33.2	108	5314	35.8	9.0	101	7942	38.0	13.4	107	6441	40.5	10.9	114
WHITE	146081	45996	89.0	31.5	102	13032	87.8	8.9	101	18665	89.3	12.8	103	14299	89.8	9.8	103
BLACK	17974	4238	8.2	23.6	77	1350	9.1	7.5	85	1625	7.8	7.8	73	1263	7.9	7.0	74
OTHER	3672	1439	2.8	39.2	127	=462	3.1	12.6	142	=618	3.0	16.8	135	=359	2.3	9.8	103

	Total	'000	%	%	Idx	'000	%	%	Idx	'000	%	%	Idx	'000	%	%	Idx
NORTHEAST-CENSUS	37005	13259	25.7	35.8	116	4828	13.0	32.5	147	5036	24.1	13.6	109	3395	21.3	9.2	97
NORTH CENTRAL	42642	11020	21.3	25.8	84	2936	6.9	19.8	78	3959	18.9	9.3	74	4125	25.9	9.7	102
SOUTH	56777	13798	26.7	24.3	79	3428	6.8	24.6	68	5741	27.5	10.1	81	4629	29.1	8.2	86
WEST	31303	13596	26.3	43.4	141	3652	11.7	24.6	132	6173	29.5	19.7	158	3772	23.7	12.0	127
NORTHEAST-MKTG.	38125	14227	27.5	37.3	121	4900	12.9	33.0	145	5823	27.9	15.3	123	3504	22.0	9.2	97
EAST CENTRAL	24794	6248	12.1	25.2	82	1864	7.5	12.6	85	2172	10.4	8.8	70	2210	13.9	8.9	94
WEST CENTRAL	28511	7714	14.9	27.1	88	1985	7.0	13.6	79	2872	13.7	10.1	81	2858	18.0	10.0	106
SOUTH	44953	11277	21.8	23.0	75	2790	5.7	18.8	64	4439	21.2	9.1	73	4048	25.4	8.3	87
PACIFIC	27344	12205	23.6	44.6	145	3303	12.1	22.3	136	5602	26.8	20.5	164	3300	20.7	12.1	127
COUNTY SIZE A	69301	25433	49.2	36.7	119	7464	10.8	50.3	122	11009	52.7	15.9	127	6960	43.7	10.0	106
COUNTY SIZE B	50433	15024	29.1	29.7	96	4335	8.6	29.2	97	5376	25.7	10.6	85	5314	33.4	10.5	111
COUNTY SIZE C	26259	7536	14.6	28.7	93	2090	8.0	14.1	90	3125	14.9	11.9	95	2321	14.6	8.8	93
COUNTY SIZE D	21534	3680	7.1	17.1	55	954	4.4	14.1	50	1399	6.7	6.5	52	1327	8.3	6.2	65
METRO CENTRAL CITY	50014	17051	33.0	34.1	111	5441	10.9	36.8	123	6851	32.8	13.7	110	4739	29.8	9.5	100
METRO SUBURBAN	76832	25740	49.8	33.5	109	7115	47.7	105		10272	49.1	13.4	107	8354	52.5	10.9	115
NON METRO	40881	8881	17.2	21.7	71	2268	5.5	15.3	63	3786	18.1	9.3	74	2828	17.8	6.9	73
TOP 5 ADI'S	39550	15620	30.2	39.5	128	4828	12.2	32.5	138	6771	32.4	17.1	137	4021	25.3	10.2	107
TOP 10 ADI'S	54877	20897	40.4	38.1	124	6324	11.5	42.6	130	9063	43.3	16.5	132	5510	34.6	10.0	106
TOP 20 ADI'S	77516	28098	54.4	36.2	118	8242	10.6	55.5	120	11970	57.3	15.4	124	7886	49.5	10.2	107
HSHLD INC. $50,000 OR MORE	17257	6839	13.2	39.6	129	1839	10.7	12.4	120	3058	14.6	17.7	142	1942	12.2	11.3	119
$40,000 OR MORE	33235	12990	25.1	39.0	126	3728	11.2	25.1	127	5313	25.4	16.0	128	3909	24.6	11.8	124
$30,000 OR MORE	59693	22074	42.7	37.0	120	6082	10.2	41.0	115	9143	43.7	15.3	123	6849	43.0	11.5	121
$25,000 OR MORE	76275	28029	54.7	36.7	119	7840	10.3	52.8	116	11574	55.4	15.2	122	8615	54.1	11.3	119
$20,000 - $24,999	18607	5624	10.9	30.2	98	1353	7.3	9.1	82	2413	11.5	13.0	104	1859	11.7	10.0	105
$15,000 - $19,999	17175	4803	9.3	28.0	91	1327	7.7	8.9	87	1842	8.8	10.7	86	1635	10.3	9.5	100
$10,000 - $14,999	24569	6128	11.9	24.9	81	1982	7.7	13.4	91	2357	11.3	9.6	77	1789	11.2	7.3	77
UNDER $10,000	31101	7087	13.7	22.8	74	2341	7.5	15.8	85	2723	13.0	8.8	70	2023	12.7	6.5	69
HOUSEHOLD OF 1 PERSON	19441	5592	10.8	28.8	93	1762	9.1	11.9	102	2240	10.7	11.5	92	1590	10.0	8.2	86
2 PEOPLE	51803	14729	28.5	28.4	92	4491	8.7	30.3	98	6057	29.0	11.7	94	4180	26.3	8.1	85
3 OR 4 PEOPLE	66933	22232	43.0	33.2	108	6153	9.2	41.5	104	8730	41.8	13.0	105	7349	46.2	11.0	116
5 OR MORE PEOPLE	29550	9120	17.6	30.9	100	2438	8.3	16.4	93	3882	18.6	13.1	105	2801	17.6	9.5	100
NO CHILD IN HSHLD	96587	28254	54.7	29.3	95	8567	8.9	57.7	100	11397	54.5	11.8	95	8290	52.1	8.6	90
CHILD(REN) UNDER 2 YRS	10844	3472	6.7	32.0	104	719	6.6	4.8	65	1262	6.0	11.6	93	1492	9.4	13.8	145
2 - 5 YEARS	26358	8988	17.4	34.1	111	2491	9.5	16.8	107	3464	16.6	13.1	105	3033	19.1	11.5	121
6 - 11 YEARS	30453	10162	19.7	33.4	108	2684	8.8	18.1	100	4378	20.9	14.4	115	3101	19.5	10.2	107
12 - 17 YEARS	36575	11958	23.2	32.7	103	3159	8.6	21.3	98	4891	23.4	13.4	107	3508	22.0	9.6	101
RESIDENCE OWNED	117770	35228	68.2	29.9	97	9653	8.2	65.0	93	14476	69.2	12.3	99	11099	69.7	9.4	99
VALUE: $50,000 OR MORE	70166	24356	47.1	34.7	113	6767	9.6	45.5	109	10170	48.6	12.6	116	7419	46.6	10.6	111
VALUE: UNDER $50,000	47604	10872	21.0	22.8	74	2886	6.1	19.4	69	4306	20.6	9.0	73	3680	23.1	7.7	81

although heavy users of yogurt (purchase six or more cups of yogurt monthly) are more likely to live in the northeast market.

BENEFIT SEGMENTATION

In his book *Looking Out For Number One*, Robert J. Ringer shares his formula showing how people can make their lives more pleasurable by focusing on individual happiness and personal needs. In a sense, benefit segmentation uses Ringer's philosophy by asking a related question from the customer's perspective, "What is this good or service going to do for me?"

Benefits are the sum of product advantages or satisfactions that meet an individual's needs or wants. They extend beyond product features and serve to satisfy physical, emotional, or psychological needs. Two clear examples of what a benefit is are often cited in personal sales training:

- "Sell the sizzle, not the steak."
- "People don't buy drill bits, they buy round holes."

Benefit segmentation probes into users' buying motives and is linked directly to the marketing discipline of consumer behavior. A compilation of key benefits is analyzed in determining pertinent market segments. A primary benefit or a summation of benefits is often featured and used for segment identification purposes—for example, the Value Seekers. Ten benefit segments for categorizing prospective MBA students based on their educational motives/preferences are listed in Figure 5-5.

Arm and Hammer Baking Soda, a product that was in the decline stage of its product life cycle as a baking aid, has been successfully repositioned in recent years by appealing to a variety of new benefit segments. These include its uses as a refrigerator deodorizer, plaque remover, and bleach booster (for sweeter smelling clothes), to name a few additional product applications. More typically, a product will have one primary usage. However, through effective research, more than one potentially profitable benefit segment can often be identified. In many cases, the composition of benefit segments may differ markedly from demographic classifications alone.

It is only appropriate that we have previously explored psychographic and product usage bases, since benefits are closely allied to these dimensions. An individual's attitudes, values, lifestyle, and habits (past purchase behavior) toward a product generally have a great impact on subsequent

Figure 5–5:
10 MBA Benefit Segments

10 MBA benefit segments

BY GEORGE MIAOULIS and MICHAEL D. KALFUS

HERE ARE THE 10 BENEFIT SEGMENTS identified in a recent survey of candidates for the MBA degree.

1. QUALITY SEEKERS desire the highest quality education available in their communities. They are generally part-time students pursuing the MBA several years after their undergraduate education. They believe a first-rate education will benefit them throughout their business lives, ultimately leading to job advancement or career change. They seek an AACSB-accredited MBA program.

2. SPECIALTY SEEKERS desire a specialized education to become experts in their fields (insurance, health care, etc.). Concentrated, no-frills programs will fit their needs, and they will seek out institutions that offer them.

3. CAREER CHANGERS want different job positions or employers and believe the MBA degree will give them the opportunity for career advancement and mobility. They have worked for several years and typically perceive themselves to be in dead-end jobs, so the benefit they seek is career flexibility. They are part-time students who take one or two courses per term.

4. KNOWLEDGE SEEKERS want to learn and feel knowledge will lead to power. They believe a graduate MBA education will be an asset to any activity they undertake in their social, community, political, or corporate lives.

5. STATUS SEEKERS feel that graduate MBA coursework will lead to increased income and prestige. The MBA program which is conveniently located and inexpensive best fits their needs.

6. DEGREE SEEKERS believe the bachelor's degree is insufficient and that the MBA is essential to being "job-competitive" in today's business environment. They want programs which are "credible" and conveniently located. More than any other, this segment tends to have the highest proportion of full-time students. They are active, self-oriented, and independent.

7. PROFESSIONAL ADVANCERS strive to climb the corporate ladder. They want professional advancement, higher income, job flexibility, and upward mobility. They're serious, future-oriented, and want to build careers within their current corporate structures.

8. AVOIDERS seek the MBA programs which require them to invest the least effort. They feel all schools will give them essentially the same education. Their motivation is "other-directed" and they select low-cost, low-quality programs.

9. CONVENIENCE SEEKERS enroll in the MBA programs that are located near their homes or jobs and have simple registration procedures. They are interested in any school with these characteristics and low cost.

10. NONMATRICULATORS want to take MBA courses without completing formal application procedures. They are attracted to schools that allow them to begin the MBA program without GMAT or formal application. They want the opportunity to evaluate whether they really should participate in an MBA program. They are part-time students and typically take one course during their first year.

Reprinted with permission of the American Marketing Assn. George Miaoulis and Michael D. Kalfus, "10 MBA Benefit Segments," *Marketing News*, August 5, 1983, Section 1, p. 14.

benefits sought by that person. As expected, the more positive these experiences are, the more likely that the potential customer will seek those satisfactions. Recognizing the renaissance of the marketing concept (placing customer satisfaction first, while generating a profit), more and more companies are now cultivating the long-term, benefit-seeking customer.

Advantages of Benefit Segmentation

The prudent use of benefit analysis provides the marketer with a new perspective and added insight into market situations. When properly executed, this approach is widely acknowledged as one of the best ways to segment markets. Some of the benefits of the benefit dimension are:

1. It is an appropriate segmentation base for both consumer and industrial markets.
2. Unlike most other segmentation bases, benefit segments are based on causal factors rather than descriptive factors. Since benefits recognize why people buy, their purposes and product desires, a direct, or cause and effect, relationship exists between motivations and purchasing patterns.
3. Benefit segmentation is a method with great flexibility.
    a) Benefit segments can be identified through a variety of techniques, including but not limited to focus groups, the Delphi approach (a group of expert opinions), in-depth interviewing, and quantitative research (mail surveys, telephone and personal interviews). Analytical methods for forming benefit segments can span the gamut from basic tabulation of opinion to advanced multivariate, computer-generated analysis.
    b) Common or custom segment classifications can be used in the study. In past segmentation studies, some generic benefit segment groups have been called the Rational Man, Swingers, Hedonists, Elitists, Young Socialites, Worriers, and a host of other explanatory segment names. Custom segment classifications (add in the results of past research projects where relevant) should be used to maximize the value of the findings.
    c) Benefit segmentation can be used in conjunction with several other closely related segmentation bases/variables. These include product/firm loyalty, psychographics, perceptions, preferences, purchase intention, and purchase situations/occasions.

Limitations of Benefit Segmentation

In some respects the shortcomings of benefit segmentation resemble those of psychographic research—namely, problems in data collection and analysis, and cost factors. A further limitation to the effectiveness of arguably the most powerful segmentation base available to marketers is human behavior. The reality of the situation is that although individuals may seek certain rational benefits from a product in the marketplace, they sometimes do not respond as they indicate, and may deviate from their expected purchasing behavior.

OTHER BEHAVIORAL BASES

So far, we have explored in some detail three of the major behavioral segmentation bases for segmenting markets: psychographics, product usage, and benefits. Although these dimensions are some of those more commonly employed in segmentation analysis, by no means are these the only options. The marketer has literally dozens of alternatives to choose from in addition to the aforementioned bases. In most segmentation studies, the use of several segmenting bases (both physical and behavioral) is recommended. A brief overview of some of the other more prominent behavioral dimensions follows.

Perceptions and Preferences. A cross between psychographics and benefit segmentation, perceptions are concerned with how individuals mentally observe and comprehend brands, product categories, or companies relative to competitors. In many cases, these perceptions can differ significantly. Often two-dimensional or multi-dimensional computerized perceptual mapping techniques will be used to better understand and graphically depict potential market segments.

Perceptions are important, but consumer preferences can be even more valuable to marketers. This knowledge can greatly assist you in tailoring products to specific segment needs and wants. Table 5-5, for example, shows how five market segments rate the "ideal frankfurter" based on nine product attributes. A major advantage of perceptual and preference research is that they are extremely useful for developing marketing positioning strategies.

Situations/Occasions. Perhaps a "sleeper" in market segmentation analysis, situations and occasions are generally used as secondary methods, but they can often add great insight into the purchase decision area. One problem with this technique is that every market studied is so unique, and as a result, these bases are often difficult to measure accurately.

These dimensions recognize that individuals act differently depending on the situation they are involved in at a given time, or the occasion for which a product is being purchased. For example, a purchasing agent may

Table 5–5:

The Ideal Frankfurter—Mean Scores by Product Segments (Among Packaged Frankfurter Users Only)

"10" Rating Means:	Packaged Users Total	Product Segments I	II	III	IV	V
Saltiness (Very Salty)	2.9	3.3	(1.4)	2.1	3.8	2.9
Seasoning (Very Highly Seasoned)	4.2	4.8	(3.3)	3.6	(2.9)	[5.3]
Flavor Strength (Very Strong)	5.2	[6.1]	5.0	4.7	(2.1)	[6.1]
Garlic Flavor (Strong Garlic Flavor)	2.2	(.6)	[3.4]	1.5	(.9)	[3.8]
Color (Very Brown)	5.2	5.9	[6.9]	(4.0)	5.7	(2.2)
Outside Texture (Very Crisp Outside)	5.3	5.3	[7.0]	(2.8)	6.1	[7.1]
Inside Texture (Very Firm Inside)	5.2	5.7	6.0	(2.6)	6.0	[7.8]
Width (Very Thick)	5.9	5.2	5.5	[7.8]	[7.1]	6.2
Length (Very Long)	6.3	6.2	7.2	6.8	(4.7)	6.8
CLIENT BRAND SHARE	14%	10%	17%	12%	7%	25%

NOTE: All the attributes contributed significantly to differentiating the segments. Among the most important are color, inside texture (firmness), outside texture (crispness), and garlic flavor.

Boxed or circled ratings are statistically significant.

Reprinted with permission of Applied Research Techniques, Inc., Parsippany, NJ.

be a very conservative, fact-seeking buyer at the office, and at home be a rather impulsive free-spender. Similarly, a woman who shops for her wardrobe at a discount clothing store may not think twice about spending $60 for a bathing suit at a specialty shop, if she is planning a Caribbean vacation. These segmentation bases acknowledge the complexities, and at times contradictions, evidenced by all people to varying degrees.

Florists and card shops are two businesses built around special occasions. As Table 5–6 indicates, approximately 90% of florists' sales come

Table 5-6:

Sales by Occasion

(Single and Multi Ownerships Metro and Non-Metro Locations)

1980

MEDIAN PERCENTAGES*

OCCASIONS	U.S. SINGLE OWNERSHIPS			U.S. MULTI OWNERSHIPS		
	Top Metro	Other Metro	Non-Metro	Top Metro	Other Metro	Non-Metro
Funeral/Memorials	25%	28%	37%	23%	26%	34%
Holidays	25	24	24	25	24	24
Illness/Maternity	16	17	14	16	19	15
Birthdays/Anniversaries	14	12	10	14	14	10
Weddings	11	10	10	9	8	9
No Occasion At All	5	4	4	7	7	4
Business Gifts	5	4	3	6	5	4
Thank You/Hospitality	3	3	2	4	3	2

*Because of rounding error, all column percentages may add up to slightly under or over 100%.

from holidays (Valentines Day, Easter, Mother's Day, and Christmas), memorable days (birthdays, anniversaries, and weddings) and illness or funerals. Figure 5-6 shows how florists' dependency on funerals has lessened in recent years, as four other areas have increased in importance.

Media Exposure   One of the strongest influences of the twentieth century has been the impact of the various media on the American public. It has been stated that the average individual is exposed to several hundred or more advertising messages daily through television, radio, newspapers, magazines and periodicals, billboards and signage, direct mail, and other media classes. Armed with the knowledge of which media vehicles people are exposed to (the specific radio station listened to or trade journal read, for example) it is then relatively easy to reach prospective market segments. Given our media-driven society, it is not surprising that segmentation by this variable has grown significantly in recent years. In addition, media exposure/preference is particulary helpful as a complementary dimension to enhance other segmentation findings. This base is very helpful for demographic analysis and most types of behavioral studies (e.g., psychographics, product usage, benefits, etc.).

Marketing Mix Factors.   Markets can be segmented based on the marketing controllables: product, promotion, price and distribution. Some possible approaches to be used include:

Product—Segmenting on product features or attributes, perceived qualities, brand loyalty, innovativeness of new product acceptance, and/or purchase intentions. Previously we discussed product usage and perceptions and preferences which could also be considered in this context. Additionally, product segmentation can occur through analyzing the five senses (sight, sound, smell, taste, and touch). Consider the impact the senses can have on food products and related purchase behavior. Is the packaging attractive? Does it have snap, crackle, and pop? Is the aroma pleasing? Do you like the taste? Do the melons feel ripe?

Prior to the emergence of market segmentation as an important marketing discipline, product differentiation (still a viable strategy in many markets) was the primary means of concentrated marketing.

Promotion—Media exposure, the flagship promotional segmentation base, has previously been described. Other segmentable promotional avenues include sales territories (usually analyzed as a geographic base), possible copy platforms and sales appeals, and promotion acceptance/response rates (e.g., premiums, coupons, special offers, etc.).

Price—Markets can be segmented by price sensitivity/elasticity, price/

Figure 5–6:

Breakdown by Occasion for all FTD Shops, U.S., 1970–1980

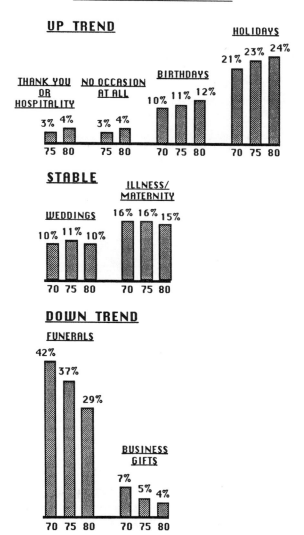

MEDIAN PERCENTAGES

Source: 1970, 1975, 1980 FTD Member Census

Table 5–6 and Figure 5–6 are reprinted from the FTD Flower Business Fact Book, pp. 27–28, with permission from the Florists Transworld Delivery Association.

quality relationships, and the importance of various price incentives on the purchase decision.

Distribution—Channels of distribution alternatives can serve to segment markets. Some examples of marketing channel strategies aid in illustrating this approach:

- selling direct to consumers (bypassing traditional channel members)
- wholesaling and retailing (taking on another channel member's function, vertical integration)
- selling via mail order (adding a new distribution method)
- selling to the government (penetrating new markets).

MANAGING THE BEHAVIORAL SEGMENTATION STUDY

At this point, marketing decisions need to be made in three areas related to behavioral attribute segmentation. These issues are selecting appropriate bases, determining the goals of the study, and whether or not outside assistance should be used.

Selecting Bases

As you can clearly see, there are many alternatives to consider as behavioral dimensions for segmentation analysis. No one choice is necessarily better than the next until it is carefully evaluated in a real world setting. Table 5–7, A Behavioral Segmentation Matrix, provides a valuable guide to assessing and evaluating all of the bases discussed in this chapter.

In a majority of projects multiple bases should be utilized, both physical and behavioral (don't neglect creativity as well—remember the car radio dial segmentation example in Chapter 1). Figure 5–7 lists some recommended behavioral dimensions and variables for use in market segmentation for a dental practice.

Goals of the Study

The ultimate objective of the segmentation study is to assist your firm in increasing its number of customers, and in turn, your revenues and profits. This can be accomplished in one of three ways: by attracting non-users to the product or service, increasing the usage of existing customers, and/or developing new markets. There are five important questions that you must answer prior to authorizing a segmentation study. These key discussion points are listed in Figure 5–8.

Table 5-7:

A Behavioral Segmentation Matrix
(Pros and Cons of the Alternative Bases)

Base	Primary or Secondary	Importance As a Base	Difficulty To Measure	Cost
Psychographics:				
• Custom	P	4	5	5
• Syndicated	S	2	1	3-4
Product Usage	P,S	5	2	2-3
Benefits	P	5	4	5
Perceptions and Preferences	P,S	4	4	4
Situations/Occasions	P,S	4	4-5	3-4
Media Exposure	S	3-4	3	3-4
Marketing Mix:				
• Product features/ attributes/qualities	S	3	3	3
• Brand loyalty	S	3	3	4
• Innovativeness	S	2	4	4
• Purchase intentions	S	4	4	4
• Sales territories	S	3	2	2
• Copy appeals	S	2	4-5	4
• Promotion response	S	1	4	4
• Price sensitivity/ quality trade-offs	S	3	4	3
• Price incentives	S	1	4	3
• Distribution channel functions/methods	S	1	3	3
• Distribution markets	S	3	3	3

Notes: P represents a primary segmentation base, while S stands for a secondary base. P,S means the base is frequently used in both applications. The three other measures are on a 1 to 5 scale; with 5 being the most important, difficult, or costly base, and 1 being the least important, difficult, or costly base relative to the other behavioral options. Also, a base that scores "low" here should not necessarily be disregarded. These are general guidelines only, and it is possible that such a dimension may be useful in the right market situation.

Figure 5–7:

Typical Behavioral Variables for a Dental Practice

Variables	Categories
Lifestyle	Traditional family, single parent family, single/ married professional, upwardly mobile, status seeker.
Benefits sought	Economy, convenience, prestige, dependability, enhanced appearance.
Patient status	Non-patient, potential patient, new patient, regular patient, occasional patient, former patient.
Frequency of dental visits	Three or more times a year, twice a year, once a year, once every eighteen months, once every two years, less than once every two years.
Loyalty to practice	None, medium, strong, absolute.
Dental health I.Q.	Low, medium, high.
Motivation to seek regular care	Low, medium, high.
Fear of dental treatment	No fear, mildly fearful, very fearful—but manageable, dental phobic.

Reprinted from the Dental Marketing Planner, 1983, pp.69–70 with permission of the American Dental Association.

Outside Assistance

Finally, there is the issue of whether or not to use outside assistance in designing, implementing, and evaluating the behavioral study. This type of research is more complex than physical attribute segmentation. In most cases (unless of course, you have someone in-house that can handle all or part of the project), it is advisable to use a skilled marketing research firm or marketing consultant in the project. Figure 5–9 lists twenty key questions to ask your research supplier prior to contracting for a behavioral study.

Figure 5–8:

Segmentation Checklist

Goals/Key Questions for the Behavioral Study

1) Have the ten planning and research guidelines (Chapter 3) been reviewed and acted upon?
2) How do you presently define your customer?
3) What alternative marketing strategies do you feel may be viable?
4) What value do you expect from the segmentation analysis?
5) How much is this answer worth to you?

Figure 5–9:

Segmentation Checklist

Contracting for Behavioral Research

1) Does the research firm have experience in this market or a related one?

2) How do they view the purpose of the project?

3) From a research perspective, what is involved in this segmentation study?

4) Will the research company work closely with you in the project?

5) What types of primary and secondary segmentation bases are advised?

6) Have all appropriate bases and variables been considered?

7) Will secondary or syndicated data and/or physical attribute dimensions be used?

8) Are national data bases required?

9) What data collection methods will be employed?

10) Will the survey instrument be pretested?

11) What size sample will be used?

12) Is the research product-driven?

13) Is the research design based on causal, descriptive, or exploratory factors?

14) What analytical methods will be employed?

15) How reliable will the findings be?

16) How practical will the information be?

17) Is assistance available in understanding and implementing the findings?

18) What information will be provided, analysis only or analysis plus recommendations?

19) Will there be an oral and written report of the findings?

20) How much will it cost?

SEGMENTATION SUMMARY SHEET: BEHAVIORAL ATTRIBUTE SEGMENTATION

Major bases: psychographics, product usage, and benefits
Other important bases: perceptions and preferences, situations/occasions, media exposure, and marketing mix factors

Psychographics:

- PSYCHOGRAPHICS = Personality Traits + Lifestyles (AIOs)
- Advantages of psychographics
  1) understanding markets
  2) explaining consumer behavior
  3) strategic marketing
- Limitations of psychographics
  1) problems in data collection and analysis
  2) costly
- Note ten guidelines to conducting psychographic studies
- Consider syndicated lifestyle research such as The Monitor or VALS

Product Usage:

- Classify users into specific consumption categories
  a) non-users vs. light users vs. medium users vs. heavy users
  b) light half vs. heavy half
  c) recognize the 80/20 rule and the 80/50 corollary
- Advantages of product usage analysis
  1) useful for consumer or industrial markets
  2) can increase consumption of heavy users in moderately competitive markets
  3) can increase consumption of light and medium users in highly competitive markets
  4) by providing additional benefits or focusing on neglected segments, non-users can be attracted to the product
- Limitations of product usage analysis
  1) product usage segments are often difficult to explain through demographics only
  2) there are problems with targeting the heavy user segment: competition, different buying motives, and lack of loyalty

3) there are definitional problems (e.g., what constitutes a heavy vs. medium user)

Benefit Segmentation:

The sum of product advantages/satisfactions that meet a specific need or want—more than a feature or attribute (what the product will do for the customer)

Advantages of benefit segmentation

1) useful for consumer or industrial markets
2) based on causal as opposed to descriptive factors
3) flexibility in research techniques, classification schemes, and works well with other bases

Limitations of benefit segmentation

1) similar shortcomings as psychographics (data collection and analysis, and cost)
2) human behavior—people don't always respond as they say they will

Other behavioral bases:

• see Table 5-7, The Behavioral Segmentation Matrix

Managing the behavioral study:

• selecting bases, goals of the study, and the use of outside assistance

APPENDIX 5-1:

Image-Concept Segmentation

Consumers are often driven by emotional needs. Consumer purchase decisions are usually made on the basis of non-rational influences rather than rational ones. Some examples of emotional needs and product categories that satisfy those needs are:

Emotional Need	Product Category
Need to be happy/feel good	Beer
Need to be successful/a winner	Business opportunity seminars
Need to be physically attractive/beautiful	Cosmetics
Need for love and affection	Flowers
Need to belong	Fashions
Need for adventure/ fantasy	Travel

Every product has a unique image, whether favorable or unfavorable. The marketer should consciously attempt to build and/or improve the image of his product or service. One way to do this is through researching the emotional needs and clustering the market segments according to what consumers wish the product or service will do for them.

Charles Revson once said, "In the factory we make cosmetics, in the drugstore we sell hope." This quotation is the quintessence of image-concept segmentation. Image-concept segmentation examines the other segmentation bases (physical and behavioral), and then supplements these with non-rational appeals. This process develops a more complete image of your product or service.

Image-concept segmentation relates well to advertising/promotional themes, particularly those using television as a medium because of its power to influence consumer behavior. However, other media have been used effectively as well. Through promotional efforts, a unique image can be projected for your good or service. This image should relate to the fulfillment of both rational and emotional needs consumers want your product to satisfy. Additionally, image-concept segmentation can also be used to enhance corporate identities.

Some prime examples of image-oriented messages for consumer goods include:

Television:
- The Pepsi Generation
- The Certs Encounter
- Have an Aviance Night
- Who says you can't have it all? (Michelob Light)

Radio:
- Molson Golden Ale

Print:
- The Marlboro Man

In summary, a more comprehensive approach to market segmentation planning, analysis, and strategy is offered by image-concept segmentation.

METHODOLOGY FOR IMAGE-CONCEPT SEGMENTATION

Step 1: Qualitative research—focus groups or in-depth interviews.

Step 2: Quantitative research—personal interviews, phone surveys, or mail/self-administered questionnaires. (Note, this is primarily an attitude-type research project, but other segmentation dimensions are incorporated into the analysis as well.)

Step 3: Develop an image-concept premise (ICP) through data analysis/reduction.

Step 4: Pre-test ICP.

Step 5: Strategic planning—develop promotional campaigns, refine distribution mix, and review pricing strategy. Make tactical decisions. (Note, the good or service offered is held constant.)

Step 6: Test market ICP-based marketing program.

Step 7: Monitor ICP-based program for performance/control. Revise, fine-tune, expand as indicated.

This appendix prepared by Art Weinstein and Marvin Nesbit, faculty members at Florida International University and partners in the marketing consulting firm, Pro-Mark Services.

APPENDIX 5–2:

The Yankelovich Monitor 1985
(Fifty-two social trends relevant to consumer marketing)

Trend Number	Trend Name
1	Personalization
1A	Social Pluralism
2	Physical Self-Enhancement
3	Physical Fitness and Well-Being
3A	Concern About Mental Well-Being
3B	Future Health Orientation
4	Social/Cultural Self-Expression
4A	Conspicuous Cultivation
5	Personal Creativity
6	Defocus on Money
6A	Toward Intangibles
7	Meaningful Work
8A	Reverence for Science
10	New Romanticism
11	Introspection
12	Novelty and Change
14	Return to Nature
16	Anti-Bigness
20	Living for Today
21	Hedonism
22	Away from Self-Improvement
24	Liberal Sex Attitudes
25	Blurring of the Sexes
26	Acceptance of Drugs
27	Anti-Hypocrisy

28	Rejection of Authority
29	Tolerance for Chaos and Disorder
30	Female Careerism
31	Away from Familism
31A	Need for Depersonalized Relationships
32	Concern About Environment
33	Concern About Privacy
34	The New Cynicism
36	Search for Community
36A	Ethnic Orientation
37	Concern About Personal Safety
38	Acceptance of Purposelessness
42	Reinstatement of the Social Contract
43	Need for Ideological Orientation
44	Flirtation With Danger
45	Simplification Through Technology
46	Commitment to Buy American
47	Responsiveness to Fantasy
48	Need for Self-Sufficiency
49	Hunger for Personal Feedback
50	Toward Divisiveness
51	Respect for Age and Experience
52	Accomodation to Technology
53	Emphasis on Winning
54	Accommodation to Wit and Wisdom
55	Away from Clutter and Complexity
56	Belief in Consumer Power

Reprinted with permission of Yankelovich, Skelly, and White, Inc. from the Yankelovich Monitor 1985, *Technical Description Reference Book*, June 1985. The firm is presently known as Yankelovich Clancy Shulman.

APPENDIX 5–3:

The VALS Typology
Nine Lifestyle Types

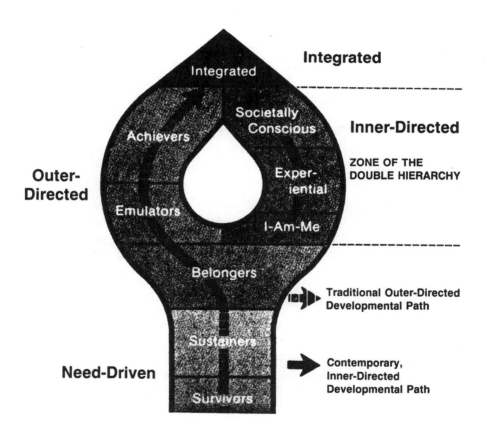

Reprinted with permission of SRI International, Menlo Park, CA.

CHAPTER SIX

Special Considerations in Segmenting Industrial Markets

In developing our industrial strategy for the period ahead, we have had the benefit of much experience. Almost everything has been tried at least once.

Tony Benn, 1974

The two previous chapters discussed major segmenting dimensions, both physical and behavioral, from a consumer-oriented marketer's perspective. Consumer market segmentation applies to retailers, personal service firms (banks or hair salons), and professional services (doctors or dentists) whose goal is to sell their products or services to the ultimate consumer. But what about the manufacturer, wholesaler, or business service firm (printer or marketing research company) whose products or services will be used by another company, as opposed to the individual consumer? In several respects this is a different marketing problem and, as such, requires a different planning, analysis, and strategic marketing approach. In this chapter, we will explore the unique needs of the business-to-business marketer, appropriate bases upon which markets can be segmented, and other considerations of industrial segmentation analysis.

WHY INDUSTRIAL MARKETS ARE DIFFERENT

Prior to designing the industrial segmentation research plan, it is important to recognize the major differences between consumer and industrial markets. The differences are:

- The Scope of the Geographic Trade Area
- Product/Market Factors
- The Nature of the Purchase Decision
- The Closeness of the Customer

Scope of the Geographic Trade Area. The area an industrial marketer serves is typically larger than the one served by local retailers or personal/professional service firms (of course, there are many national retailers such as Sears and McDonald's and services such as Merrill Lynch and H & R Block). However, most retailers and service firms generate a majority of their business from a relatively small geographic trade area, as shown in Appendix 4-2.

It is not uncommon for the industrial firm to conduct business in several counties, states, regions, or occasionally in international markets. Despite this larger trade area focus, the customer base of the industrial firm is generally highly concentrated. To illustrate this point, a client of mine in the industrial pumps and motors business serviced accounts throughout the Southeast, but the majority of his sales came from his own backyard (South Florida).

It should also be noted that industrial market areas are often easier to quantify and target than consumer markets. A distributor of graphic supplies can identify a target market (advertising agencies, for example) through readily obtainable trade directories. In addition to providing sales leads by name and location, these sources often list other vital marketing data such as the size of the company, key management personnel, and the products or services offered.

Product/Market Factors. Most industrial sales are larger than those in consumer markets. Of course, there are consumer purchases of automobiles, boats, or houses. But for individuals these are rare purchases. Most consumer sales are relatively small compared to industrial sales of equipment, materials, components, products, or services (periodic reorders of industrial parts and supplies may be small orders, however).

As a corollary to this, there are generally fewer potential customers for the company to target in industrial markets. At times, this smaller customer pool can play havoc with the best laid marketing plans. Dependency on a small core of customers often leads to large variations in revenues and profits (greater peaks and valleys), as the firm acquires or loses a major account. Industrial sales come from derived, not final, demand, which makes the industrial firm more susceptible to cyclical market pressures.

Steel producers, for example, are greatly dependent on automobile sales.
Nature of the Purchase Decision.   A complex consumer decision may
be a joint one between a husband and wife to buy new bedroom furniture.
In industrial markets complex decision making occurs on a regular basis.
Often, many people will be involved in purchase decisions. Special justifica-
tions, authorizations, and approvals will be needed, and months can pass
before a sale is transacted. The industrial salesperson is confronted with
more intelligent, calculating, and rational buyers than are typically found
in the consumer sector. On the positive side, once a customer has been
"sold," loyal, lasting customers are often the result.
Closeness of the Customer.   In Peter's and Waterman's book, *In Search
of Excellence*, they stressed the importance of getting close to customers
and listening to their needs and wants. This was one of their major criteria
for "excellence." Industrial companies are naturally closer to their
customers, although their satisfaction levels will vary from poor to excellent
depending on how well they implement the marketing concept (customer
satisfaction at a profit). Closeness in industrial markets is nurtured because:
personal selling is the most effective promotional strategy, the sales force
typically goes on-site to the buyers' premises, and long-term customer
relationships often develop. In addition, it is easier to stay in touch with
your market through trade journals that comprehensively cover industry
news and views, trade directories that provide detailed marketing information about firms, and trade associations that share knowledge about
markets. But, action—a responsive, customer-centered marketing program—is needed to truly meet the needs of the customer.

BASES FOR SEGMENTING INDUSTRIAL MARKETS

The segmenting dimensions for the industrial marketer are essentially
the same as for the consumer marketer, with some changes and a couple
of new additions. We have previously reviewed the following bases:
geographic, demographics, psychographics, product usage, benefits, and
other behavioral bases (perceptions and preferences, situations/occasions,
media usage, and marketing mix factors). These are important—to varying
degrees—in segmenting industrial markets. The difference between consumer and industrial market segmentation is the specific variables used
as part of these dimensions. Demographics provide a good example of
this point. Let's assume the variable in question is income. In consumer

markets, our concerns may be household, family, or per capita income. In industrial markets, our interests would turn to basic financial statistics about the organization (e.g., total revenues, sales by division or product line). Additionally, in this section, we will introduce two other segmenting bases particularly suited for industrial markets, SIC codes and product end-use analysis.

The Physical Dimensions

Geographic Bases. Geography, the starting point in an industrial segmentation study, is used to divide markets by market scope factors and geographic market measures. As discussed in Chapter 4, the market scope factors include global, national, statewide, and local scope breakdowns, while geographic market measures include population density (potential customer density for industrial markets), climate-related factors, standardized market areas, and census classifications. These latter two measures are of primary importance to the business-to-business marketer. Also, such sources as *Sales and Marketing Management*'s "Survey of U.S. Industrial and Commercial Buying Power" and the business census reports (see Appendix A, Part III - Business Demographics) allow the firm to target their efforts to specific industries, states, and counties. Through these resources, industrial marketers can better identify market areas, define and measure sales area potential, direct promotional activities, and evaluate the success of strategic marketing initiatives.

Demographic Bases. The next step, after geographic bases have been specified and determined, is to analyze a battery of relevant demographic variables. These "business demographics" are similar in concept and purpose to consumer demographics, but vary as to their application. Let's compare business demographic bases and variables to the more traditional consumer demographics. Table 6-1 shows the relationship between these two groupings using the basic framework developed in Chapter 4.

Note that two other demographic categories—Men and Women; and Race, Nationality, and Religion—were not considered in Table 6-1, since there was no relationship between those consumer demographics and comparable business demographics. This is not to say that these factors should never be considered in analyzing business markets. They can and should be used for a higher level analysis. Once all business data has been collected (business demographics plus product usage, benefits, SIC and end-use information, where appropriate and available), the marketer will

Table 6–1:

Business vs. Consumer Demographics

Category	Business Demographics	Consumer Demographics
Market Size	number of potential customers, number of stores/locations/ plants for a firm, the number of employees in a company	population, number of households or families, family or household size
Age and Stage	number of years firm has been in business, stage of product/ industry life cycle firm is in	age distribution, family life cycle
Monetary Factors	financial factors (revenues, sales volume, profits), type of business in (products and services), management style/ structure	income, occupation, education
Ownership Factors	own building/property vs. lease, type of establishment (storefront, office, plant, warehouse), length of time at facility	homeowner vs. renter, type of dwelling, house- hold mobility/ stability
Social Class (Industry Stature)	market/industry position, high tech vs. low tech	lower/lower to upper/upper, cluster approach

seek personal information about the decision maker—hence, back to consumer demographics.

However, at this time the issue at hand is business demographics. Where can you obtain this information? Table 6–2 shows the availability of key business demographic sources, based on a survey of libraries throughout the United States. You are also advised to refer to Appendix A: Sources of Marketing Information, Part III for brief summaries of some of the best business demographic references.

Table 6–2:

Library Demographics, Business Sources

Reference	% Libraries Available At
County Business Patterns	86%
U.S. Business Census Reports (e.g., Wholesale Trade)	77%
Sales and Marketing Management's Survey of U.S. Industrial and Commercial Buying Power	77%
Business Demographics from State Agencies	36%
State Business Censuses	32%
Business Demographics from Local/County Agencies	32%
Dun's Census of American Business*	18%
Other (eight additional business demographic sources were cited)	N/A

*This source was not on the original questionnaire. As a result, it is highly likely that this reference is more widely available than the survey figures indicate.

The Behavioral Dimensions

Product Usage. Analyzing consumptive patterns of existing and potential customers can be an important segmenting dimension in industrial markets. The first step is to divide the market into two groups: users and non-users. Next, workable classifications and definitions of users must be determined. Some possibilities include:

- heavy vs. medium vs. light users (based on unit or dollar sales, or number of orders)
- users of your product or service vs. users of competitors'
- loyal vs. non-loyal customers (the degree of loyalty shown)
- the applications of product usage by user group

- geographic differences by market (comparing customer penetration and growth patterns of two or more market areas)

As these categories indicate, the product usage dimension is by no means limited to a buy or no-buy decision. Through careful research, a wealth of valuable data can be gathered about past purchase behavior. Often this information is close at hand—customer invoices and credit records can be checked, industry directories and trade papers studied, and primary or secondary data collected where needed. Equipped with this knowledge, you are in a much better position to develop strategies to target various user segments of the industrial market.

Benefit Segmentation.   What is a business looking for when it considers purchasing an office copying machine? There are a number of possible factors that may enter into this purchase decision. These may include: price, special features offered (e.g., the ability to enlarge or reduce, make colored ink copies, produce a large number of copies quickly, etc.), service, including the maintenance required and company support provided, and reputation of the seller (is it a Xerox or an unfamiliar brand?). A benefit to one customer (enhanced features) may be perceived as a drawback to another customer (higher price).

By segmenting an industrial market through analyzing benefits sought, marketing strategy (e.g., personal selling techniques and promotional campaigns) can be tailored to the needs of specific customer sectors. Hence, customer action (interest, inquiries, and sales) and post-sale satisfaction are more likely to result through this approach than through unfocused marketing initiatives. You are advised to review the sections of Chapter 5 discussing product usage and benefit dimensions. The approach for these two segmentation bases is basically the same in consumer and industrial markets, but they are explored in greater detail there.

Psychographics.   Lifestyle and personality factors are not that critical in an initial segmentation study for an industrial market. The bases described previously in this chapter, plus some others to be discussed shortly, SIC codes and end-use analysis, play a more important role in the analysis. However, since individuals ultimately make all purchase decisions, psychographics can be an important dimension in understanding purchase behavior and influences. This higher level analysis assumes that the industrial marketer already has a good perspective on the market situation, and wants to expand the analysis to include characteristics of the target firm's decision maker(s).

Other Behavioral Bases.   Four additional behavioral bases were discussed in Chapter 5. These included perceptions and preferences, situations/occasions, media exposure, and marketing mix factors. Perceptions is a base requiring an understanding of individuals' awareness and attitude levels for a particular product, service, or company. In industrial markets, the key people to analyze for perceptions and preferences include purchasing agents, users, influencers, and decision makers. Similar in some respects to psychographics, these dimensions are typically not used in basic segmentation studies, but they can be incorporated into advanced analyses, where personal characteristics are of prime concern. End-use segmentation (to be discussed in the next section) is often used in lieu of situations/occasions in industrial markets.

As in consumer markets, media exposure can be an important secondary segmenting dimension. In industrial markets, however, personal selling is a more important promotional strategy than advertising. Industrial advertising is generally used to build a company's image, to remind customers and potential customers about the firm's products and services, and to generate leads for the sales force. A paramount media mix often employed in industrial marketing might include direct mail, trade journals, and trade shows (although the latter is really a sales promotion method, rather than an advertising media vehicle). Given the small market base and the relative ease with which potential customers can be reached, media exposure/preference analysis can be very effective in supplementing other segmentation findings.

The marketing mix factors described in the previous chapter—product, promotion, price, and distribution—can also be quite useful in industrial applications. The reader is advised to review that section, since it is applicable here as well. There is one major difference, however. In industrial markets, customized products for very specific applications are frequently needed. In this case, precise product requirements must be met, negotiation of price is a factor, face-to-face communication is critical, and distribution changes from a product movement function to one of service delivery.

Special Industrial Dimensions

Standard Industrial Classification (SIC) Codes.   One of the simplest and most important industrial segmenting bases, SIC codes have evolved from a statistical government data collection facilitator to a customer/

supplier classification tool for industrial marketers. The *Standard Industrial Classification Manual*, a publication of the U.S. Government Office of Management and Budget, is the master reference for defining industries.

This publication is periodically revised (every ten years or so, although the 1972 version is not scheduled to be superseded until 1987) and spans the gamut of U.S. economic activities including, but not limited to, the divisions of agriculture, mining, construction, manufacturing, transportation, communication, wholesale trade, retail trade, finance, services, and public administration. Major two-digit groups (e.g., wholesale trade are categories 50 and 51, durables and nondurables, respectively) are the first industry level breakdown. Table 6–3 provides a list of all of the two-digit SIC codes. Next, a three-digit industry group code is assigned (e.g., 501 represents the wholesaling of motor vehicles and automotive parts and supplies). Finally, a four-digit industry-specific number indicates an even finer distinction (e.g., 5012 is the appropriate category for the wholesale distribution of automobiles and other motor vehicles). The beauty of the SIC system is its widespread acceptance. A number of marketing references both public and private use the SIC code as a basic data gathering unit. Therefore, market analysis through multiple sources is possible.

The SIC system does have some major shortcomings, however. First, the basic manual is updated infrequently. Since the 1972 manual was the latest one available at the time of this publication, many high-tech industries such as computers, telecommunications, and robotics are not well represented as specific markets or industries. Furthermore, most marketing professionals feel that the SIC system is not responsive to today's service-based economy. Second, classes don't always correspond with marketer's needs. Some four-digit codes may have ten, twenty, or more subcategories. Let's examine SIC 5012 again. In addition to automobiles, other vehicles are included such as buses, campers, motorcycles, taxicabs, and trucks. With the SIC system, you are forced to "buy" the whole code—you cannot select specific segments of a predefined industry. A final limitation is the nondisclosure rule imposed by government publications. This means that information for an individual establishment in a geographic area cannot be released. If that firm was a potential customer of yours, you would not have access to data from public sources about that company. *Sales and Marketing Management*'s "Survey of U.S. Commercial and Industrial Purchasing Power" is not governed by the nondisclosure rule and provides important SIC-related data for industrial marketers. Figure 6–1 offers a brief guide to using this important industrial reference.

Table 6–3:
The Two-Digit SIC Codes

SIC Code #	Industry Description
01	Agricultural production—crops
02	Agricultural production—livestock
07	Agricultural services
08	Forestry
09	Fishing, hunting, and trapping
10	Metal mining
11	Anthracite mining
12	Bituminous coal and lignite mining
13	Oil and gas extraction
14	Mining and quarrying of minerals
15	Building—general contractors
16	Other construction—general contractors
17	Special trade contractors
20	Mfg. food and kindred products
21	'' tobacco
22	'' textile mill products
23	'' apparel and fabric products
24	'' lumber and wood products
25	'' furniture and fixtures
26	'' paper and allied products
27	'' printing and publishing
28	'' chemicals
29	'' petroleum refining
30	'' rubber and plastics
31	'' leather and leather products
32	'' stone, glass, clay, and concrete
33	'' primary metal industries
34	'' fabricated metal products
35	'' machinery, except electrical
36	'' electrical/electronic machinery
37	'' transportation equipment
38	'' measuring/controlling instruments

Table 6–3 (continued)

SIC Code #	Industry Description
39	Miscellaneous manufacturing industries
40	Railroad transportation
41	Highway passenger transportation
42	Motor freight transportation
43	U.S. Postal Service
44	Water transportation
45	Air transportation
46	Pipelines, except natural gas
47	Transportation services
48	Communication
49	Electric, gas, and sanitary services
50	Wholesale trade—durable goods
51	Wholesale trade—nondurable goods
52	Retail building materials, hardware, garden supply, and mobile home dealers
53	Retail general merchandise stores
54	'' food stores
55	'' auto dealers and gas stations
56	'' apparel and accessory stores
57	'' furniture/home furnishings
58	'' eating and drinking places
59	Miscellaneous retail
60	Banking
61	Credit agencies
62	Security and commodity brokers
63	Insurance
64	Insurance agents, brokers, and service
65	Real estate
66	Combinations: real estate, insurance, loans, law offices
67	Holding and other investment offices
70	Hotels and lodging places
72	Personal services
73	Business services
75	Automotive services
76	Miscellaneous repair services

Table 6–3 (concluded)

SIC Code #	Industry Description
78	Motion pictures
79	Amusement and recreation services
80	Health services
81	Legal services
82	Educational services
83	Social services
84	Museums, art galleries, botanical and zoological gardens
86	Membership organizations
88	Private households
89	Miscellaneous services
91	Government
92	Justice, public order, and safety
93	Public finance, taxation, and monetary policy
94	Human resources programs
95	Environmental quality and housing programs
96	Administration of economic programs
97	National security and international affairs
99	Nonclassifiable establishments

Source: *Standard Industrial Classification Manual* 1972, Office of Management and Budget.

End-Use. With this approach, the final application of the product is the segmenting base. Industrial products can take many forms, including raw materials, work-in-process, and finished goods. The end use of the product has a definite impact on the purchase decision (is it a relatively insignificant, perhaps replaceable part or is it a critical component of a machine?).

Related to the product application in industrial markets is a technique known as input-output analysis. This recognizes that most industrial transactions pass through a channel of users. By analyzing a series of intermediary sales, a company can more accurately focus in on their actual target markets. You now know how much of your product is being used, and by whom. This production/consumption data is available from such sources as *The U.S. Industrial Outlook, County Business Patterns, Survey of Current Business, Sales and Marketing Management,* Department of Commerce publications, trade associations, and private research firms.

Figure 6–1:

Guide to Using S&MM's Survey of Industrial & Commercial Buying Power

Guide to using S&MM's Survey of Industrial & Commercial Buying Power

B D E F G H

A

C

County SIC	Industry	Establishments		Shipments/ Receipts ($ Mil)	% Of U.S Ship / Recpt	% In Large Estab
		Total	Large	1983 (S&MM Est.)		
Marshall	All mfg.	73	25	928.6	.0477	71
2016	Poultry-dressing plants	7	5	346.3	3.7624	93
2328	Men's & boys' work clothing	3	2	61.0	1.2591	97
Mobile	All mfg.	190	55	2,999.4	.1541	72
2621	Paper mills, except building paper	2	2	589.4	2.8255	100
2819	Industrial inorganic chemicals n.e.c.	7	5	162.7	1.3896	93
2869	Industrial organic chemicals n.e.c.	5	3	373.7	1.0163	84
3731	Ship building & repairing	8	4	157.3	1.7724	93
7011	Hotels, motels, & tourist courts	10	1	71.1	.4078	82
8062	General medical & surgical hospitals	8	6	219.0	1515	97

A. Counties with at least one establishment of 20 or more employees in any 4-digit manufacturing SIC or any of the *SICBP's* selected 4-digit nonmanufacturing SICs are listed alphabetically, by state. In each county, individual 4-digit SIC industries with an aggregate employment of 1,000 or more are listed below the corresponding county name. Industries are identified at the 4-digit level of the **Standard Industrial Classification (SIC)** system used by the federal government, since this is the level of detail most often used by marketers. For a more in-depth discussion of the SIC system, see the article that begins on page 48. CAUTION: The county "All mfg." totals *will* add up to the U.S. total, although the individual 4-digit SIC industry totals for counties *will not* add up to the U.S. totals shown in **Section A** (page 50), since an industry will not appear under a county if it has less than 1,000 employees.

B. The "All mfg." line that appears for each county listed refers to the overall total for all of the manufacturing establishments in that

county with more than 20 employees. If there are no 4-digit industries employing 1,000 or more people in a particular county, the "All mfg." line will be the only data listed for that country.

C. The 4-digit SIC codes listed under a county name indicate that this industry has an aggregate employment of 1,000 or more in that county. The industry definitions for each 4-digit code are found to the right of the number. Nonmanufacturing entries are printed in italics. A more complete listing of all SIC coded industries and their titles is in the *Standard Industrial Classification Manual* (U.S. Government Printing Office, Washington, DC 20402; price: $15). It should be noted, however, that the *Survey* lists a few more 4-digit industries than the SIC manual, since we have retained certain industries that have been merged by the federal government into catchall groups.

D. The total number of establishments with 20 or more employees. For a detailed definition of

what constitutes an establishment, see the SIC article on page 48. The *Survey* lists establishments with 20 or more employees because these locations typically account for 90%–95% of an industry's activity.

E. Large establishments are locations with 100 or more employees. Since they generally account for a greater share of a county's total activity, a separate total of such establishments is provided. They can most often be considered the key selling prospects in a county.

F. The total shipments/receipts figure is the dollar value of the goods produced or distributed, or the services provided. Shipments is the term commonly used in mining and manufacturing industries; receipts in all other industries. Figures are shown in millions of dollars.

G. The figure showing the percentage of U.S. shipments/receipts indicates a county's importance relative to others, either in the "All mfg." area or in separate SIC industries. The two ratios make it easier for marketers to pinpoint those counties that are most important to their product or service. It should be noted, however, that the "All mfg." percentage figures pertain to a county's share of total U.S. shipments/receipts, whereas the percentage figures for 4-digit SICs refer to the county's share of the U.S. total *in that particular industry only.* Thus, within a county, percentages for 4-digit manufacturing industries will not add up to the percentage total for "All mfg.".

H. The portion of a county's business volume accounted for by large establishments (100 or more employees), suggests the necessary level of sales coverage. Normally, the higher the percentage, the fewer salespeople required.

Reprinted with permission from Sales and Marketing Management's Survey of Industrial & Commercial Buying Power, April 23, 1984, p. 54.

DESIGNING INDUSTRIAL SEGMENTATION STUDIES: SPECIAL CONSIDERATIONS

How do industrial segmentation research designs compare to consumer ones? There are some differences, but essentially they are similar in concept and in practice. The first step is to understand the "nature of the beast." In the beginning of this chapter, the issue of how industrial and consumer markets differ was addressed. The next step is to review the ten required elements (and note differences, where appropriate) of the segmentation design, presented earlier in Chapter 3. Recapping, these included:

1) Establish research objectives
2) Specify target population measurement units
3) State relevant definitions
4) Recognize segmentation viability/segment formation criteria
5) Select segmentation bases
6) Choose appropriate data collection methods
7) Employ sampling procedures
8) Analyze the data
9) Consider budgetary constraints
10) Know how the information will be used

Elements one through three are clear enough and require no further explanation. The major difference between industrial and consumer segmentation analysis is the segmentation bases (the heart of this chapter). You have now been exposed to these tools and can choose appropriate dimensions for your situation. The 4 Rs (rating the market, realistic in size, reach, and responsiveness) are often easier to assess in industrial markets, while segment formation criteria largely depend on the segmentation bases selected. Elements six through eight, the research procedures, generally are less complex (more clearly defined because of the personal interaction with the customer) in industrial markets. Since the company more often than the individual is the focus of the research, there is less of a need for psychographic and perceptual bases, and as a result, multivariate analytical techniques are seldom employed. Finally, cost factors and possible benefits of the information should be carefully evaluated prior to authorizing an industrial segmentation study.

Figure 6–2 provides two brief summaries of industrial market segmentation situations.

Figure 6–2:

Two Segmentation Capsules

Example 1:

Medic-Aid is a computerized healthcare forms processor specializing in Medicaid and Medicare reimbursements. The firm's primary market has been pharmacies, although hospitals, physicians, nursing homes, and other medical-related providers can benefit from this billing service. Major advantages of this service are:

1) Labor costs are reduced since additional employees/labor hours are not needed to code and enter prescription data.

2) Payment reimbursements are expedited.

3) The denied billing rate is substantially reduced.

Based on the nature of the service, market needs, and initial marketing efforts, the firm has further defined its primary target market as independent drug stores in areas with a large concentration of poor and/or elderly people.

Example 2:

CompuRent is a company that rents and leases computer equipment to banks, hospitals, schools, nonprofit organizations, and industry. The consumer market is a secondary market for the firm. Benefits of renting/leasing versus purchasing include:

1) You can try before you buy.

2) You may only have a short term need for the equipment.

3) Cash flow is controlled.

4) Expenditures can be applied toward purchase, if desired.

Recognizing the proliferation of computer retailers and the subsequent market shakeout, CompuRent was able to carve a niche in its local market by providing an alternative approach to computerization in our information dependent society.

Note: The two profiles above are based on marketing projects conducted for clients. The company names have been changed.

SEGMENTATION SUMMARY SHEET: INDUSTRIAL MARKETS

How industrial markets differ:

- the scope of the geographic trade areas (large, but concentrated)
- product/market factors (large sales, fewer customers)
- the nature of the purchase decision (more complex)
- the closeness of the customer (frequent personal contact)

The physical dimensions: see Table 6–1, business vs. consumer demographics

The behavioral dimensions:

- Important bases (product usage, benefits, media exposure, and marketing mix factors)
- Used for a higher level analysis; psychographics and perceptions and preferences

Special industrial dimensions: SIC codes and end-use analysis

Advantages of the SIC system:

1) simple
2) widespread acceptance
3) a customer/supplier classification tool

Limitations of the SIC system:

1) infrequent updates
2) product/service classes don't always match marketer's needs
3) the nondisclosure rule

End-use:

- the final application of the product is the segmenting base (similar to consumer situations/occasions)
- input-output analysis examines the series of intermediary sales transactions through the distribution channel

Segmentation design differences:

- segmentation bases are the major difference (reviewed as the focus of this chapter)
- segmentation viability, the 4 Rs (rating the market, realistic in size, reach, and responsiveness), easier to assess in industrial markets, generally
- less complex research procedures required

CHAPTER SEVEN

A Practical Approach To Segmenting Markets

Small opportunities are often the beginning of great enterprises.
Demosthenes, 343 B.C.

As we have alluded to throughout the book, there is no singular approach to conducting a market segmentation analysis. Therefore, it is impossible to state exactly what steps are necessary in segmenting markets. If we look at other disciplines, it is often possible to clearly identify procedures for accomplishing a specific task. Let's take photography, for example. The basic steps invariably are, 1) load the camera (insert film, and/or batteries and flash), 2) focus on the subject, 3) shoot the picture, and 4) develop the photographs. Segmentation is more difficult because every business situation is different, requiring specific manipulation of company resources, research tools, and analytical methods.

THE 8–S FORMULA

Nonetheless, a general flexible model can be used to facilitate the market segmentation process. This practical approach to segmenting markets consists of eight steps, which can be called the **8-S Formula**. The eight Ss are:

- Select market to evaluate
- Segmentation planning
- Secure information
- Segment formation I
- Situational segmentation
- Segment formation II
- Select target markets
- Strategy formulation

To illustrate how a market can be segmented using this approach, a segmentation study conducted for Hoffman Cosmetic Dental Studios will be featured. Segmenting markets via behavioral attributes will be discussed later in this chapter.

HOFFMAN COSMETIC DENTAL STUDIOS: A DEMOGRAPHIC EXAMPLE

As its name implies, Hoffman Cosmetic Dental Studios (HDS) is not your typical "drill 'em," "fill 'em," and "bill 'em" dental practice. Founded by Dr. Howard J. Hoffman in 1977, this two-dentist, ten-employee, North Miami, Florida practice has undergone a progressive transition process. Starting as a traditional dental practice (Howard J. Hoffman, D.D.S), it evolved into a full-service center (Hoffman Dental Center), and is presently an aesthetically-oriented practice (The Studio). Although preventive and remedial dentistry are still provided, the practice's major marketing thrust has been toward cosmetic services (e.g., bonding and implants).

Pro-Mark Services conducted a demographic market segmentation study for HDS to identify, quantify, analyze, and rate major market segments as to their relative potential. The objective was to develop appropriate marketing strategies to increase the overall market share of the practice by concentrating on selected target markets. This was of major importance, because in the highly competitive South Florida dental services market, dentists must be able to evaluate, anticipate, and react to changing market structures to survive.

The Analysis

A review of how Pro-Mark used the 8-S Formula in the market segmentation study for Hoffman Cosmetic Dental Studios follows:

Step 1—Selecting the market to evaluate. Prior to segmenting a market, it is necessary to precisely define the trade area in which a company competes. Based on a consultation with Dr. Hoffman, and an in-depth examination of pertinent county and zone maps, the market area was defined. This definition was based on four geographic market measures: census tracts, zip codes, municipalities, and area boundaries. Census tract data was the primary information gathering unit in this analysis. Figure 7-1 lists the thirty-two census tracts comprising HDS's service area.

Figure 7-1:

The HDS Service Area

(by Census Tract)

1.03	4.01
1.04	4.02
1.05	4.03
1.06	4.04
2.01	4.05
2.02	4.06
2.03	4.07
2.04	11.01
2.05	11.02
2.06	11.04
2.07	12.02
2.08	12.03
3.01	12.04
3.02	38.00
3.03	97.01
3.04	97.02

Step 2—Segmentation planning. Once the market for the study has been determined, then the analysis should be carefully planned out. The ten key planning guidelines for a segmentation study were detailed in Chapter 3. Let's examine these issues briefly as they relate to the HDS study.

1. Research objectives: The three primary objectives of this analysis were:
   a) to analyze the present market area (determine basic demographic statistics and short- and long-term growth patterns).
   b) to segment the market into distinct market segments, so unique and effective/efficient marketing programs could be designed.
   c) to profile and assess the relative strength of the cosmetic sector.
   A secondary objective of this study was to analyze the competitive environment in the HDS service area. Figure 7-2 summarizes the competitive situation in the market area.
2. Target population measurement units: Prospective patients were the measurement unit for the consumer analysis. The American Dental Association (ADA) Directory and the Yellow Pages were used for the competitive analysis—a listing of other dentists/dental practices.

Figure 7–2:

The Competitive Analysis

An important factor in analyzing market potential is the competition in an area. One method of measuring competitiveness is the resident-to-dentist ratio. The resident-to-dentist ratio for the southeastern United States averages 2,252 to 1 and in Dade County 1,665 to 1, based on 1983 population estimates.

The following table indicates the resident-to-dentist ratios by zip code in the defined market area of this study. The GP column indicates the ratio when only general practitioners are considered. The total column provides the ratio when both general practitioners and specialists are combined.

Zip Code	1983 Population	Resident-to-Dentist Ratio*	
		GP	Total
33138	27,891	2,145 to 1	1,550 to 1
33160	28,670	1,303 to 1	1,247 to 1
33161	39,027	1,858 to 1	1,561 to 1
33162	37,880	1,082 to 1	789 to 1
33167	17,562	17,562 to 1	17,562 to 1
33168	21,018	5,255 to 1	5,255 to 1
33180	11,020	1,102 to 1	918 to 1
33181	17,507	1,459 to 1	1,347 to 1

* Calculated by dividing the 1983 population estimate for each zip code by the number and type of dentists with offices located in that zip code. The information on the number, classification, and location of dentists was gathered from the *American Dental Association Directory*. The higher the ratio, the more favorable competitive situation in that area.

3. Relevant definitions: No unusual definitions were necessary.
4. Segmentation viability/formation criteria: The viability of segmenting dental markets has previously been documented in several trade publications. As discussed earlier (see Figures 4–5 and 5–7), the ADA endorses market segmentation as a strategic positioning tool. Additionally, articles such as Peter M. Sanchez's "Concepts and Strategies for Dental Services Marketing," which appeared in the 1983 American Mar-

keting Association publication, *Emerging Perspectives on Services Marketing,* provide a framework for segmenting dental markets. Dental markets also pass the **4Rs** test described in Chapter 3. They can be rated, are realistic in size, can be reached, and are responsive to marketing initiatives. Actual segment formation criteria will vary depending on the segmentation bases and variables used in the analysis.

5. Segmentation bases: Physical attributes were employed in analyzing the market for HDS and dental services. Geographic, demographic, and socioeconomic bases were used.

6. Data collection: The consultants relied heavily on public demographic information.

7. Sampling: Since behavioral attributes were not considered, sampling procedures were unnecessary. A census of the area was obtained through the appropriate sources of information used (see step 3).

8. Data analysis: Numerous market worksheets were developed to explore relationships among dozens of possible variables. Hundreds of calculations were performed to test for associations or differences for the key factors.

9. Budgetary constraints: Given the limited research budget for this project, behavioral attributes such as psychographics, purchase patterns, and perceptions were not considered.

10. How the information was used: Dr. Hoffman turned the research findings over to his advertising/public relations consultant for selected implementation.

Step 3—Secure information.   Given the scope of this project, syndicated and primary data were not used. Secondary demographic sources employed included U.S. Census Bureau reports, Dade County Planning Department data, and Donnelley's *Market Profile Analysis* for Dade County. A cluster-based segmentation design was used in the analysis. A battery of relevant demographic and socioeconomic variables were considered. Major demographic factors explored included population, household size, median age, and growth trends. Socioeconomic characteristics included median household income, home values, household mobility/turnover, and education levels. Other basic data was gathered in the course of the analysis which was not critical in eventual segment formation. This marketing planning information included data on sex, race, occupation, and comparative city and zip code demographics. Figure 7–3 depicts an overall market profile of the HDS service area.

Step 4—Segment formation I.   During this phase, an initial or rough classification scheme is devised. In the HDS analysis, the composite characteristics of the thirty-two census tracts under study act as basic segment-

Figure 7–3:

Market Analysis: HDS Service Area

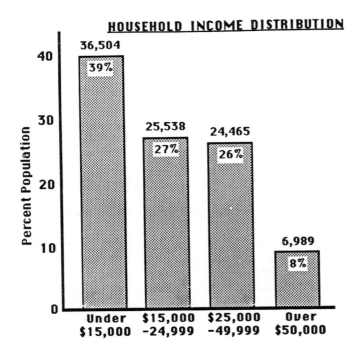

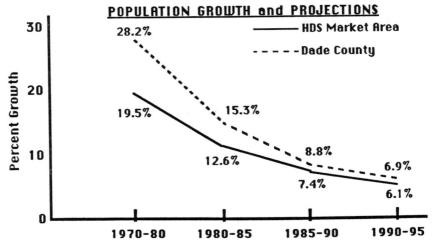

Figure 7–3:

Market Analysis: HDS Service Area (continued)

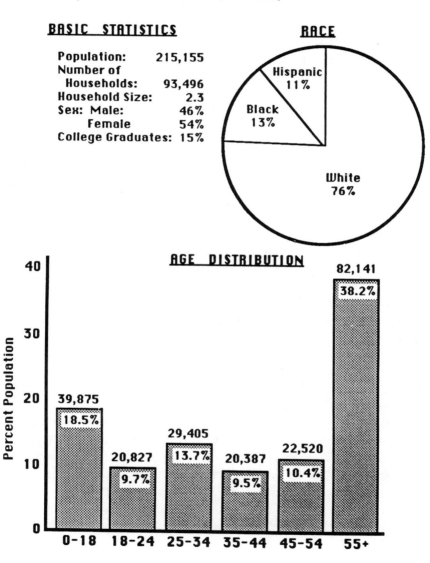

BASIC STATISTICS

Population:	215,155
Number of Households:	93,496
Household Size:	2.3
Sex: Male:	46%
Female	54%
College Graduates:	15%

RACE

Hispanic 11%
Black 13%
White 76%

AGE DISTRIBUTION

Percent Population

Age	Count	Percent
0-18	39,875	18.5%
18-24	20,827	9.7%
25-34	29,405	13.7%
35-44	20,387	9.5%
45-54	22,520	10.4%
55+	82,141	38.2%

ing units. A comparative tract-by-tract analysis serves to reduce the individual geographic areas into eleven similar market segments.

Step 5—Situational segmentation.   The next step is to decrease the number of market segments to a more manageable number. This is done by isolating appropriate segmentation variables. In this study, five variables— median age, median household income, home value, mobility/turnover ratio, and education—were key differentiating factors (segment formation criteria).

Step 6—Segment formation II.   Once the critical elements have been determined, further simplification of the market segments is possible. In this study, segment formation II reduces the eleven segments to six (see Figure 7-4, the six segments). One tract, #1.03, is unclassifiable due to the many inconsistencies of its population base (relative to the segment formation criteria). Appropriate names have been given to each segment based upon salient attributes of each group. Names facilitate segment recognition and are helpful in further marketing planning.

Step 7—Select target markets.   Based on the market segmentation analysis conducted for HDS, six segments were identified after segment formation II. Three segments, The Up-and-Comers, American Dream, and Home Base, were deemed as potentially profitable segments. Figures 7-5 and 7-6 provide an overall segment profile and census tract composition for the Up-and-Comers. Two other sub-markets, Opa-Locka and The Squeezed Seniors, were cited as unprofitable potential segments. The dental philosophy and business mission of HDS are not compatible with serving the lower economic stratum characterized by the Opa-Locka area. Major shortcomings of The Squeezed Seniors segment are its geographic location (not in close proximity to the office) and low per capita incomes. The consultants recommended that no marketing investment be directed toward these segments. This does not imply that patients should be turned away from these areas, but rather efforts should be concentrated on the stronger market segments. A final segment, The Condo Dwellers, was viewed as a borderline case. While the analysis revealed that this segment was potentially profitable, the marketing investment required to reach and persuade this group to utilize HDS's dental services would be quite costly in both time and dollars. Therefore, no immediate marketing efforts to this segment were advocated.

A sound market segmentation analysis, such as the one outlined here, requires strategic choices. The objective is to pursue the most attractive

Figure 7–4:

The Six Segments

(by Census Tracts)

Up-and-Comers
11.04, 12.02, 97.01

American Dream
2.04, 2.05, 3.01, 3.02, 3.04, 4.01, 11.01, 11.02

Home Base
2.01, 2.02, 2.06, 2.07, 2.08, 3.03, 12.03

Condo Dwellers
1.04, 1.05, 1.06, 12.04, 38

Opa-Locka
4.02, 4.03, 4.04, 4.05, 4.06, 4.07

Squeezed Seniors
2.03, 97.02

Note: Census tract # 1.03 was unclassifiable due to the many inconsistencies of its population base.

target market opportunities (using differentiated marketing strategies and
tactics) at the possible expense of less desirable segments.

However, segments not targeted for marketing activity might still, at
times, respond to marketing initiatives. The segmentation spillover effect
means that consumers in non-targeted segments may relate to the promotional message, for example, and wish to take advantage of the product
or service offered.

Step 8—Strategy formulation.   The final step in a good segmentation
study is to develop short- and long-term strategies based on the findings.

Figure 7–5:

Basic Findings—Segment Profiles

Up-and-Comers Profile

1. This segment is characterized by professionals, managers, and administrators who are heading toward or at their earnings peak.

2. This segment is comprised of census tracts 11.04, 12.02, and 97.01.

3. The geographic location of this segment is in Miami Shores [11.04 and 12.02] and the Ojus area [97.01].

4. The total population in this segment is 21,873.

5. The total number of households in this segment is 8,397.

6. The average household size of this segment is 2.6 persons, which is above the market area average of 2.3.

7. The distribution by age for this segment is:

<18	18–24	25–34
5,290 [24.2%]	1,663 [7.6%]	2,775 [12.7%]
35–44	45–54	55 and over
2,982 [13.6%]	2,976 [13.6%]	6,187 [28.3%]

8. The household income distribution for this segment is:

<$15,000	$15–$24,999	$25–$49,999	$50,000
2,196 [26.1%]	1,562 [18.6%]	2,816 [33.6%]	1,823 [21.7%]

9. 70% of the residences are single family units and 82% of all residences are owner occupied.

10. This segment has an average mobility turnover ratio of .22, which is well below the county average of .32.

11. 28.4% of this segment are college graduates, which indicates an education level significantly above the market area, with 14.6%.

12. This segment is projected to have virtually zero growth from 1980–85 with the exception of tract 97.01, which is slightly above the county average.

Figure 7–6:
Up-and-Comers
Census Tracts

	11.04	*12.02*	*97.01*
83 Population	4,324	6,898	10,651
83 Household Size	2.3	2.2	3.1
Median Age	47	47	34
83 Median Household Income	25,744	25,828	34,316
% Difference County Median Income	34.5	35.0	79.3
80 Home Value	70,958	82,676	117,510
Mobility Turnover Ratio	.25	.24	.19
% College Graduates	15	28	34
% Growth 1980–85	0	1	18

This will be discussed in the next chapter. In our in-depth study for Hoffman Dental Studio, general marketing recommendations in the areas of planning, strategy, and evaluation were provided, since no previous marketing research was undertaken (note Figure 7–7). However, specific target market recommendations were the focus of the strategic marketing work performed. Examples of marketing strategies designed for The Up-and-Comers segment are provided in Figure 7–8.

THE BEHAVIORAL SEGMENTATION STUDY

The HDS example illustrates a "typical" demographic segmentation study based on the physical attributes discussed in Chapter 4. But what about the potentially more powerful behavioral dimensions explored in Chapter 5? Will the **8-S Formula** work in this type of segmentation analysis? The answer, I am pleased to report, is yes. There are some minor

---

Figure 7–7:

General Recommendations

Planning:

— Use market research from this analysis as a foundation in development of a comprehensive marketing plan.

— Compare demographics of existing patients with segment profiles.

— Measure visitation patterns of existing patients with classification by frequency, services rendered, etc.

— Establish marketing objectives and budget for marketing efforts by segment and promotional activities.

Marketing Strategy:

— Implement sales training/patient relations program for staff.

— Develop a patient survey to assess present product/services and pricing strategies.

— Use promotions to attract new business as well as for reminder purposes.

— Expand telemarketing efforts to attract new business, increase visitation frequency, and promote patient goodwill.

Evaluation:

— Use computer as a marketing information system (demographics, visitation patterns, direct mail).

— Promotional efforts need to be measurable.

---

differences between the two major classes of studies, however. Let's look at the **8-S Formula** as it applies to behavioral attribute segmentation.

Step 1—Selecting the market.   In a behavioral study, the market to be evaluated is often not a geographic one. While physical areas play a part in the market definition, behavioral studies often define the market as a "state of mind" or "state of action" (e.g., the fashion-conscious woman, the traditional savings account customer, or the frequent flyer).

Figure 7–8:

**A Summary of Recommended Marketing Strategies
for the Up-and-Comers Segment**

Overall Strategy: Promote high quality family dentistry as well as the
benefits of cosmetic dentistry.

Marketing Rationale: Patients in this segment are likely to have at least
two needs for dental services. First, they are seeking the "best" available care for their family. A second major need of these young professionals is to improve their appearance, often to enhance their careers.

Appropriate Type of Dentistry: Preventive and cosmetic dentistry.

Promotional Appeals: Aesthetics, vanity, attention, and humor.

Promotional Tactics:

a) advertising—highly targeted advertising to this upscale market is
required. Appropriate media vehicles include a community magazine with reader demographics geared to the cosmetic thrust (upper
income, expensive homes, substantial net worth, mostly managers
or professionals, and primarily college graduates ages 25–54) and
an affluent homeowners mailing list.

b) promotions—new promotional incentives should be considered for
this segment. Possibilities include gold-plated toothbrushes, dental travel kits (containing toothbrush, toothpaste, and floss), pens,
calculators, and restaurant or club passes.

c) patient relations—the dentists should treat these patients as peers.
The dental staff and office should reinforce an image of high quality professionalism.

Step 2—Segmentation planning. There is little difference between
research objectives and target population measurement units for physical
and behavioral attribute segmentation analyses. Both of these planning elements need to be specified in a successful study. Relevant definitions,
however, are more problematic in a behavioral project. These might include
trade area definitions (physical and non-physical); measures for evaluat-

ing lifestyles, benefits, or perceptions; consumptive classifications; defining marketing mix elements in terms of segmentation variables; etc.

Segmentation viability and formation criteria can be more difficult or easier to assess and construct, depending on the segmentation base(s) employed. For example, psychographics is generally more complex, while a product usage analysis may only require basic tabulation by consumption into user groups. As far as actual dimensions are concerned, there are many more options available to the marketing analyst, with creative approaches to "old" problems often possible.

The research process itself is usually more complicated, since most of the information gathered is primary in nature. This may require designing survey instruments, developing field procedures to collect data, using sampling methods to provide representative findings, and employing computer-assisted analytical methods.

Also, behavioral projects (depending on the scope of the research) often are many times more costly than demographic studies. Since the research results may differ markedly from what is expected, a good marketing manager should be flexible and open-minded.

Step 3—Secure information. Marketing research might tell us that the automobile market can be subdivided into five segments; the status/luxury, performance, utility, economy, and used car markets. While behavioral studies rely greatly on primary data, the incorporation of syndicated data, particularly in the lifestyle area, is gaining in popularity. Secondary data almost lives up to its nomenclature in behavioral studies, since it is relegated to a supporting role (this is not by choice, but rather by the research limitations of this information).

Step 4—Segment formation I. In many behavioral studies, there may be some historical precedent for segment formation. A past study may have been conducted by your company, aspects of a competitor's planning strategy could have been featured in a trade journal article, or information might have been obtained through a trade association presentation. Sometimes valuable lessons can be learned from other companies operating in similar, but distinct, industries. A good example of this is the marketing strategies that hospitals have adapted from the hotel industry (e.g., both industries are dependent on room occupancy, work closely with intermediaries—doctors or travel agents, are highly labor-intensive, and are in extremely competitive markets). A prior knowledge base can be used as a foundation for building a new segmentation model.

The dental market research reviewed earlier (e.g., the ADA information and the Sanchez article) are "information building blocks." Rather than trying to reinvent the wheel, researchers should utilize other valuable findings, expand on them, and adapt the research to their situation at hand. The overall assessment of other marketing studies is that they should be incorporated into the new project wherever feasible. They can provide a basic understanding of a market, its driving forces, and perhaps input on customer needs. Russell I. Haley's classic benefit segmentation description of the toothpaste market (the sensory segment, the sociables, the worriers, and the independent segment) documented demographic strengths, key behavioral characteristics, brands favored, and personality and lifestyle factors for these four market classifications.

Hypotheses and hunches should also be explored. "Gut feel" is often sound business judgment based on an aggregation of years of experience. A priori determinations for testing can also be useful in providing the segmentation model direction.

Step 5—Situational segmentation.   A major difference between physical and behavioral segmentation is that in the latter study, an explanatory link to purchase behavior (the dependent variable) is obtainable through the employment of key segmentation factors (independent variables). Independent variables can include all demographic characteristics, and behavioral variables such as lifestyle data, benefits, perceptions/preferences, situations/occasions, media exposure, and marketing mix factors. Dependent variables are generally related to consumptive measures of a market (e.g., sales by units, customer category, product or brand, etc.). This causal relationship can be expressed mathematically as:

$$aX1 + bX2 + cX3 + dX4 + \ldots + nXn = Y$$

(where X1 is the first independent variable, X2 the second, and Xn the nth; a, b, c, or n is the degree of impact of that variable; and Y is the dependent variable).

Demographic analysis does fall short, in that only general characteristics of a population are surveyed. It is also important to gauge product-driven and situation-specific factors to complete an overall market picture.

Step 6—Segment formation II.   At this stage, new segmentation findings have been added to previous segmentation classifications. Final segment formation is now imminent. A couple of key points to remember. First, analyze segments by chosen segmenting dimensions. If these factors are consistently evidenced in all segments (or a vast majority), they are not good segmenting dimensions, but perhaps, market descriptors.

Second, seek a unique segmenting dimension as a competitive edge. Table 7–1 provides a rating of ten product characteristics desired by potential buyers of a desk lamp. This table will be used to clarify these two points.

Four consumer markets can be identified using the findings above. Segment 1, The Price Shoppers, want an acceptable desk lamp at the lowest cost. Segment 2, The Quality Shoppers, are most concerned about the brand name or manufacturer, the type of lighting provided, and the style of the lamp. Segment 3, The Special Features Seekers, view desk lamps as being essentially the same commodity. Their purchase choice depends primarily on what unique advantages one lamp provides over another as it relates to their needs (e.g., adjustability, space requirements, and/or special lighting features such as high intensity lighting or a hi/lo switch). Finally, there is Segment 4, The Light Conscious. These consumers are most interested in a product that offers them the best possible lighting. These people spend

Table 7–1:

Purchasing a Desk Lamp

Benefits Sought	Segment 1	Segment 2	Segment 3	Segment 4
Adjustability			X	X
Brand Name		X		X
Color		X		
Fluorescent Lighting		X	X	X
Functional	X	X	X	X
Has a Hi/lo Switch			X	X
High Intensity		X	X	X
Minimal Space Requirements			X	X
Price	X			
Style		X	X	

a lot of time at their desk and will carefully shop for a desk lamp that meets their rigorous standards.

As you will note from Table 7-1, the desired product characteristics of fluorescent lighting, functional, and high intensity would not be good segmenting dimensions since these benefits are sought by most or all of the segments. Also, if most of the desk lamp manufacturers and distributors were targeting the Price and Quality Shoppers segments, potential might exist in pursuing the Special Features or Light Conscious segments (of course, further research into the size and accessibility of these segments would be necessary).

Steps 7 and 8—Select target markets and strategy formulation. There are no major differences between physical and behavioral attribute segmentation as they relate to these steps. Both are logical extensions of research findings, whereby specific marketing opportunities are pursued. Target market selection and strategy development will be stressed in the next chapter.

SEGMENTATION SUMMARY SHEET:
A Practical Approach to Segmenting Markets

The **8-S Formula** is a general flexible model to facilitate the market segmentation process. It is useful for both physical and behavioral attribute segmentation studies.

The eight Ss include:
- Select market to evaluate
- Segmentation planning
- Secure information
- Segment formation I
- Situational segmentation
- Segment formation II
- Select target markets
- Strategy formulation

Step 1—Selecting the market: geographic, state of mind, or state of action measures.

Step 2—Segmentation planning: specify the ten key planning elements of a good segmentation study.

Step 3—Secure information: primary, secondary, and/or syndicated data sources.

Step 4—Segment formation I: devise an initial or rough classification scheme, utilize other valuable findings, expand on them, and adapt to your present marketing situation. Produce a basic market segment structure for the industry and/or company.

Step 5—Situational segmentation: decrease the number of segments to a more manageable amount, isolate appropriate segmenting variables, determine independent and dependent variables, and analyze product-driven and situation-specific factors.

Step 6—Segment formation II: further simplification of the market segments, name the segments, analyze by chosen segmenting dimensions, and seek a unique segmenting dimension.

Step 7—Select target markets: choose potentially profitable segments cognizant of marketing investment required, competitive actions, and resources. Use differentiated marketing strategies and tactics, and products or services (where necessary) toward target market opportunities.

Step 8—Strategy formulation: see Chapter 8.

PART THREE

Translating Segmentation Findings Into Strategy

CHAPTER EIGHT

Target Market Strategy

*Take time to deliberate, but when
the time for action has arrived,
stop thinking and go in.*

Napoleon Bonaparte, 1815

Market segmentation can be informative, insightful, and even interesting. But its real value lies in its ability to create profitable business opportunities from similar market situations. Market segmentation analysis and strategy development can be likened to playing cards in several respects.

All players (the companies competing in a given industry or market) must abide by the same rules and are dealt cards from the same deck (overall market conditions). Each player must decide how they will play their hands (the strategy) given their resources (financial, skills, strengths and weaknesses, etc.). Some players might be financially strong and can outspend their competitors, while others may be aggressive and win on their business savvy (knowing how to bluff, when to get out, etc.).

Market segmentation recognizes that all hands (marketing opportunities) should not be played equally, but rather the players (the companies) should concentrate on those efforts which provide them the best chance for success. In marketing, success is most likely to come from the best prospects for your goods or services—your target markets. Strategic marketing, the subject of this chapter, is a difficult issue to address since there are so many interrelated factors (marketing, managerial, and financial) that impact it. We will examine strategy from the market segmentation perspective. That is, the strategic process necessary to translate segmentation findings into an actionable plan, and how the marketing mix must be tailored to segment needs and desires.

THE THREE BASIC STEPS TO STRATEGY FORMULATION

A three-step process can be used to achieve the first half of this objective. This consists of the following components:

1) Identify market segments
2) Target market segments
3) Position the segments

Identify market segments.   The first seven chapters of this book developed a framework for planning and conducting a market segmentation analysis. The end product of such a study is the determination of a given number of homogeneous market segments based on selected segmentation variables and criteria. Now the market has structure, and marketing decisions will change from analytical to strategic in nature. Figure 8–1, for example, depicts a perceptual map of six benefit segments of Americans who are potential vacation travelers to Canada.

Target market segments.   The first major strategic decision is to select from the alternative market segments one or more groups you want to target for marketing activity. Each of the individual segments needs to be evaluated on its own merits and in conjunction with the capabilities and environmental situation surrounding the firm. Such an evaluation will recognize that the options are distinct and unique from one another, and have varying degrees of attractiveness to the company. Although several sub-markets may be worth pursuing, the firm must balance a multiplicity of tangible and intangible factors. This list must include customer needs, the internal environment (in particular, financial and other resources), the external environment, an assessment of opportunities versus problems, and corporate objectives. A measure of segment potential can then be determined. At this point, the company has decided what sectors of the market to go after.

Position the Segments.   It is next important to formulate a unique marketing strategy to appeal to the customers you are trying to reach. Although a "me-too" or copycat strategy has worked at times for some firms, in the majority of cases, a new perspective or fresh approach to marketing is required to stand out from the crowd and be successful.

Let's assume, for example, that research findings from a psychographic segmentation study for an automobile dealer indicate that they can target either young professionals or middle-age consumers for their new sports car. If most of their competitors will be pursuing the Yuppie segment,

Figure 8-1:

Map of the Six Benefit Segments

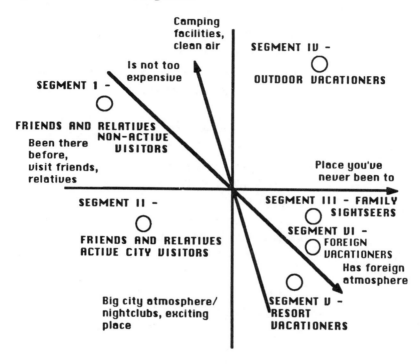

Reprinted with permission of the American Marketing Assn. Shirley Young, Leland Ott, and Barbara Feigin, "Some Practical Considerations in Market Segmentation," *Journal of Marketing Research*, August 1978, pp. 405–412.

the firm should strongly consider the alternative sub-market. A "fountain of youth" strategy, allowing mature adults to combat a mid-life crisis or restore some of their younger days, might be called for. Such a positioning strategy might be just what the doctor ordered in a highly competitive market.

The overall marketing strategy employed, which includes the manipulation of the marketing mix (the 4 Ps), is the positioning aspect of strategic implementation. The basic premise behind positioning is that the firm must have a competitive advantage or advantages to survive or prosper in the marketplace. These advantages can be real (e.g., a better product or lower price) or perceived (e.g., a product that is built to last or backed by a company's reputation). Positioning is sound marketing decision making based on the facts—the segmentation study findings—plus business creativity. This creative process might call for searching out unique marketing advantages, seeking new market segments which competitors are not cultivating, or developing new approaches to "old" problems. Figure 8-2 provides a model for incorporating the three-step strategy formulation process into a company's marketing plan for selected target markets. The goal of the positioning strategy is to carve out a market niche for the firm.

Nichemanship: Strategic Marketing Management at Its Best

Nichemanship is the process whereby a company integrates marketing and management activities to optimize its strategic position in a given market. The development of a positioning strategy for a targeted market segment (evolving from a segmentation study) is a major part of nichemanship, but other key factors play an important role as well. Nichemanship resembles market segmentation in many respects, but there are some additional qualities found in the firm aggressively pursuing niches in the marketplace. These activities include:

1) The company determines the products or services it can best provide cognizant of market needs and wants.
2) They design differentiated products and services to meet these demands.
3) By only focusing their energies on specific target markets, they are much more efficient in satisfying their customers.
4) Change is sought. These companies are not looking to conduct business like everyone else, but rather find a new and (hopefully) better way to do things.
5) A management commitment to excellence in all endeavors is the company's underlying operating philosophy. An environment for growth is fostered.

Additionally, firms that practice nichemanship are customer-driven, trend setters/trend spotters, product and market innovators, and creative marketing strategists. True niche-based firms also recognize the value of sound research and stand the test of time. Apple Computer and McDonald's are two such firms. While the former might be a more obvious choice to many, the latter company also fits this bill. In 1955, McDonald's had only one hamburger restaurant. Thirty-plus years later, "The Golden Arches" have served billions of hamburgers, revolutionized the fast-food industry, and created a worldwide empire.

It is in the scope of their areas of responsibility that nichemanship and market segmentation differ. Nichemanship is a broader concept encompassing management direction, overall marketing strategy, and product

Figure 8–2:

The Strategy Formulation Process

Step 1: Identify Market Segments
(list the sub-markets from the market segmentation study)

Market Segment A _____
                                    segment name

Market Segment B _____
                                    segment name

Market Segment C _____
                                    segment name

Market Segment D _____
                                    segment name

    ,,   ,,   _____
                                    segment name

Market Segment X _____
                                    segment name

Step 2: Target Market Segments
(select key segment or segments for marketing activity)

Primary market _____
                                    segment name

  Target market profile and needs:

Secondary market _____
                                    segment name

  Target market profile and needs:

Step 3: Position the Segments
(formulate a unique marketing strategy)

Primary market _____
                                    segment name

  Competitive advantages:

  Positioning strategy:

Secondary market _____
                                    segment name

  Competitive advantages:

  Positioning strategy:

differentiation. Segmentation, on the other hand, is a more clearly defined marketing discipline designed to discern and respond to customer needs in the marketplace. Since market segmentation is a strategy unto itself, it is directly related to managerial policy making and decisions and the company's marketing plan. Product differentiation, mentioned briefly in Chapter 1, will be explored later in this chapter as an alternative to market segmentation in selected business situations.

STRATEGY DEVELOPMENT

Marketing strategy was touched upon in Chapter 2 (the marketing planning section). Segmentation strategy is the process whereby a firm maximizes the marketing controllables (the 4 Ps) toward satisfying a target market's needs. Marketing strategy recognizes the dynamics of markets, and the objectives, resources, and "personality" of a company. Personality means the company's business character (its organizational philosophy and management style) and the importance of people functions in the marketing plan.

Hence, a master marketing program must mesh with your company's business style, and be appropriate for the firm given its present situation. Marketing is not a business function to be undertaken by only the marketing researchers, advertising department, or sales force. It is an ongoing series of activities that permeates all levels of the company, from president to part-time help. Similarly, all levels of the company must be apprised of appropriate strategies or tactics relevant to their areas of responsibility.

Successful segmentation strategy consists of two phases. First, the strategic position (niche) in the marketplace must be pursued. This three-step process, described earlier, sets out the overall strategic direction the company will follow. Next, primary and secondary marketing mix elements must be reviewed, formulated, or revised. These are the weapons used to win the "marketing war."

In specifying marketing strategies for a target group, three broad business areas must be carefully analyzed. They are customer needs, and internal and external marketing factors. Customer needs must consider how segments are defined based on the typical physical and behavioral segmentation dimensions and variables; product uses and usage patterns (note: since consumptive measures frequently are dependent variables, it is advisable to separate out this base); present levels of product satisfaction;

etc. As a starting point, the Strategic Environmental Scorecard, Figure 8-3, can be used as a comparative measure of strength or weakness for a number of internal and external marketing factors.

Product Strategy

In segmentation studies, the customers' views toward the product are the driving force in shaping appropriate product strategies. In developing these strategies, a firm must analyze all of the goods or services it offers. This includes individual product items, brands, product lines, and the product mix the business handles. In segmentation strategy decisions, we are more concerned with specific product units or families of products than entire product classes, markets, or industry sales volume.

Factors that impact product strategy decisions include the nature of the product, the product and industry life cycle, the classification of goods, product policies, and the role of product differentiation.

The nature of the product refers to the basic characteristics of the good or service. Some important product questions to ask are listed in Figure 8-4. Once these issues are resolved, the firm has a good understanding of the intricacies of the product, its applications, and the market it is competing in—a key toward strategy formulation.

Life cycles provide another useful tool for analyzing products prior to strategy development. Like people, industries and products have an aging process. This five-phase life cycle consists of birth, growth, maturity, decline, and death. It is important to assess where the industry is, and where the industry is heading. Also, determine where your product is in its life cycle. At the introductory and early growth stages of a market, products will appeal to innovators and the early adopters. As the industry develops and matures, competition will intensify and new segmentation strategies will be needed to find a niche in the marketplace. Finally, at the decline stage, the customer pool has been severely depleted, and the remaining market segments must be nurtured and cultivated for efforts to remain profitable.

The classification of goods framework divides consumer and industrial products into groupings of similar products based on their inherent qualities or characteristics. Convenience, shopping, specialty, and unsought goods comprise the consumer goods classification. Table 8-1 shows the role market segmentation takes on for the various types of consumer products. Industrial goods can be classified into capital purchases (such as build-

Figure 8–3:

The Environmental Scorecard

Factors	Strength +	Neutral 0	Weakness −

Internal Situation

Resources:
    People
    Financial
    Facilities
    Equipment
    Computers
    Other (list)

Past performance:
    Company
    Division
    Product line
    Product

Constraints:
    Objectives
    Commitment
    Policies (list)

Present marketing mix:
    Product
    Promotion
    Pricing
    Distribution

External Situation

The industry:
    Size of the market
    Industry structure
    Homogeneity of market
    Market potential
    Growth trends
    Opportunities/problems

Competition:
    Number of competitors
    Strength of competitors

Environmental factors:
    Economic conditions
    Social/lifestyle trends
    Technology
    Political environment
    Legal environment

Note: This checklist can be used as a guide to major environmental factors affecting a firm. An in-depth marketing audit and situation analysis is recommended. Additionally, the factors will have varying degrees of significance, and this must be assessed to provide a complete picture of the firm's environment.

Figure 8–4:

Segmentation Checklist

The Nature of the Product

1) What type of product is it?

2) What is it primarily used for?

3) Are there any other applications for the product?

4) Who uses the product?

5) Why do they use it?

6) What benefits are customers seeking?

7) Is there anything customers or potential customers do not like about the product? Why?

8) Is the product branded?

9) Does it have any other favorable proprietary positions (i.e., patents, copyrights, and/or trademarks)?

10) How is the product manufactured?

11) How is the product distributed?

12) How is it promoted?

13) How is it priced?

14) What is the product's past performance (sales figures, strengths, and weaknesses)?

15) Does the company produce any related products?

16) What is the competitive environment like?

ings or heavy equipment), tools and other equipment, raw materials, parts and materials, supplies, and industrial services. Chapter 6 addressed the area of industrial market segmentation.

Product policies relate to the firm's business mission and operating philosophy. These are constraints or guideposts which govern product decisions. Product policies serve to limit product choices in a number of strategic areas. The first consideration is the markets to compete in and the broad product offerings to compete with. Other product policies can relate to the company's product testing program (planning efforts, research and development, and test marketing), new product policies (a product

Table 8–1:

Market Segmentation and Consumer Goods

Type of Goods	Example	Importance of Segmentation	Overall Assessment
Convenience Goods:			
• Staples	Grocery products	2-4	These products are widely distributed and low-cost. Mass marketing is generally more important than market segmentation. Segmentation, however, can be important for branded goods in competitive markets.
• Impulse	Breath sweeteners	2	Ease of purchase and preferred display are major success factors for impulse items. Since these purchases usually are unplanned, segmentation has little impact on the buying decision.
• Emergency	Automotive repair service	1	An unexpected purchase, consumers will opt for quick solutions to their problems.
Shopping Goods:			
• Homogeneous	Toaster	3	Although consumers will exert some effort for these products, these goods essentially are perceived as being similar. Price is often the determining factor in the purchase decision.
• Heterogeneous	Videocassette recorder	4	These products are viewed as related, but different. Styles or unique features are sought by consumers. Segmentation can be very important for these markets.

Table 8-1:

Market Segmentation and Consumer Goods (continued)

Type of Goods	Example	Importance of Segmentation	Overall Assessment
Specialty Goods:			
	Exotic perfumes	5	These products are only available through limited or exclusive outlets. Consumers will search for the products or brands they want, and will not settle for substitutes. Segmentation is very important for these goods.
Unsought Goods:			
• New	Videotex	2	While some segmentation efforts can be pursued (targeting the innovators and early adopters), the majority of the market are not good prospects, since they are unaware of the product's existence or they cannot personally justify its benefits.
• Existing	Cemetery plots	1	While consumers are aware of these products (and often their benefits), it is a decision that is frequently avoided—many times until the need for such a product arises. It is extremely difficult to segment this type of market.

Notes: a) The importance of segmentation is listed on a 5-point rating scale. A 5 means segmentation is most important and a 1 means segmentation is least important. A 3 indicates average importance.

b) This table provides general guidelines only. All consumer products and markets must be evaluated individually for possible market segmentation, and the actual importance of this procedure may vary somewhat in selected markets.

innovator or imitator), product mix decisions (including branding and product line extensions or deletions), packaging, warranties, and service.

The four product factors we have explored so far have provided some direction for a market segmentation program—adapting the product or service to meet the unique needs of selected target markets. But in some cases, product differentiation—emphasizing the product differences rather than the customer needs (if the needs for a product are basically the same)— is the more important marketing strategy. The Strategy Selector, Figure 8–5, can be used to assist in this decision process.

The soft drink industry is a clear example of a market in which seg-

---

Figure 8–5:

The Strategy Selector

Marketing Variable	Market Segmentation More Important			Product Differentiation More Important	
Size of the market	Large				Small
	1	2	3	4	5
Customer sensitivity to product differences	Low				High
	1	2	3	4	5
Product life cycle	Saturation			Introduction	
	1	2	3	4	5
Type of product	Distinct Item			Commodity	
	1	2	3	4	5
Number of competitors	Many				Few
	1	2	3	4	5

Adapted with permission of the American Marketing Association. R. William Kotrba, "The Strategy Selection Chart," *Journal of Marketing,* July 1966, pp. 22-25.

mentation is the preferable strategy. According to the criteria in the Strategy Selector, it would score a 1, 3, 2, 2, and 1 respectively. On the other hand, hearing aids are a product where product differentiation is the more advisable strategy. Since its market is relatively small, and the product is always used for the same purpose (to amplify sound), product superiority is more important than market segmentation. Its scores using this model might be 5, 4, 3, 4, and 3 respectively. These results do not mean that either strategy should be used in isolation. Product differentiation is still important in the soft drink industry—there are regular vs. diet products, colas vs. non-colas, caffeine-free products, and a variety of package sizes, to name a few distinctions. Also, segmentation would be used to reach the audiologists (a prime decision maker for selecting hearing aids).

Although five key factors affecting product strategy have been discussed, an overall product strategy must still be formulated. Each of these five areas can play a major role in designing specific product strategies. Also, the product decisions are closely linked to the other marketing mix elements (promotion, pricing, and distribution). Based on the analysis of the product factors, product-oriented strategies will surface. These might include the introduction, modification, or elimination of products. Modification can be minor or major. The objective is to reposition, reformulate, or repackage the goods or services to appeal to new segments of the market or strengthen the firm's market position with existing segments. Another option, at times viable, is no change. If the analysis indicates that the present product mix is strong, strategic marketing changes may be called for in other functional areas. In addition to prescribed overhauls for overall product strategy, sometimes dozens of tactical product decisions may need to be made to fine-tune a company's product offerings.

Promotional Strategy

A company can reach and persuade its target markets by using a mix of the four promotional elements—personal selling, advertising, publicity, and sales promotion. The Definitions Committee of the American Marketing Association defines these promotional tools as follows:

Personal Selling—An individual promotional means characterized by face-to-face two-way communication about a good or service.

Advertising—Any paid form of nonpersonal presentation of ideas, goods, or services by an identified sponsor.

Publicity—News about a product, service, institution, or person not paid for by the sponsor.

Sales Promotion—All activities which supplement advertising and personal selling efforts, such as exhibitions, displays, demonstrations, and other nonrecurrent selling activities.

Personal selling is a deceptively important promotional strategy. In the United States, annual investment in this area is approximately three times the amount spent on advertising. Selling is where the actual dollars change hands, irregardless of the market (consumer, industrial, government, etc.). Good selling is matching the needs of the customer to a firm's goods or services. If this is accomplished, a sale will be made, a satisfied customer established, and a potential long-term relationship will be started. The beauty of personal selling is that its objective parallels that of market segmentation—tailoring products to meet customers' needs.The one major weakness plaguing this promotional approach is its high costs. The February 17, 1986 issue of *Sales and Marketing Management* featured the "1986 Survey of Selling Costs." This source estimated that the cost of a single sales call is $131.40. To offset this limitation, the other mass promotional techniques can be employed to generate highly qualified inquiries and leads to make personal selling more efficient (hence, improve the closing ratio).

Advertising is a dynamic, interesting, and at times glamorous field which is often misunderstood by the American public. It is also a very complex area with many interrelated components affecting its overall business impact (e.g, media options, budgets, media selection and scheduling, message preparation, the role of the advertising agency, and measurement techniques). Depending on a company's promotional focus, advertising can span the gamut from being virtually nonexistent to being a major factor in determining a firm's success or lack of success. From a segmentation perspective, advertising is an excellent, but not inexpensive, means of reaching out to the firm's most likely prospects, their target markets.

Successful advertising calls for investing your dollars wisely. Advertising expenditures should be allocated to those media vehicles which can best deliver target markets. There are dozens of different media that can be used (one advertising professional claims that more than 14,000 choices exist). Obviously, most of these media are obscure, impractical, or unimportant. For simplicity, media can be divided into three major classes: broadcast (radio, television, film, and other electronic media), print (newspapers and many types of periodicals), and other media (direct, directory, outdoor, transit, specialty, etc.). The "etc." are those remaining 14,000 options. In addition to the media classifications, there are thousands of media vehicles to choose from. Some are highly selective and well suited to reaching designated market segments. Consider these examples.

- Cable TV: The Entertainment and Sports Programming Network (ESPN) can deliver upscale men.
- Business publications: Regional business magazines can provide business professionals in desired geographic areas.
- Direct Mail: More than 25,000 different mailing lists can be purchased. The ABCs of Direct Mail includes available lists for accordian players (professional ones, of course), bird cage manufacturers, and Chinese launderers, for starters.

Other media vehicles are more general in nature. They reach large numbers of potential consumers, but are poorer at delivering the desired market profile. In addition to media considerations, creative and copy platforms must be developed in meeting segment needs.

Publicity is somewhat related to advertising but is a different promotional strategy. Unlike advertising, which is company sponsored, publicity is placed by an outside organization and is perceived as being more objective. Excluding PR initiation costs, publicity is free promotion, and its exposure can provide a most favorable response to the firm. In addition to the targeted media vehicles used in a well executed publicity campaign, speaking engagements, written materials, and special events are typically featured.

Finally, sales promotion activities such as samples, consumer price incentives, premiums, contests and sweepstakes, point-of-purchase displays, and trade shows and exhibits can be used to supplement other promotional efforts. The underlying question to answer prior to the use of any and all promotional strategies and tactics is, "Is it right for the market segment you are trying to attract?"

Pricing Strategy

How much should you charge your customers for your product? This question is one of pricing strategy. Setting prices for your goods or services is not a simple issue. There are many marketing and financial factors affecting this decision. Price also can be viewed from several perspectives, in addition to the marketer's concept of price. Table 8-2 shows how other business professionals view price.

Table 8–2:

The Many Faces of Pricing Decisions

Business Professional	Techniques Used in Determining Price	How Price Is Set
Accountant	Analyze fixed and variable costs Perform breakeven analysis	Cost plus markup
Financial Analyst	Analyze past and proforma financial statements	Payback, return on investment
Economist	Analyze supply and demand	Where marginal revenue equals marginal cost

Financially-based pricing methods are important considerations in setting prices, but from a marketing standpoint, other factors besides price must be considered. These include the firm's operating philosophy, the image it is trying to convey, the competitive situation, other external factors, the target market the company is pursuing, customer price expectations, product factors, promotional strategies employed, and distribution channels used. Price/quality tradeoffs may exist or be perceived by target markets (some customers feel that because a product is more expensive, it is a better product—this may or may not be true).

Pricing is not a unidimensional variable. For many products, price may be composed of several elements. Take the real estate market, for example. The rise of creative financing methods in recent years recognizes the dynamics of the key pricing components of this market. The consumer contemplating buying a house today must understand the home's list price, interest rates, closing costs such as points and builder's costs, a variety of mortgage options, buydowns (if any), taxes, insurance, etc.—all part of the pricing package. In other business situations, the price may also be affected by finance charges, delivery expense, trade discounts, consumer price incentives, and/or service fees. The bottom line is that price setting is not something to be taken lightly. Like other strategic aspects of the marketing plan, careful research is vital in this area.

Overall pricing strategies for a company can take one of four directions.

1) *Beat their price:* This strategy depends on high volume, as offering low price implies operating on low margins.

2) *Meet their price:* This competitive pricing strategy recognizes market forces. In this instance, the firm competes on some nonprice issues in an attempt to differentiate itself from the other firms. This can include having a better product, an improved image or reputation, offering post-sale servicing, etc.

3) *Do not compete on price:* If a higher priced strategy is being used, the firm must provide additional benefits to their customers or convince them that they are purchasing "top quality." High prices may be justified where there is limited competition, high costs associated with new product development, exclusive products offered, or limited consumer resistance.

4) *Retreat due to price:* In some circumstances, the firm may not have the economies of scale or other operating efficiencies to compete profitably in a market situation. In this case, the recommended strategy might be to cut your losses and get out of that market, and allocate those resources toward other more attractive market opportunities.

Which strategy is best? Again, it depends on the firm's market situation. Pricing research is an area that should also be addressed as part of the market segmentation analysis.

Distribution Strategy

Channels of distribution, a sometimes neglected marketing controllable, need to be periodically evaluated (although less frequently), as do the other marketing mix elements. A marketing channel is an exchange pathway through which goods are moved, flowing from the production point to intermediaries, and finally to the ultimate consumers. A channel might include a manufacturer, one or more middlemen, retailers, and customers, although much shorter channels are evident in many business situations (for example, mail order).

While marketing channel decisions tend to be well entrenched (it is a relatively fixed marketing variable), present strategies should be analyzed to determine if they are the most efficient ones possible. Sometimes minor changes such as using a new supplier can have a favorable impact on a company's distribution program. Some distribution strategy options for the firm include:

Long vs. short channels—A long channel uses several intermediaries to handle storage, sorting, transportation, promotion, and related functions.

The other extreme is the short channel, which implies a direct relationship. An example of this is the customer who buys direct from a manufacturer.

Wide vs. narrow channels—If the objective is to get the product into as many outlets as possible, a wide channel strategy is employed. Building an extensive distribution network is necessary if mass marketing tactics are used. Narrower channels recognize the value of market segmentation. One example of this channel strategy might be to establish an exclusive product in selected "fine stores."

Push vs. pull strategies—If the product is promoted to other channel members (manufacturers to wholesalers to retailers, for example), a push strategy is used. If the end user is targeted directly, as grocery product manufacturers promote their goods to consumers, then a pull strategy exists.

Imitate vs. innovate—Traditional channels of distribution are the obvious, safe, and uncreative approach. Many times it is the way to go. However, if a new or modified channel can be found, a competitive edge may arise.

The above strategies are polar extremes. Not everything in life and in marketing is black or white. Varying degrees of greys also occur. Therefore, a channel may be shorter or longer, wider or narrower, etc. Combinations of push and pull, and imitation and innovation may also be required. Additionally, several of these channel strategy options may be happening simultaneously (e.g., short, narrow channels).

TARGET MARKET STRATEGY FORMULATION: MAKING THE PLAN WORK

Ideally, market segmentation findings can be readily translated into workable strategic programs. But this is not always the case, and strategy formulation is not an easy process. Although many segmentation studies are data-based, strategy development almost requires a sixth sense. There are intangible factors such as experience and creative insight that also play a major role in strategic design. Given the limitations of one chapter, this book could only present a framework for general strategy development. Marketing elements will have different levels of importance in various segmentation analyses. For one company, product factors may be the primary consideration, while in another, promotion or distribution can be the central issue. Secondary elements should not be neglected either, since their impact can also be crucial to developing the new marketing program.

Specific strategies and tactics must be adapted to particular situations (market segments). Figure 8-6, the Target Market Strategy Worksheet,

Figure 8–6:

Target Market Strategy Worksheet

Market Segment Name: _____

Opportunities:

    1.

    2.

    3.

Threats:

    1.

    2.

    3.

Goals:

    <u>Marketing</u>   <u>Financial</u>

Overall Marketing Strategy:

Marketing Mix Strategies:	Present Strategy	Recommended Strategies	Potential Impact
Product			
Promotion			
Pricing			
Distribution			

Marketing Mix Tactics:	Present Tactics	Recommended Tactics	Potential Impact
Product			
Promotion			
Pricing			
Distribution			

Evaluation/Control Measures:

provides a model for identifying key strategic issues and capitalizing on them. An in-depth strategic plan is the recommended next step. The goal is to produce a consistent, information-backed document with synergism created among all of its components. Such a project can be implemented, and then monitored for performance.

SEGMENTATION SUMMARY SHEET: TARGET MARKET STRATEGY

The three steps to strategy formulation:

1) Identify market segments (options from segmentation study)
2) Target market segments (select key segments for activity)
3) Position the segments (seek competitive advantages and a new market niche)

Overall Strategy:

- research customer needs
- internal factors (resources, performance, constraints, present marketing mix)
- external situation (the industry, competition, and environmental factors)

Product strategy factors:

- the nature of the product (segmentation checklist)
- product and industry life cycles
- classification of goods
- product policies
- product differentiation vs. market segmentation

Promotional strategy:

- the right mix of personal selling, advertising, publicity, and sales promotion techniques

Pricing strategy:

- price setting factors include the firm's operating philosophy, the image it wishes to project, the competitive situation, external factors, its target market, customer price expectations, the other marketing controllables, and cost considerations
- strategies available—beat, meet, do not compete, or retreat

Distribution strategy:

- long vs. short channels, wide vs. narrow channels, push vs. pull, imitate vs. innovate

Making the plan work:

- use a planning framework
- recognize primary and secondary issues
- add the intangible ingredients into the formula (experience and creative insight, plus the research)
- adapt strategies and tactics to your situation (fine-tune the marketing mix)
- monitor the plan and make necessary changes

CHAPTER NINE

Enhancing Segmentation's Value — Some Guidelines

The business executive is by profession a decision maker.
Uncertainty is his opponent. Overcoming it is his mission.

John McDonald, 1955

The market segmentation study has been conducted, findings specified, and strategies developed. Is our segmentation work complete at this
juncture? Almost, but not quite. Two important areas must still be
addressed. First, there is the implementation and evaluation of the action
plan. Secondly, and more importantly, is the creation of an internal marketing environment conducive to maximizing the value of market segmentation analysis.

IMPLEMENTATION AND CONTROL

Bringing "life" to the segmentation analysis is the function of implementation. No longer are we concerned with "what ifs?", now we "do it."
Successful implementation of prescribed marketing strategy will require
the skills and expertise of many professionals. Marketing researchers,
analysts, planners, strategists, advertising and public relations personnel,
the sales team, consultants, and marketing managers must all work in con-
cert to accomplish specific goals and objectives. Additionally, the marketing department must interface with corporate management to ensure
that strategic thrusts are compatible with organizational policies and values.
Assuming all systems are go, a "master implementation switch" is turned
on, and plans now become actions.

Are actual results meeting expectations? Probably not. In most business situations, there will be a number of unforeseen occurrences impact-
ing the product—some good, some bad. The objective is to maximize your
strengths (opportunities) and circumvent your weaknesses (threats). This

is where the essential, but too often overlooked, evaluation program takes over. For top effectiveness, a system of controls should be built prior to implementing marketing strategy. This mechanism leads to quick detection of potential problems and advantageous situations. Implementation and control is a major part of a sound overall marketing program.

GUIDELINES FOR SEGMENTATION STUDIES

Market segmentation can reward your firm with some or all of these riches—new customers, better customers (a segment of the market desired), more satisfied customers (designing products more responsive to their needs), increased sales, the identification of potentially profitable marketing opportunities, and improved market share. This process takes considerable time and effort, however. Successful segmentation requires well conceived research and planning, and strategies formulated based on the study's findings and monitored for performance.

The following guidelines are tips to assist and improve the value of your firm's market segmentation efforts. This list is divided into two parts. The first set of guidelines are procedural in nature. These are helpful "how-to" pointers geared toward conducting segmentation studies. The second group of recommendations are management-oriented. Their purpose is to provide direction for segmentation's role in your company's marketing plan.

Procedural Guidelines

Here are five valuable tips designed to assist you in performing segmentation analysis.

1) Plan, plan, plan.   Successful segmentation projects are based on planning. The major objective is to obtain usable information. Will it assist in solving specific marketing problems? Determine what is presently known about your market, and what you need to know about your market. The difference is the focus of the research. The planning guidelines presented throughout this book (e.g., the 4Rs, the ten required elements of segmentation design, the 8-S Formula, and various segmentation worksheets and illustrations) are one such aid. This information can be used to supplement company, industry, and general planning guidelines.

2) Consult key references.   Thorough research is the backbone of the segmentation project. There is a wealth of free and low-cost secondary sources of information that can be used. Tapping these sources can often answer many of your initial market information questions at a fraction of the cost of primary information (see Appendix A: Sources of Marketing Information). Past industry and company research can also prove instrumental in the new project. The segmentation researcher must be a "student of the market." You should regularly follow movements and market trends, the industry structure, overall market performance, the competitive environment, and related factors. The quest for market insight should go on continuously—not just when the need for specific information arises.

3) Recognize the dynamics of the market. Just as no two people are identical, neither are two markets or companies. It is critical to acknowledge the uniqueness of business entities and situations, and act accordingly. Consumer markets differ markedly from industrial ones; personal services are not the same as professional or business services. Similarly, within broad industry groups, clothing retailers are not the same as grocery retailers, and so forth. Within industries, individual firms must target and pursue their own niches in the marketplace. A multitude of forces are simultaneously inter-reacting and must be understood for market opportunities to be fully exploited.

Market segmentation analysis should be integrated with other marketing studies where feasible. Additionally, non-customer marketing issues can be addressed in segmentation projects. This cyclical treatment of market segmentation and marketing planning can help the marketer to recognize and respond to changing market conditions.

4) Use a cluster of segmentation bases and variables. To provide the most realistic profile of a market, several physical and/or behavioral dimensions should be used for defining markets. Also, one or two variables within these bases are generally insufficient for segmenting markets. An analysis of all potentially useful variables should be planned prior to beginning the analysis. Syndicated services analyze a battery of key factors to better understand markets. Your company should also recognize the benefits of the cluster approach.

5) Get down to basics. The segmentation study should be designed to provide information needed for marketing decision making. Traditional approaches to market segmentation often emphasize theoretical methods and multivariate analysis. The end result of such a study is a complex segmentation model understood only by the researcher—and seldom utilized by management. Practical segmentation should be strived for. This stresses a systematic planning framework, minimizes quantitative analysis, involves management in the study, and provides findings that are readily translatable into marketing strategy.

Managerial Guidelines

Segmentation is a planning tool, but it can also be the foundation upon which successful overall marketing strategies are developed. The eight guidelines presented below will assist you in managing the market segmentation function in your firm.

1) Integrate market segmentation with other marketing management activities.   Market segmentation is not an activity that should be undertaken in isolation. Segmentation findings should be incorporated into your company's marketing plan, as are product descriptions and specifications, and promotional tactics. The nichemanship concept, discussed in the last chapter, broadens the scope of market segmentation by recognizing management's input on marketing decisions. Additionally, all levels of the organization need to be involved in marketing the company, as well as its products.

2) Get involved in the project.   Ideally, the project manager should work closely with the researchers, planners, analysts, and/or consultants on the study. This will provide information that is practical and answers today's hard-hitting questions. Furthermore, it precludes possible misunderstandings at a later date. Frequent meetings and regular, two-way communication between management and the project team can lead to better quality studies.

3) Be realistic in your expectations.   The prudent manager sets reasonable goals. Segmentation analysis is not a substitute for other marketing or managerial deficiences. Used properly, however, it can be a basis upon which more effective customer-related decisions can be made, which can favorably impact the bottom line. Costs and potential benefits must be weighed, with short- and long-term paybacks evaluated. Some patience must be exercised in assessing segmentation's value. Unlike an advertising blitz, which may bring immediate results, the segmentation project may bridge several weeks or months, from the research and analysis to the strategy implementation phase.

Also, other marketing elements can greatly influence purchase behavior, making the reconcilement of the study's findings and actual consumption more difficult. Hence, the need for coordination of marketing efforts is critical.

4) Listen to the results.   Research should be welcomed as a learning opportunity. It provides another chance to deeply probe into the market in which the firm competes. Some information may be new, while other findings build on and refine the existing knowledge pool. The research should be acted upon as circumstances dictate. The use of such insight can be the competitive edge necessary to survive and prosper in emerging or established markets.

5) Dare to be different. Although segmentation studies can provide fresh perspectives on a situation, in most cases, the translation of findings into strategy is not a crystal clear picture. Strategists should look at the findings from various angles, adding business judgment and the "new idea" into their marketing planning scenarios. Sometimes, this means some risk—going out on a limb. Innovators, however, can be leaders. The bold new approach may help to secure a favorable market position, while the follower may get lost in the crowd.

6) Request frequent updates and projections. The marketing environment is a constantly evolving one. Market segmentation studies should not be thought of as one-shot projects. Staying current with market conditions is a means of detecting changing trends, and is helpful in both short- and long-term planning.

7) Get professional assistance where necessary. Segmentation analysis is not something that can be learned overnight. It is advisable to consult with experts to assist in research design, obtaining data, interpreting the findings, and strategy development where necessary. Consultants can analyze situations objectively and are more efficient for short-term projects than hiring additional staff.

8) Treat market segmentation analysis as an investment. Management should recognize that market segmentation is a beginning, not an ending point. The completed study sets in motion a series of recommended marketing activities contributing to a customer-centered marketing plan.

Market segmentation will continue to gain prominence in the next few years as more and more companies, large and small, acknowledge the importance of the marketing function. In a January 31, 1986 article in *Marketing News* entitled "Strategic Marketing Top Priority of Chief Execs," 64% of the top executives surveyed stated that marketing was the most important management area, up from only 29% in 1983. Furthermore, segmentation's role in the marketing plan will increase significantly. Firms in all industries are discovering the power of this strategic marketing tool for attracting and keeping customers in competitive markets. How about you?

PART FOUR

Segmentation Strategy Cases

The following four case histories provide in-depth examples of how market segmentation analysis and strategy was used successfully by leaders in their respective industries. Each of the companies profiled; AMI Parkway Regional Medical Center, Barnett Banks, Burdines (a Federated Department Store subsidiary), and Publix Super Markets, Inc., compete in rapidly changing and highly competitive markets.

These companies have effectively used market segmentation techniques to differentiate themselves from their competition and take maximum advantage of market opportunities. By reviewing these cases, you can learn more about the types of planning and research that goes into segmentation analysis, the market factors with which these firms must contend, and the strategic decisions made and marketing initiatives implemented by management.

AMI Parkway Regional Medical Center

AMI Parkway Regional Medical Center, Inc. is a full-service hospital in North Miami Beach, Florida. It is situated in the northeast quadrant of Dade County, convenient to several major expressways and access roads, and approximately three miles south of the Broward County line.

Recognizing the dynamics of the tri-ethnic South Florida market (white, black, and Hispanic populations), AMI Parkway is attempting to increase its penetration into the large, and potentially lucrative, Latin market.

BACKGROUND

AMI Parkway Regional Medical Center is a 412-bed acute care hospital with a board certified or board eligible medical staff of 420 physicians, representing more than forty medical specialties. An additional 1,000-plus employees assist in treating close to 12,000 patients annually, which accounted for nearly $100 million in revenue in 1984. As the largest employer in North Dade, over $17 million is expended on payroll, while over $7 million is spent on supplies yearly.

AMI Parkway began as a ninety-four-bed community hospital in 1961. Since 1969, under the leadership of American Medical International, Inc. (AMI), AMI Parkway has grown considerably, and expanded its commitment to the community it serves. An example of this is the recently completed program of modernization and development, which included expansion of the Emergency Department, state-of-the-art critical care units, a cost-saving ambulatory surgery unit, and facilities for outpatient and community education programs. Other important recent innovations include the Center of Arthritis and Rheumatic Diseases (unique in the State of Florida), the Rehabilitation Center, and the state-certified Level II Trauma Center. This latter project, part of the new South Florida Trauma Network, was pioneered by AMI Parkway in response to the need for such services in its service area.

AMI Parkway is one of six AMI hospitals in South Florida (four in Dade, one in Broward, and one in Palm Beach County). AMI, a Los Angeles-based health care conglomerate, is a publicly held corporation with over 40,000 employees in the United States and a dozen other countries throughout the world. AMI owns 100 hospitals and three dozen other health care facilities nationwide (see Exhibit I, AMI Vital Statistics).

Organizational Structure

Due to environmental pressures, AMI Parkway, like many hospitals throughout the country, has taken on a more aggressive marketing posture in recent years. To broaden its marketing base and expand its service mix, its name was recently changed from Parkway General Hospital to AMI Parkway Regional Medical Center. In keeping with this newfound marketing orientation, a patient-centered philosophy was adopted, and a structural reorganization of major hospital divisions was undertaken.

The marketing function has been elevated to one of the six major hospital divisions. The Marketing and Business Development Division now has equal stature with the Finance, Professional Services, Administrative Services, Patient Services (Nursing), and Human Resources divisions. Weekly meetings among representatives of all of these divisions are held to coordinate and synthesize the planning objectives of the various hospital units.

The six assistant administrators report to the hospital executive director, who in turn works closely with AMI Parkway's Board of Directors. The present board consists of seven physicians, four AMI executives, the hospital administrator (the executive director), and a college professor. Three additional lay people from the business sector will also be added to the board in the near future. In Exhibits II and III, the organizational charts for the hospital and the Marketing and Business Development Division are depicted, respectively.

Exhibit I:

AMI Vital Statistics

Owned hospital bed size range: 48 to 586.

Founded investor-owned health care industry in 1960.

Total number of licensed beds: about 20,000.

Net Revenues, fiscal year 1984: $2,048,996,000.*
  9% revenue growth in FY 1984.

Net Income, fiscal year 1984: $155,162,000.
  20% net income growth in FY 1984.

Earnings Per Share: $1.85.*
  15% per share growth in FY 1984.

Health Care Centers

Hospitals in the United States	100
Single day surgery centers	18
Industrial medicine clinics	3
Substance abuse recovery centers	12
Psychiatric hospitals	3
DOMESTIC TOTAL (17 states)	136
Owned internationally	20
Managed internationally	11
INTERNATIONAL TOTAL	31**
TOTAL HEALTH CARE CENTERS	167

  *excluding merger costs

**Australia, Brazil, Canada, Ecuador, England, France, Greece, Saudi
  Arabia, Scotland, Singapore, Spain, and Switzerland.

  Source: American Medical International, Inc., 6/27/85

Exhibit II:

Parkway Regional Medical Center

Table of Organization

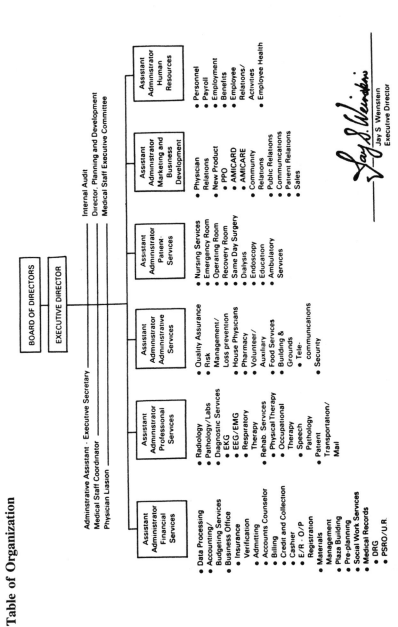

Exhibit III:
Parkway Regional Medical Center
Marketing and Business Development Division (July 9,1985)

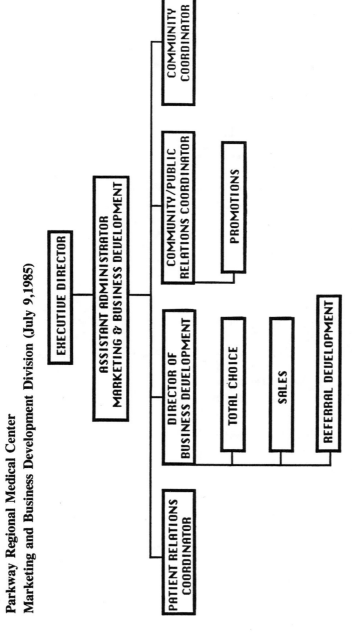

Goals and Objectives

After decades of service to the community, AMI Parkway understands the level of personalized and high quality care its patients expect and deserve. As described in John Naisbitt's book *Megatrends*, AMI Parkway is striving for the perfect combination of modern technology and human caring—high tech/high touch.

In a May 20, 1985 memorandum to the Board of Directors, Jay S. Weinstein, the executive director (no relation to the author), outlines the objectives that were developed for AMI Parkway for 1986. They include:

1. Reduce costs through reducing the average length of stay
2. Increase markets
3. Develop physician participation/joint ventures
4. Protect the franchise through the development of new programs and new markets
   a. Expand the Center of Excellence concept
   b. Cardiac Catherization Facility
   c. Oncology Center
   d. Hand Program
   e. Foot Program
   f. Diabetes Outreach
   g. Obstetrics/Gynecology/Pediatrics/Women's Center
   h. Medical Office Building II
   i. MRI Facility (Magnetic Resonance Imager)
   j. Lithotripter
   k. Psychiatric and Substance Abuse
5. Improve medical staff relations
6. Improve employee relations
7. Improve quality of care/patient relations
8. Develop marketing blitz
9. Improve efficiencies and reduce costs to become competitive with third party programs
10. Develop business plans as required
11. Develop networking

In addition to overall annual hospital objectives, the Marketing and Business Development Division and key individuals within the department are very active in the marketing planning function. One of the identified goals relating to AMI Parkway's need to gather marketing information is listed below.

Goal: Determine the wants and needs of the hospital's customers, physicians, patients, employees, and employers.

Objective:

- Conduct sound, systematic ongoing research.
- Research new products or services prior to implementation.
- Determine long term viability of existing products/services.

Measurement: Conduct annual research of physicians, patients, and industry. Research key market segments as needed.

THE CHANGING ROLE OF MARKETING IN HOSPITALS

The healthcare industry has experienced dramatic changes and challenges during the past decade. As this major shakeout in healthcare delivery has transpired, hospitals have faced pressures from several fronts, affecting not only their profitability, but their individual survival as well. The major factors that have negatively impacted the market for hospital services include:

1. Consumer lifestyles: Americans are healthier than ever, as millions of individuals are more exercise- and fitness-conscious, concerned with nutrition and wellness, and better educated about their healthcare options than the generations preceding them.
2. New forms of competition: In the past, hospitals were the "only game in town." Today there is formidable competition from health maintenance organizations (HMOs), preferred provider organizations (PPOs), walk-in medical centers, physicians, and other healthcare professionals/providers. This new competition forces hospitals to compete with each other for a shrinking share of the market.
3. Improved technology: There have been some notable medical advances in recent years which have reduced the need for, and shortened the length of, hospital stays for many patients. Examples of these are found in the areas of cardiac care, cancer treatment, and the early detection/diagnosis of other potentially serious or life-threatening diseases.
4. Escalating costs: Hospitals are faced with the ever increasing costs of conducting daily operations, purchasing state-of-the-art equipment, and personnel.
5. Reductions in Medicare and insurance reimbursements: Cost-cutting Medicare measures, including the development of Diagnosis-Related Groups (DRGs) and smaller third-party (insurance companies, HMO and PPO plans) payments have severely hindered hospitals' profitability.

Fighting Back: Discovering Marketing

To combat these environmental pressures, hospital executives are turning to marketing in droves. They recognize that a marketing orientation (placing the patient's needs first) is critical to their success. And they are hoping that this business discipline will be the key to improving their operations by attracting new patients and better satisfy existing ones.

Michael Marquez, former Assistant Administrator and director of Marketing and Business Development at AMI Parkway, stresses that patient care is the key element. He states, "Since equipment and physician services are basically the same (generally high quality) at most hospitals, the objective is to make patient stays as pleasant as possible. In the final analysis, how well service is delivered (patient relations) is the difference as to how a hospital is perceived."

A recent trend that has emerged is the shift in leadership of marketing departments in hospitals. According to Marquez, marketing directors have evolved from either community relations/PR positions or operations backgrounds. The next wave in this evolution is the hiring of marketing professionals. Hospitals are learning that marketing is a lot more than an occasional advertisement or fancy slogans. They are seeking well rounded professionals that understand the entire scope of marketing—including research, planning, strategy formulation, implementation, and evaluation. Paralleling this trend has been the increased availability of pertinent marketing literature/information for hospital administrators. An example of this is the recent inauguration of the Academy for Health Services Marketing division of the American Marketing Association.

AMI PARKWAY'S MARKET POSITION

AMI Parkway is the thirteenth largest hospital in South Florida in terms of bed size, according to the *South Florida Business Journal.* It's main competition comes from non-AMI hospitals in North Dade and South Broward counties. AMI Parkway is located in North Miami Beach, a municipality with a high concentration of senior citizens. As a result of this, approximately 65% of their patients are on Medicare, with the balance, a younger set, typically commercially insured.

South Florida is a difficult area for hospitals and many medical professions. Marquez puts the situation into perspective. "This is one of the most hotly contested healthcare markets. It is over-bedded, overphysicianed, and over-serviced," he says. Given this fierce competitive environment, AMI Parkway's occupancy rate averages slightly more than 60%. Ideally, this figure would be 80-90%.

To increase the hospital's utilization, research is conducted periodically to assess new potential markets and improve the service delivery of present target markets. Tangible results of such market research are readily apparent. Consider the following projects:

1. A transportation system for the elderly was analyzed. This program was proven feasible, and in November 1984, three vans transporting senior citizens to and from the hospital were implemented. It presently serves more than 550 patients per week.
2. A research project analyzing the development and cultivation of the Latin market was completed in August 1985. As the central issue of this segmentation case, this topic is discussed in detail next.

TARGETING THE LATIN MARKET

The Hispanic community in Dade County is a major force. In fact, the 1980 U.S. Census indicated that Latins accounted for 36% of the county's population. More significantly, this market segment is growing rapidly. According to the Dade County Planning Department, the latest population update (1984) showed more than a 5% Hispanic increase to a 41.3% share of the market. The hospital, well aware of this growth, both county-wide and in its service area, wants to prepare for necessary changes in marketing strategy.

AMI Parkway's northeastern location, however, is away from the heavy concentration of Latins (primarily Cubans), which is mostly in the central part of the county. This includes the large cities of Miami and Hialeah, which together house most of these residents. Preliminary findings based on an analysis of relevant 1980 census tracts indicate that the Latin population in the hospital's service area hovers around 10%. Presently, only 1% of the patients that AMI Parkway cares for are of Hispanic origin. Marquez felt that any additional Latin patients that AMI Parkway can attract will be incremental business. Therefore, the overall goal of the segmentation research was to design a marketing plan to increase the number of Latin patients using AMI Parkway Regional Medical Center.

Research Objectives

Specific objectives of the research study were:

1. To better understand the Hispanic market regarding healthcare needs.
2. To provide an overview of Hispanics' attitudes and perceptions about hospitals/medical facilities. In particular, their:
   a. needs and wants
   b. hospital awareness levels
   c. hospital utilization rates
   d. opinions on hospital image/the competitive environment
   e. level of concern regarding the ethnic background of staffs
   f. insurance coverage plans
3. To determine hospital selection criteria and satisfaction levels.
4. To determine what Hispanics are looking for in a medical facility.
5. To determine key services Hispanics prefer, and what changes will be necessary to attract them to AMI Parkway.

Methodology of Study

A three-tiered research plan was used for analysis. This included the following survey instruments:

- a brief questionnaire distributed to the Latin doctors associated with AMI Parkway
- qualitative research of Latin consumers conducted through focus groups
- quantitative consumer research via telephone surveys.

The physician survey was administered in-house through AMI Parkway's marketing department. This was sent to the seventy Spanish-speaking doctors associated with the hospital. The qualitative and quantitative research was conducted by Strategy Research Corporation, a marketing research firm specializing in the Latin market.

The focus group format was selected in the qualitative phase as a means of generating in-depth marketing information and potential alternative marketing approaches. The focus group was also a valuable tool for developing a questionnaire for use in the second stage, the quantitative study. Two focus groups of eleven Hispanic participants each were selected. These individuals had to reside in AMI Parkway's market area and be at least eighteen years old. Other qualifiers included not having participated in a focus group during the past year, and not being employed in a research or medical capacity. A demographic breakdown of the focus group participants is listed below in Exhibit IV.

The quantitative research technique employed the telephone interviewing format with a sample of 200 Hispanic individuals. The random digit sampling method was used. A summary of key demographics of respondents in this sample is provided in Exhibit V below.

Major Findings

The results of the research conducted revealed many interesting facts about the Hispanic healthcare market. Most of the data collected provided general information about attitudes toward hospitals. Some AMI Parkway-specific information also was gathered in the course of the study.

General Information:

- Awareness levels of area hospitals: Very high
- Hospital selection criteria: For non-emergencies, physician consultation was the primary means of selection, with relative referral a distant second. For extreme emergencies, patients seek the closest hospital,

---

Exhibit IV:

Focus Group Demographics

Sex: Male - 8, Female - 14
Age: Under 36 - 11, Over 36 - 11
Ethnicity: Cuban - 12, Other Hispanic - 10
Income: Under $20,000 - 11, Over $20,000 - 11

Exhibit V:

Telephone Survey Demographics

Sex: Male - 50%, Female - 50%
Age: 25-54 = 66%
Income: $10,000 - $30,000 = 50%, no response = 26%
Length of Residency: More than 10 years - 50%
                     More than 4 years - 85%

while for non-extreme emergency room treatment, the reputation of
the facility may be a factor.

- Hospital satisfaction rates: More than 90% of the respondents rate
  hospitals as good or very good for nursing services, physician care,
  and in-patient treatment.
- Importance of bilingual staff: Close to 90% of consumers and doctors
  feel that this is important.
- Insurance coverage: Most are covered by insurance. They want
  policies that provide freedom in doctor and hospital selection.
- Most important services: Emergency room, surgery, and cardiology.
- The ideal hospital: Although this varied among individuals to some
  degree, characteristics most frequently cited by respondents included;
  emergency room treatment/capabilities, competent specialists (similar
  to Jackson Memorial, a University of Miami teaching hospital in central
  Miami), more humanistic attitudes by nurses and staffs (treat with
  dignity and respect), and advanced technology.

AMI Parkway—Specific Information:

Overall, AMI Parkway's services were perceived as good. In particular,
the emergency room was rated very high, with specialists also faring well.
The major problem repeatedly mentioned was that AMI Parkway was the
most costly hospital in the area.

Although AMI Parkway was the second most used hospital in the qualitative sample, it only ranked eighth according to the larger quantitative sample. This is surprising given the fact that it was second based on total
awareness scores. As far as hospital image was concerned, AMI Parkway was about neutral. North Miami General and Palm Springs were considered "warmer," while Jackson was viewed as more advanced. On the
other hand, the hospital was perceived more favorably than several other
local competitors.

MARKETING IMPLICATIONS: THE LATIN MARKET

Based on the completed research, AMI Parkway geared up to target the
Latin market. In a September 25, 1985, memorandum to the executive
management staff, Marquez stated: "The Latin market research study clear-

ly indicates an opportunity for AMI Parkway to significantly increase market share in this expanding market segment.''

Recommendations

This is the ten-point marketing plan outlined by Marquez to the executive management staff:

1. Conduct a linguistics survey to assess departmental bilingual resources available and determine future needs in this area.
2. Develop bilingual capabilities at all department levels to facilitate easier communication with Latin patients and visitors.
3. Identify physicians at AMI Parkway and competing hospitals with substantial Latin practices that are not supporting the hospital. Make every effort necessary to shift these physicians' practice patterns.
4. Develop advertising and promotional campaigns in Spanish promoting AMI Parkway as a quality, technologically advanced, caring, bilingual institution.
5. Conduct a direct mail campaign to Latin households in the service area.
6. Provide hospital informational brochures in Spanish upon admission.
7. Develop monitoring mechanisms to accurately measure AMI Parkway's Latin market share, the success of various marketing programs, and the healthcare needs of this market.
8. Review with Mr. Paul Cejos, new board member, the research study results and recommended action.
9. Take a leadership position within AMI's South Florida hospital network in promoting the network hospitals as receptive to the needs of the Latin population.
10. Prior to implementing external marketing plans, the internal resources needed to successfully impact the external plans must be in place.

Some additional marketing initiatives recently undertaken have included:

- the dissemination of press releases about AMI Parkway's services to the Latin news media.
- recruiting efforts for an advertising agency specializing in Spanish language promotion. This agency will work with both AMI Parkway Regional Medical Center and Palmetto General Hospital (an AMI hospital located in Hialeah).

BARNETT BANKS OF FLORIDA, INC.*

Florida is probably the most diverse and competitive banking market in the U.S. today. More than 400 banks and 120 savings and loans seek to share the state's $146 billion deposit base as of mid-year 1985, while countless billions of dollars are held by other financial institutions. At the same time, with the advent of regional interstate banking, new competitors are entering the market through acquisitions, creating both challenges and opportunities.

A LOOK AT FLORIDA'S BANKING LEADER

Barnett Banks of Florida, Inc. was founded 108 years ago and has emerged as the state's foremost banking organization. The Bank has developed an extensive range of financial services delivered through the state's most comprehensive network of offices, systems, and people. It has 373 offices and 338 automated teller machines serving 164 cities in forty counties.

Barnett Banks also is recognized as Florida's most consistent, high-performance bank in market share, profitability, and earnings growth, as evidenced by:

- Ten consecutive years of increased earnings.

---

*This case was prepared by Marvin Nesbit, a faculty member at Florida International University, Miami, and President of Pro-Mark Services. It is printed here with the author's permission.

- A five-year asset growth rate of 28%, creating a financial institution with $13.2 billion in assets at mid-year 1985.
- Compound growth of 16% in earnings per share for the past five years, from $1.57 to $3.31.
- Consistent market-share gains through internal growth and acquisitions resulting in a solid 17.81% of all bank deposits in Florida.
- A market-share position of first, second, or third in thirty-seven of forty-two Florida counties where over 95% of the population resides.

Barnett Banks' highly decentralized structure is unique in Florida's banking industry. While the largest banking institution in the state, Barnett is really a close-knit assembly of thirty-one local, community-oriented banking affiliates. Each of these banking affiliates has its own chief executive officer and board of directors. These banks range in size from $20 million to $3.5 billion in assets. There are also ten non-banking affiliates, including insurance, brokerage, mortgage, credit, international finance, and trust operations.

In retail banking, Barnett Banks has long been acknowledged as Florida's premier institution. The company asserts that a Barnett office is within ten minutes of more than 90% of the state's residents. Some of the accomplishments in this sector include:

- The largest account base in the state, with 1.5 million customers.
- The leading consumer lender in the state, originating more than one of every five consumer loans made at a Florida bank.
- More than $2.3 billion in deposits as a result of a Senior Partners program, a special combination of services for persons 55 and older.
- A network of bankers who implement Barnett's Newcomer programs, introducing new residents to available programs and services.

Although Barnett's primary emphasis has been in the retail banking sector, it has responded to Florida's growing industrialization by intensifying its corporate banking presence. This has resulted in:

- An increase in market share of commercial loans among Florida banks to almost 13%.
- A 19% market share of commercial real estate loans, larger than any other Florida bank.
- Business relationships with nearly one-quarter of the Florida corporate marketplace.
- A lending limit that now exceeds $100 million, the largest in the state.

- A complete product line of sophisticated cash management services, delivered through a system of eight regional centers staffed by specialists and equipped with the latest computer technology. Today, 1,300 companies use these services.
- Expanded international capabilities that include a full range of trade-related services delivered through four regional centers for the growing number of Florida companies engaged in overseas trade.
- An intensified national calling effort, resulting in banking relationships with over 550 out-of-state companies having business interests in Florida.
- A corporate trust organization providing trustee, registrar, or paying-agent services for more than $5 billion in fully registered bond issues.

THE REASON FOR THE SEGMENTATION STUDY

There were three primary reasons why the segmentation study was conducted. First, deregulation has caused Barnett Bank to more clearly define the segments of the market it wants to serve. Second, bank management felt Barnett should strategically position itself with certain markets since it could no longer afford to be all things to all people. Finally, the study was used to identify the niches that presented the best opportunities for Barnett. The 55-and-over segment was identified as one of these opportunities.

THE SENIOR PARTNERS PROGRAM

The Senior Partners program was introduced by Barnett Banks on a statewide basis in 1984, after two years of extensive research and testing. This program catered to the 55-and-over market, and was tested in eight cities in southwest and south central Florida.

According to the Director of Marketing at Barnett Bank of South Florida, marketing research played an important role at four major decision points during the development of the Senior Partners program.

First, the company had to decide whether or not to target the segment of the market referred to as the "Seniors Segment" (55 years and older).

Second, if the segment identified above was targeted, the company had to decide what to offer the market segment.

Third, customer satisfaction must be monitored to provide feedback for future product development and modifications.

Finally, the program must be tracked to determine the viability of the segment measured against the program's objectives.

EXPLORING THE DECISION POINTS

Four important questions that needed to be answered were at the crux of these decision points. As the development of the Senior Partners program progressed, marketing research was used to gather information to use in answering these questions.

Should We Target the Seniors Segment?

The segments of the consumer financial services market are fairly natural and obvious. Banks nationwide are well aware of the importance of the senior market as a source of deposits. In Florida, this importance is augmented by the sheer magnitude of this market residing in the state. At this stage of the program's development, marketing research provided data to answer these questions:

- What are the patterns of usage of financial services among seniors, and how do they differ from other segments of the market?
- What are the financial needs and attitudes of seniors?
- What is the typical portfolio of services held by senior customers, and how can Barnett enhance its share of the senior household's portfolio?

Barnett needed to know not only the types of accounts seniors have, but how much money they have in those accounts. This was not easy information to obtain. Surveys that ask consumers to detail their financial holdings are not only extremely sensitive, they are also lengthy and expensive to administer. For these reasons, Barnett relied heavily on national multi-subscriber research conducted by SRI International of Menlo Park, California.

SRI provided household asset and liability data from a large-scale survey of U.S. consumers. The survey also collected attitude data on a variety of areas in consumer banking. Barnett used the data to determine how the financial behavior and attitudes of seniors differ from those of other market segments. The information gave valuable clues for the design of an appealing package of financial services. The financial data allowed Barnett to "model" the dollar value of a typical senior relationship with a bank, compare the model with the known value of existing relationships, and set financial goals for the segmentation program.

What Should We Offer the Target Market?

The product developers designed a financial services package with a variety of alternative features. At this stage, research helped answer the following questions:

- What are the most attractive components of the package?
- How should the eligibility requirements—or the price—of the package be set?
- What should the service be called?

Barnett described the package concept to seniors in focus groups. The groups discussed their usage of banks and bank services, as well as the needs they expected their personal financial program to meet. The respondents also indicated their interest in each of twenty-nine possible components of a senior financial package. The findings from these groups helped Barnett design the final program and set minimum balance requirements (see Exhibit I).

A statewide telephone survey among senior consumers collected data on the prospects' preferences among various suggested names for the package. The most popular name was "Senior Partners."

Are Customers Satisfied With the Program?

Barnett tracks consumer response to the program through an annual customer satisfaction survey conducted by mail. The company also holds focus groups with customers to learn more about why they signed up for the service, how they use it, and how they might like to see it improved.

How Is the Program Performing?

The market segmentation program has two fundamental purposes: (1) to increase the bank's penetration of the target market, and (2) to enhance the bank's relationships with customers in the program. Barnett tracks its penetration of the senior market on a county level by comparing the number of Senior Partners customers in the market with demographic estimates of the number of prospects in that area. General consumer surveys also provide estimates of the bank's penetration of target segments.

Focus group interviews provide information on how customers might react to changes in the program. If a change in the package is seriously considered, mail surveys help the marketing managers forecast customer response to those changes.

Exhibit I:

The Senior Partner's Program

As a member of Barnett's Senior Partners, a customer receives the following benefits and services:

Financial Services

Free Checking Account—New customers can choose either a traditional checking account or an Interest-on Checking account without any balance requirements or service charges. Current customers may use their existing accounts, which will also have no balance requirements or service charges.

(Customers may use a Money Market Checking account in the Senior Partners Program; however, the $10.00 fee will *not* be waived if the balance drops below $2,500.)

Free Personalized Checks—Customers will receive free personalized wallet-style checks as well as a Senior Partner checkbook cover.

Free Traveler's Checks and Cashier's Check—Customers can request traveler's checks and cashier's checks free of charge.

Monthly statement summarizing all related deposit accounts—Customers will receive a monthly statement summarizing all their related deposit accounts (DDA, NOW, or MMC, all their savings accounts, MMI, and all their CDs, including IRAs).

Insurance Coverage Provided—Senior Partners (primary transaction account owners and co-owners) are automatically covered by a common carrier accidental death policy. This policy provides for the payment of $100,000 in the event of death while traveling by common carrier (planes, trains, boats, buses, taxis) as defined in the Certificate of Insurance. Senior Partners will be issued a Certificate of Insurance when the relationship is established.

*Loan Services—From time to time, individuals who qualify for Senior Partners may have a need to borrow money for special reasons and opportunities. If such a need exists, our loan officers will provide prompt and courteous assistance.

*Discount Brokerage—Individuals who qualify for Senior Partners may be experienced investors and may want to use our discount brokerage service. By using the direct line to our discount brokerage service, Senior Partners can make their investments and save up to 70% on commissions.

*Access to Trust Service—Individuals who qualify for Senior Partners may also be potential trust customers. When a need for trust services is identified, we will arrange for a meeting (by phone or in person) with a representative from Barnett Trust Company.

Exhibit I:

The Seniors Partner's Program (continued)

*Bank-by-Mail and Direct Deposits—Although these services are available to all customers, they can be especially attractive to individuals who qualify for the Senior Partners and are therefore included in the package as optional convenience features.

*Services not unique to Senior Partners

Non-Financial Benefits

Financial Planning Guide—Customers are given this thirty-six-page Financial Planning Guide free of charge when they join our Senior Partners Program.

Periodic Communications—A communication called the Senior Partner Pipeline will be periodically published. Its purpose is to provide Senior Partners with a wide range of useful information to keep them informed about new products and services at Barnett, enhancements to the Senior Partners Program, and other valuable information.

Membership Card—Senior Partners will be issued a membership card at the time the relationship is established. This card should be used by customers when taking advantage of the free benefits offered with the Senior Partners Program.

Free Copying Service (except in Palm Beach County and South Florida)—Senior Partners are welcome to use our copy machines, without charge. A limit of ten copies per visit is applied.

IMPLEMENTATION

Several promotional strategies were used to bring the program to market. Television, radio, and newspaper advertising were used to deliver the Senior Partners message. Media targeted specifically to the 55-and-over market were selected. Additionally, one million Floridians in this same age range received a personalized direct mailing from a local Barnett banker that promoted the program. The initial wave of advertising and promotional efforts for Senior Partners was conducted over a fourteen-week period.

The program was introduced during the presidential election campaign of 1984. The ads used this event as their leitmotif. Capitalizing on the election media coverage and the fact that both presidential candidates were over age 55 resulted in an ideal situation for the initial campaign.

The television spots depicted the White House on a Florida beach while "Hail to the Chief" played throughout. The voice-over announcer discussed the fact that both presidential candidates were eligible for the program and described some of the Senior Partner program benefits. Two versions of this spot were produced—one that aired before the election, and another for the post-election period. Exhibits II and III contain the copy for the two television commercials.

Exhibit II:

Copy for White House TV Ad

VIDEO	AUDIO
CLOSE-UP OF WHITE HOUSE. PULL BACK THROUGHOUT COMMERCIAL TO REVEAL MORE AND MORE OF THE WHITE HOUSE AND ITS LAWNS.	(MUSIC UNDER: HAIL TO CHIEF) ANNCR: Since both presidential candidates are over 55, their economic advisors should tell them about Barnett's Senior Partners program. You see, people 55 and over can qualify for checking, traveler's checks, travel insurance, and a lot more—all without service charges. Now, if Florida has an economic policy like that, shouldn't the White House make a move like this?
CONTINUE PULL BACK TO REVEAL THAT WHITE HOUSE AND LAWNS HAVE BEEN RELOCATED IN FLORIDA, ON THE BEACH.	
LOGO BEGINS APPEARANCE ON SCREEN. SUPER: BARNETT IS FLORIDA'S BANK. MEMBER FDIC	Senior Partners. One more reason Barnett is Florida's bank.

Exhibit III:

Copy for Post-Election TV Ad

<u>VIDEO</u>	<u>AUDIO</u>
CLOSE-UP OF WHITE HOUSE. PULL BACK THROUGHOUT COMMERCIAL TO REVEAL MORE AND MORE OF THE WHITE HOUSE AND ITS LAWNS.	(MUSIC UNDER: HAIL TO CHIEF) <u>ANNCR</u>: The people have spoken . . . and once again they've elected a president over 55. If he lived in Florida, he'd be eligible for Barnett's Senior Partner's Program: Checking, traveler's checks, travel insurance, and a lot more— all without service charges.
CONTINUE PULL BACK TO REVEAL THAT WHITE HOUSE AND LAWNS HAVE BEEN RELOCATED IN FLORIDA, ON THE BEACH.	If you're 55 or over, it's one of the reasons for moving here.
LOGO BEGINS APPEARANCE ON SCREEN.	Senior Partners. One more reason Barnett is Florida's bank.
SUPER: BARNETT IS FLORIDA'S BANK. MEMBER FDIC	

The radio commercials were lifted directly from the television spots. Newspaper ads supported the broadcast media with the White House illustration and program benefits. Exhibit IV is a copy of the newspaper ad.

At the local level, certain banks have sponsored a Senior Olympics program. This includes many competitive events such as bowling and shuffleboard. There have been over five thousand participants in this program in South Florida alone. The participants are all given special T-shirts and the various event winners provided with trophies.

Exhibit IV

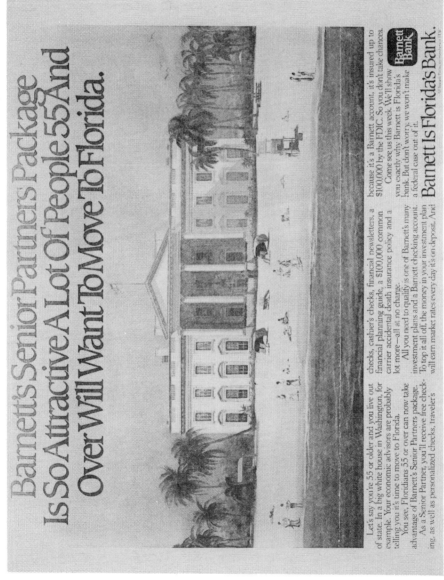

Barnett's Senior Partners Package Is So Attractive A Lot Of People 55 And Over Will Want To Move To Florida.

Let's say you're 55 or older and you live out of state. In a big white house in Washington, for example. Your economic advisors are probably telling you it's time to move to Florida.

You see, Floridians 55 or over can now take advantage of Barnett's Senior Partners package.

As a Senior Partner, you'll receive free checking, as well as personalized checks, traveler's checks, cashier's checks, financial newsletters, a financial planning guide, a $100,000 common carrier accidental death insurance policy and a lot more—all at no charge.

All you need to qualify is one of Barnett's many investment plans and a Barnett checking account. To top it all off, the money in your investment plan will earn money market rates every day it's on deposit. And because it's a Barnett account, it's insured up to $100,000 by the FDIC. So you don't take chances.

Come see us this week. We'll show you exactly why Barnett is Florida's Bank. But don't worry, we won't make a federal case out of it.

Barnett Is Florida's Bank.

THE RESULTS

A total of 21,000 Senior Partners relationships and $275 million in new deposits were generated during the initial campaign period. Every promotional dollar expended brought in approximately $100 in new deposits.

Burdines Mayfair

Burdines, a Florida department store chain and subsidiary of Federated Department Stores, recently opened a new type of shopping concept different from all other Burdines in Florida. Before introducing this store, called Burdines Mayfair, much research was conducted and observations made on its viability. The objective was to determine the need for this revolutionary approach to fashion retailing, given the unique market conditions existing in the Coconut Grove area of South Florida.

COMPANY BACKGROUND

In 1898, the first Burdines was started by Mr. William M. Burdine in Miami. At that time, the city's population was about 1,000 and the tiny shop was little more than a frontier trading post.

Burdines: The Early Days

This original store relocated in 1900, and began to prosper. But in 1911, Mr. Burdine died, and his son Roddey became president at age 24. Twelve years later, he made history by erecting Miami's first skyscraper (Burdines occupied two of the five floors). By 1925, Burdines had become the largest volume retail department store in the southeastern United States. That year, they also opened their first branch store on Miami Beach. Under the leadership of William M. Burdine, Jr., the company grew to five stores by 1956.

Burdines has always been a strong fashion leader. In 1914 fashion shows began, and in 1928, Burdines invented a "Revue of Fashion," resulting from buyers' first trips to Europe.

The Affiliation with Federated Department Stores

On July 28, 1956, Burdines became affiliated with the nation's largest department store conglomerate, Federated Department Stores, Inc. Federated, a 57-year-old company, is diversified into thirteen major department store chains (e.g., Abraham and Straus, Bloomingdales, Filenes, Rich's, etc.) consisting of 225 retail stores. Additionally, this national company operates five other divisions, including specialty shops, mass merchandisers, and a supermarket chain. According to the August 1984 issue of *Chain Store Age Executive*, Federated is the seventh largest retailer in the United States.

Federated's first priority, company-wide, is "serving its customers." Customer needs and wants, once easily identifiable, are now more complex to measure, as consumers' lifestyles, values, age distribution, and income levels continue to change. The identification of target markets for each of its retail operations, and tailoring strategies to meet the specific expectations of these customers, is a critical part of the Federated "success formula." This trend toward more market segmentation was described in the 1985 Annual Report.

> "We believe this will remain the central challenge of retailers throughout the remainder of this decade. That is why we have planned and made a number of strategic moves directed at serving the changing needs of our customers in all of our lines of business."

Many of Federated's department store chains, including Burdine's, have become pioneers in their respective retail markets. Operating in some of the choicest markets in America was no accident. Expansion of department store franchises occurred geographically, taking advantage of suburban and regional growth opportunities in selected markets. The Annual Report adds,

> "Recognizing and consistently meeting expectations of our target customers is the heart of our headquarters department store strategy. It is also key to our strategic objective of building market share within existing markets for each of our department store divisions."

According to Value Line, the direction of future growth for many retailers lies not in new store expansion, but in expansion of existing stores.

Federated responds to this trend by striving to provide desired merchandise offerings, high levels of customer service, and attractive store environments. The common denominator linking the various store chains is value. Federated customers demand and receive quality and value in the products they buy.

In addition to Burdines, Federated runs three other divisions in South Florida. These include Bloomingdales (an upscale department store chain), Richway (a mass merchandiser), and The Children's Place (a specialty shop). This strategy allows Federated to maximize market share in a volatile retail market.

The Growth of Burdines

With Federated's support, Burdines underwent and is still enjoying extensive growth in Florida. Four new department stores were opened in the 1960s, eight added in the 1970s, and ten more through the end of 1985, stretching from Cutler Ridge (in the south) to Gainesville (in the north). To date, Burdines operates twenty-seven department stores and two clearance centers in the state (see Exhibit I). They have no intention of expanding outside of Florida.

Typical store sizes range from 105,000 to 225,000 square feet. Burdines' revenues are larger than its top three Florida competitors combined. Federated's 1985 Annual Report stated that Burdines' sales for 1984 were $691.5 million.

Burdines' Marketing Philosophy

Burdines strives to keep in close touch with its customers. The tropical market and lifestyles of Floridians are studied in depth. Buyers reside locally, and are familiar with the special needs of Florida living. This includes the latest styles, fabrics, colors, and looks; not only in clothing, but in furnishings too.

According to David Dyer, Vice President and Director of Marketing,

"Burdines is the fashion store for the Florida lifestyle. Our target market is consumers with an above average income and interest in fashion. We view ourselves as a family store—we make a statement for every age group. We're updating a person's look, home, and lifestyle. That's what fashion is all about."

Mr. Dyer stated that there are three "drivers" that differentiate Burdines from other department stores. They are: 1) fashion (the products offered),

Exhibit I:

Burdines The Florida Story

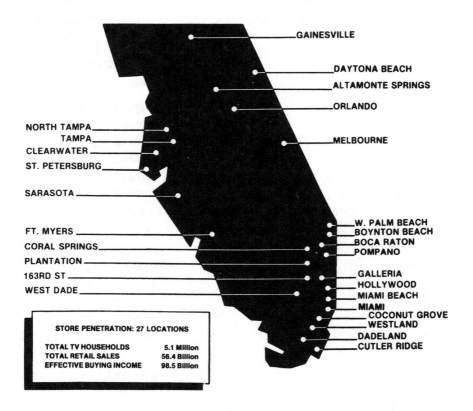

GAINESVILLE

DAYTONA BEACH
ALTAMONTE SPRINGS
ORLANDO

NORTH TAMPA
TAMPA
CLEARWATER
ST. PETERSBURG

MELBOURNE

SARASOTA

W. PALM BEACH
FT. MYERS   BOYNTON BEACH
CORAL SPRINGS   BOCA RATON
PLANTATION   POMPANO
163RD ST   GALLERIA
WEST DADE   HOLLYWOOD
                                                MIAMI BEACH
                                                MIAMI
                                                  COCONUT GROVE
                                                WESTLAND
                                                DADELAND
                                                CUTLER RIDGE

STORE PENETRATION: 27 LOCATIONS	
TOTAL TV HOUSEHOLDS	5.1 Million
TOTAL RETAIL SALES	56.4 Billion
EFFECTIVE BUYING INCOME	98.5 Billion

2) the environment the products are presented in, and 3) the superior customer service provided.

THE INDUSTRY

Department stores are typically known for their large selection of clothing offered. The National Retail Merchant's Association stated that apparel sales accounted for 56% of their business industry-wide. However, department stores also carry home furnishings, housewares, and a multitude of other product lines which affect their profitability. Consumer electronics, computer products, and personal services are some of the recent departments introduced, as large retailers look for competitive advantages.

Current Situation

According to the U.S. Department of Commerce, department store sales totaled $115.5 billion in 1983, representing 10% of all retail sales. Chains of eleven or more stores accounted for 96% of the industry revenues.

Many people think of general merchandisers such as Sears, Penney's, and Ward's when discussing department stores. These three stores record about a third of industry sales, but the growth segments are not in this mid-priced market. Rather, the industry has polarized to a large degree, and the demand for high quality merchandise and discount goods have simultaneously expanded. Burdines specifically, and Federated generally, compete for the more affluent and fashion-conscious department store shopper.

Major pressures faced by department store chains at this time include lower gross margins dictated by increased competition and higher operating expenses, and expensive land and construction costs. This has forced many chains to implement stringent inventory control systems and other cost-cutting measures, and to curtail new store expansion and concentrate on improving productivity in existing selling space. In this highly seasonal business, more than a quarter of annual sales occur in November and December.

The Competition

Federated's major national competitors include three of the largest retailers in the U.S.: Allied Stores Corporation, Associated Dry Goods Corporation, and R.H. Macy and Company.

Allied Stores Corporation has retail establishments in forty-five states, the District of Columbia, and Japan. It operates twenty-one department store divisions, six specialty store divisions, and seven regional shopping centers (five are owned by the company).

Associated Dry Goods Corporation, founded in 1916, employs approximately 59,000 people. Associated conducts business in thirty states through twelve department store divisions (consisting of 156 stores), one women's specialty shop division, and two upscale discount store subsidiaries. Lord and Taylor is one such division of Associated, and operates forty-two department stores.

R.H. Macy and Company was founded in 1858. It has five regional store groups: Macy's New York, Macy's Midwest, Macy's California, Bamberger's, and Davison's. These five divisions consist of ninety-six stores operating in fifteen states. More than 75% of the stores are located in major shopping centers, and the company also owns and manages five regional shopping centers, and has a 50% interest in five others. A comparison of some key financial statistics of the industry giants is provided in Exhibit II.

In Florida, Burdines' main head-to-head competition comes from a pair of Allied chains. Jordan Marsh has fifteen stores located on the east coast of Florida, and Maas Brothers operates nineteen west coast stores. Other statewide competitors include the general merchandisers (Sears and Penney's), Gayfers (part of the Mercantile Stores Corporation), Robinsons (an Associated Dry Goods Affiliate), and Ivey's. The recent influx of New York department stores has added Saks Fifth Avenue, Lord and Taylor, Macy's, and Bloomingdales to the crowded market. Burdines' edge over their new competitors is their knowledge of the Florida market.

BURDINES MAYFAIR: THE CONCEPT

Burdines Mayfair opened September 8, 1984. This store is no ordinary Burdines, or ordinary department store for that matter. It was the culmination of three years of research and planning which supported the need for this more upscale department store.

The Mayfair Area

Burdines Mayfair emerged in response to the unique market conditions existing in the Coconut Grove area. Coconut Grove, the oldest and one of the more charming parts of South Florida, was founded in 1873. It is a ridge of great natural beauty, overlooking the clear and bountiful Biscayne Bay. The Grove is in close proximity to the upper-income residential areas of Coral Gables, Key Biscayne, and Brickell Avenue. Also, it is midway between downtown Miami, Miami Beach, and South Dade County. Thousands of well-to-do South American and European tourists are just minutes away. This accessibility and the abundance of discretionary incomes make the Grove an attractive shopping area for merchants.

Due to its location and atmosphere, Coconut Grove has become a thriving community. It is home to nearly a dozen luxury hotels, and hundreds of expensive high-rise condominiums and townhouses, owned by young, upwardly-mobile professionals. This activity has created a large base of affluent consumers in the immediate vicinity.

Exhibit II:

Financial Data - The Industry Leaders

1984 - 1985	FEDERATED	ALLIED	ASSOCIATED	MACY'S
Net Sales	$9.7 billion	$4.0 billion	$3.7 billion	$4.4 billion
Net Earnings	$286.7 million	$141.0 million	$115.5 million	$189.3 million
Net Earnings Per Share	$6.77	$6.71	$5.95	$3.69
Dividends Paid	$2.40	$2.00	$2.10	$1.10
Return On Shareholder Equity	13.5%	14.6%	14.8%	N/A
Advertising Expenditures	$287.5 million	N/A	$132.8 million	$278.8 million

Note: All financial data extracted from company 10-K reports for the 53-week period ending January 1985. However, for the R.H. Macy and Co. data, the 10-K report was for the 53-week period ending July 1985.

A January 1981 expansion proposal for the Mayfair Shops in the Grove (pre-Burdines) described the new shopping center as follows:

> "Mayfair in the Grove is a unique potpourri of renowned fashion boutiques and fine restaurants. It offers an air of elegance to affluent shoppers. It has been created with style and fashion in mind, in a setting of unequalled ambiance in the country. On its three tiers, the Garden Level, Promenade Level, and Penthouse Level, Mayfair is distinctively different from all shopping centers. It contains forty-seven shops, four fine restaurants, and an outdoor cafe. Mayfair resembles a European village. Its facade is composed of sculptured, cast-stone arches and embellished with integral ornamentation of sculptured base relief. The two interior courtyards are the central focal points of the boutiques, featuring brick floors, mahogany ceilings, and planters overflowing with lush tropical foliage. Fountains, reflection pools, and sculpture highlight hidden areas throughout the gardens of the center."

The Burdines Mayfair Store

Burdines was a major part of the recent Mayfair expansion. In addition to the developer's desire for a high fashion department store, a retail shopping area was added, as was the Mayfair House, a 185-suite European-style hotel. This hotel was designed to add traffic to the Mayfair stores, allowing visitors to shop, dine, and relax without having to leave the Mayfair complex.

Two marketing studies were instrumental in the decision of Burdines to enter Mayfair in the Grove. A November 1981 "Shopping Habits Survey" compared Mayfair shoppers to Burdines customers at their Downtown and Dadeland stores (the two nearest Burdines to Mayfair). Research results indicated that concerns over possible store cannibalization were unfounded. A high degree of Burdines store loyalty was evidenced. Furthermore, it was determined that sales generated by the Burdines Mayfair location would be incremental business. A Burdines Task Force Analysis subsequently assessed the feasibility of this new venture by analyzing customer profiles, competition, vendor structures, product potential, buyer's responsibilities, and general concerns.

These studies, coupled with executive judgment, led to the corporate decision to proceed with the Mayfair experiment. Mr. Dyer explains,

> "Mayfair represented another marketing opportunity to build and maintain market share. We recognized competition from Saks Fifth Avenue and Lord and Taylor, and knew Bloomingdales was entering the market.

> This store was not to be just another Burdines, but a showcase accentu-
> ating the most fashionable, contemporary, up-to-date, and mostly
> European merchandise . . . . It is also a "test case" store—we can learn
> from it—and it can be a prototype for others."

Burdines Mayfair is the smallest department store in the chain. This three-
level, fashion-oriented store is only 75,000 square feet. Advanced consumer
electronics are the only hard lines carried (see Exhibit III, Burdines Mayfair
directory). The architectural style of the store blends well with the overall
Mayfair Complex theme; lots of marble, brass, and glass are used. The
merchandising, visual displays, and special windows invite pedestrians
strolling the Grove to stop in and browse. In a November 2, 1985 article
in the Miami Herald, entitled "Chic Mayfair Dresses up the Grove," the
impact of Burdines Mayfair on the overall success of the Mayfair shops
was addressed.

> "Mayfair was praised as the end of funk and the beginning of class . . . .
> But they didn't come so much to spend as to gawk, so it was decided
> there should be an anchor store to draw shoppers. But not just any anchor
> store; it had to be one with a good track record—like Burdines. This
> couldn't just be any Burdines, with such tacky items as housewares and
> furniture. It had to be exclusive and elegant, with rosewood and marble
> and couturier clothes, by-invitation-only designer trunk shows, and
> Stanley West playing the grand piano on weekend afternoons. And
> though some people argued it still needed televisions and sofas and
> Cuisinarts, they came—and they bought."

Other differences between the Mayfair store and traditional Burdines are:

- It is called Burdines Mayfair to distinguish it from other Burdines
  department stores.
- Burdines Mayfair has its own promotional budget, separate advertising
  campaigns, a distinctive logo, and features frequent fashion shows.
- Sales personnel are called sales specialists and provide superior service
  to customers.
- Different shopping bags and gift wrap are used to project an elite image.
- The store restaurant has a different name (The Paradise Cafe) and
  menu, offering fresh salad platters, fine wines and champagne, and
  elegant desserts.

In addition to Saks and Lord and Taylor, Burdines Mayfair's major competitors include the dozens of exclusive line, specialty stores located within

Exhibit III:
Burdines Mayfair Directory

C
Cameras .... Cámaras 3
Candy .... Confitería 3
Cash Office .... Oficina de Pagos 3
Cosmetics .... Cosméticos 1
Cul de Sac
　Accessories .... Accesorios 2
　Jewelry .... Joyería 2
　Shoes .... Zapatos 3
Customer Service .... Servicios al Cliente

D
Depot .... Departamento de hombres 3
Dresses .... Vestidos
　Better .... De calidad superior 2
　Designer .... De diseñador 2

F
Fragrances .... Perfumería
　Women's .... De mujer 1
　Men's .... De hombre 1
Foundations .... Ropa interior femenina 2

G
Giftwrap .... Para envolver regalos 3

H
Handbags .... Carteras
　Better .... De calidad superior 1
　Designer .... De diseñador 2
　Fendi .... De Fendi 1
　Gucci .... De Gucci 1
Hats .... Sombreros
Hosiery .... Medias 2
　Women's .... De mujer 3
　Men's .... De hombre

J
Jewelry .... Joyería
　Bridge .... De calidad superior 1
　Cartier .... Cartier 2
　Designer .... De diseñador 1
　Fine .... Fina 1
　Watches .... Relojes
Juniors .... Jovencitas 3

L
Lingerie .... Lencería
　Daywear .... Refajos, sayuelos 2
　Foundations .... Ropa interior femenina 2
　Loungewear .... Batas de casa 2
　Robes .... Salidas de cama, negligés 2
　Sleepwear .... Ropa de dormir 3
Luggage .... Valijas, Maletas 3

M
Men's .... Hombres
　Active .... Ropa casual 3
　Clothing .... Ropa 3
　Designer .... Diseñador 3
　Furnishings .... Accesorios 3
　Robes .... Batas 3
　Shoes .... Zapatos 3
　Sleepwear .... Pijamas 3
　Sportswear .... Ropa deportiva 3

P
Personnel .... Oficinas de personal 3
Paradise Cafe .... Café Paraíso 3
Personal Shopper .... Servicio de guía de compras 2
Public Telephones .... Teléfonos Públicos 3

R
Restaurant .... Restaurante 3
Rest Rooms .... Baños 3
Robes .... Batas 2

S
Shoes .... Zapatos
　Better .... De calidad superior 2
　Designer .... De diseñador 1
　Juniors .... De jovencita 2
　Men's .... De hombre 3
Stereos .... Equipos de sonido 3
Sunglasses .... Espejuelos 1
　Women's .... De mujer 1
　Men's .... De hombre 3

T
Telephones .... Teléfonos 3
Televisions .... Televisiones 3

W
Women's .... Mujeres
　Accessories .... Accesorios 1
　Activewear .... Ropa casual 2
　Better Sportswear .... Ropa deportiva de calidad superior 2
　Designer Sportswear .... Ropa deportiva de diseñador 2
　Designer dresses .... Vestidos de diseñador 2
　Dresses .... Vestidos 1
　Hosiery .... Medias 1
　Sportswear .... Ropa deportiva 1
　Swimwear .... Trajes de baño 1

W
Watches .... Relojes
　Women's .... De mujer 1
　Men's .... De hombre

Mayfair (e.g., Charles Jourdan, Ralph Lauren, and Yves St. Laurent), and at The Shops of Bal Harbour (located approximately fifteen miles northeast of Mayfair). The principal advantage Burdines Mayfair has over their Mayfair neighbors and many specialty shops is the depth and breadth of their merchandise mix. The numerous shopping malls in Dade County provide only indirect competition, since they cannot offer the exceptional quality and service that Burdines Mayfair shoppers receive.

BURDINES MAYFAIR: THE STRATEGY

The Burdines Mayfair marketing success formula is built around four major elements: knowing who the customer is, knowing what she or he wants, effectively promoting the store and its merchandise, and providing the customer with a unique shopping experience.

Customer Profile

Burdines Mayfair shoppers can be classified into three groups reflecting the lifestyle these consumers enjoy. These customer segments are the Chic Sophisticate, the Trendsetter, and the Occasional Shopper.

The Chic Sophisticate is upwardly mobile and often career-oriented, with substantial discretionary income. This shopper wants quality with fashion savvy, but is less flamboyant than the Trendsetter. They also have little available time for leisurely browsing; thus, they want to fulfill their needs and move on. Their classification of needs include wear-to-work, day-into-evening, social occasions, and weekend wear. This segment accounts for 40% of Burdines Mayfair's total sales.

Trendsetters are often (but not exclusively) non-working "ladies of leisure." They have a nouveau-riche attitude, therefore, price is rarely a consideration. They might be called "professional shoppers" since they spend a large portion of their free time shopping, and purchases are frequently based on appeal rather than need or practicality. The Trendsetter is extremely image-conscious, and is well acquainted with most major fashion publications and the latest trends. They are usually well traveled and often will purchase head-to-toe outfits (total looks) if merchandised appealingly. Their classification of needs include trendy daywear, specialty pieces/one-of-a-kind looks, party wear, and swim/active wear. This group also represents 40% of Burdines Mayfair's sales.

The third type of customer is the Occasional Shopper. This customer may or may not be a resident of the primary trade area. They are of varied age brackets and have relatively less discretionary income than the other two segments. This customer seldom shops in the Mayfair area, generally preferring the convenience of the malls. When they do shop at Mayfair, it is for the ambiance of the Grove, special purchases, or window shopping to observe the latest fashion trends. This target market provides 20% of Burdines Mayfair's sales.

Prior to the store opening, the company anticipated sales from a fourth type of shopper, the Basic Need customer. It was thought that if they could attract shoppers seeking basic merchandise, it was likely they would stay to shop fashion as well. However, this has been the one group that the store has not reached. D. Craig Miller, Director of Administration and Selling Services for Burdines Mayfair explained,

> "We have never really attracted this type of customer. People don't shop Mayfair to buy socks or underwear. As a result, many of these lines have been cut back or phased out."

A common link among Burdines Mayfair shoppers is that they are predominantly women ages 25-45 (or with a similar age mentality), are in the upper income strata, and are fashion innovators/early adopters.

The Merchandise Mix

Burdines Mayfair builds foremost upon its strength as a department store. It offers alternative shopping while maintaining an obvious fashion-forward profile. That is, customers realize that the fashions seen there are the newest and most contemporary. Classic fashion is offered, with a majority of the merchandise being trendier products that won't be found at other department stores, including Burdines. This image is a key to the store's success. The product mix is diverse, while the basic item merchandise is limited.

The pyramid vendor structure is the one most commonly used by department stores. The majority of the merchandise is considered basic lines, with a narrowing up through better and designer levels. However, the Burdines Mayfair vendor structure takes shape as a diamond. It is broad in the middle with better sportswear and dresses, and narrows up toward designer wear and couture, and narrows down to other more basic vendors. According to Mr. Miller, the merchandise mix is the number one factor in the success of Burdines Mayfair.

The Importance of Personal Service

Service is the area where Burdines Mayfair enhances its image. Historically, the strength of Mayfair's specialty shops has been in providing superior personal attention to customer's needs. To compete with these exclusive stores, the Burdines Mayfair sales specialists operate as personal shoppers. Given their high level of fashion awareness, they are able to satisfy their selective clientele.

How do Burdines Mayfair professional salespeople differ from those in other department stores (including traditional Burdines)? The sales specialists call customers to inform them about new merchandise arrivals and unadvertised one-day sales. A client service book is kept of customers (who are greeted by name) containing such information as birthdays, sizes, designer preferences, and charge account numbers (see Exhibit IV). Sales specialists follow up sales with telephone calls and thank you cards, where appropriate. Comment cards are aggressively sought to learn more about customer preferences and satisfaction levels.

About 30% of the sales staff are paid on commission, therefore, their income is dependent upon their productivity. Hiring standards are stricter at the Mayfair store than typical Burdines (four times as many potential salespeople were interviewed prior to hiring). Additionally, dress codes are more strictly enforced at this store. Sales specialists must present the image of stylish professionals that their customers expect. To insure the best possible service, ongoing sales training and testing is conducted in key areas.

Other Mayfair Differences

Burdines Mayfair has a separate advertising strategy from the balance of the department store chain. Jorge Lopez, Vice President, Advertising for Burdines, stated:

> "We run one or two separate ads per month for Mayfair. These are targeted to a much more upscale customer. Since this showcase store features top designers and products like $2,000 dresses, a different advertising plan is used in response to market needs."

In addition to print media, monthly postcards and direct mail pieces are sent to highly targeted lists (e.g., designer women's customers, credit card customers, etc.). Also, sales specialists send out announcements of new collections and special events of interest to their customers. Since the

Exhibit IV:

Burdines Mayfair Client Service Book

Burdines Mayfair	CLIENT SERVICE BOOK

DATE

NAME

BURDINES ACCOUNT NUMBER ☐ CHARGE ☐ CASH

BIRTHDAY

HOME ADDRESS	CITY	STATE	ZIP

BUSINESS ADDRESS	CITY	STATE	ZIP

HOME PHONE ( ) BUSINESS PHONE ( )

OCCUPATION TITLE

OTHER AUTHORIZED BUYERS

NECK/SLEEVE	WAIST/INSEAM	SUIT	COAT	SHIRT
SWEATER	UNDERWEAR	SOCKS	SHOES	PAJAMAS
BLOUSE	SKIRT	SLACKS	DRESS	SLEEPWEAR

PERSONAL REMINDERS/
PREFERENCES:

international customer is important to Burdines Mayfair, some Spanish-language magazines such as Miami Mensual are used to reach the Latin American consumer.

Unlike other Burdines, which typically draw from a seven- to ten-mile radius, Burdines Mayfair has a much greater geographic pull. Customers will come from all of Dade and even Broward County to experience the "Mayfair Mystique."

Another difference is the "shop concept," whereby different vendors' fashion trends, color trends, or cultural trends are displayed separately. This gives the store the look of a specialty shop rather than a department store with racks of clothing. The fixtures used are also special to Mayfair with moveable walls which allow department merchandisers flexibility in designing the different shops. The store doesn't use rounders on the selling floor and the amount of sale merchandise is minimal. Even the hangers for each department are different.

Burdines Mayfair is unique in many aspects. This uniqueness in catering to its target market is what makes the store the success it is.

Publix Super Markets, Inc.

Publix Super Markets, Inc. is a Lakeland-based grocery chain of nearly 300 supermarkets operating exclusively in the state of Florida (see Exhibit I). Despite its concentrated geographic focus, Publix is the tenth largest supermarket chain and largest privately held grocery company in the United States.

Publix executives feel that there are sufficient growth opportunities in their "own backyard," and as such, presently have no out-of-state expansion plans. This profile focuses on how Publix satisfies its Florida market by instituting the marketing concept into its everyday operations.

BACKGROUND

The key ingredient in the Publix success formula has always been its people. Publix doesn't act like the large corporation it is, but operates like a small business. Publix employees are in a sense a large family. This is not surprising, since the company started as a family-run business, and family ties among management and staff are still evidenced today. This approach is what differentiates this company from other successful supermarket chains. Bill Schroter, Vice-President, Advertising and Marketing, explains the Publix difference:

> "We are in the people business, not just the grocery business. Since Publix is totally employee-owned, every Publix person has a personal stake in the success of the overall operation (piece of the rock syndrome).

252

Exhibit I:
Publix Super Markets By Location

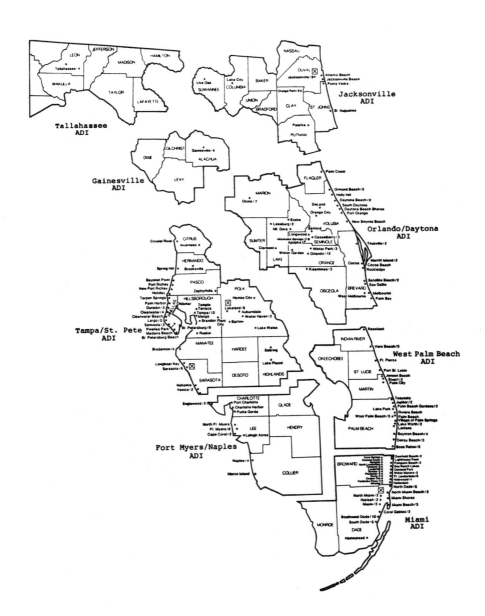

With employee-ownership comes the very strong promote-from-within policy; we do not look outside the company for management material . . . we train and promote from within, and every employee realizes it. There is a deep, personal concern about pleasing the customer—a concern that reaches from cashier and bag-person all the way up to advertising and marketing decisions, real estate and site selection teams, to company president. In other words, to truly KNOW the market and the customer.''

Words and phrases such as courtesy, friendly/smiling faces, and the personal touch are not typical descriptors of large corporate employees, but at Publix they are repeated daily by many of their millions of satisfied Florida shoppers.

Building the Publix Empire

Publix Super Markets was founded in 1930 by George Jenkins, opening the first Publix Grocery Mart in Winter Haven. Jenkins, one of the great entrepreneurs of the twentieth century, had a vision of what a "dream food store" should be like. But it took several years to pursue that dream. In 1940, Jenkins closed his two operating grocery markets, and went after his dream. This marked Publix' entry into the supermarket era. The first Publix Super Market was a store years ahead of its time. It had many features never before seen in a supermarket (which are commonplace today), such as air conditioning, fluorescent lighting, water fountains, electric-eye doors, parking lots, and of course, one of the finest grocery assortments in the country.

The next major step forward for Publix occurred in 1945. Jenkins arranged the purchase of the nineteen-store All-American grocery chain, along with its Lakeland corporate headquarters and warehouse distribution center. These stores were for the most part small, run-down, and poorly stocked. However, a liberal financing arrangement made the deal affordable, and provided Publix with a rapid growth opportunity. Also significant were the experienced grocery personnel (four future Publix vice-presidents were bought that day) and the strong customer base the stores offered. A remodeling program was immediately implemented to bring the stores up to acceptable Publix standards. A replacement program subsequently followed, whereby many of the older stores were replaced with newer, bigger, and more modern ones—similar in many respects to the first Publix Super Market.

From 1945 to 1959 Publix evolved into a major force in the central

Florida grocery industry. A chain of grocery stores had been built that stressed quality foods, cleanliness, attractive decor, uniformity, and, most importantly—pleasing the customer. In 1959, an expansion program was in full force as Publix entered, and began to prosper in, the highly competitive south Florida market. A little more than a decade later, Publix aggressively penetrated the north Florida market.

Current Situation

In 1984, Publix registered $3.23 billion in sales. This was a 14% increase over 1983 figures. According to *Progressive Grocer*, its 2.36% before-tax net was highest among the top dozen supermarket chains, and 2½ times as great as Safeway, the industry leader. Additionally, earnings increased 33% to $75 million. Prospects for the next several years are equally favorable.

As of December 1985, Publix operated 290 supermarkets. In addition, there were twelve sites under construction with seventy-six approved locations that were targeted for construction within the next three years. Publix presently employs 37,000 people through their three major divisions: the Jacksonville, Lakeland, and Southeast Coast Divisions (see Exhibit II). The corporate headquarters remains in Lakeland, with major distribution warehouses in Jacksonville, Lakeland, Sarasota, and Miami. The typical Publix Super Market is approximately 33,000 square feet, with a store size range of from 21,000 square feet (which employs fifty to sixty people) to superstores of 57,000 square feet (which employ 150 to 250 people). The company had operated two dozen Food World Supermarkets (a discount food chain) in the mid-Florida area, most of which were converted to Publix Super Markets in 1984 and 1985. The only non-supermarket venture the company has ever engaged in is a somewhat unusual, yet related business. In the late 1970s, Joe Blanton, then president of Publix, founded a pig farm to dispose of wasted produce and out-of-date bakery products.

The Publix Philosophy: Where Shopping and Working Is a Pleasure

No background discussion of Publix would be complete without addressing the Publix philosophy. Mr. Schroter, in his early days with Publix, developed the slogan that was to epitomize the Publix spirit, and challenge the employees to deliver excellence on a daily basis—WHERE SHOPPING

Exhibit II:
The Three Divisions

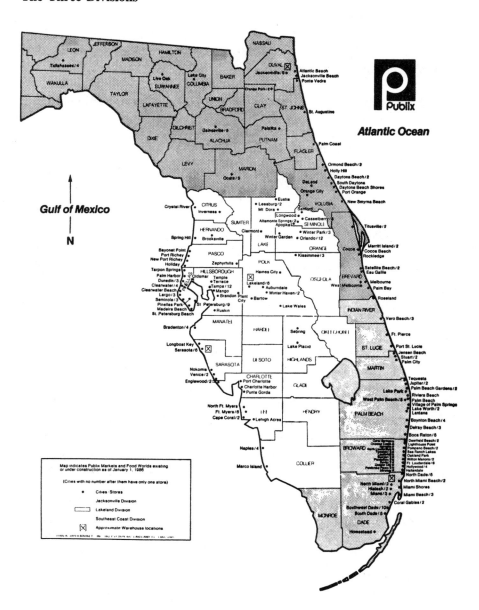

IS A PLEASURE. Some twenty-five-plus years later, Schroter expounds on this overall corporate philosophy:

> "At Publix we believe our primary responsibility is to operate the best stores possible, where shopping and working are always a pleasure, and where the customer is always provided with fair values. This philosophy does not say that Publix will be the largest chain in Florida . . . it does not say that we will be the cheapest show in town . . . it simply says what we believe and what we strive for. Note that it stresses 'value'."

Recently, Publix Super Markets was featured in the book, *The 100 Best Companies to Work for in America*, and cited for excellence by industry analysts. In an October 1985 article in *Progressive Grocer* Publix was identified as one of the "Five Chains That Stand Out."

THE GROCERY INDUSTRY

According to the *1985 U.S. Industrial Outlook*, food stores are America's largest retail industry, accounting for more than 22% of the sales in this economic sector in 1984. Grocery stores accounted for 95% of total food sales, totaling $265 billion for the year, an 8.6% rise over 1983. Large grocery chains were responsible for nearly 60% of total grocery sales. *Progressive Grocer's 1986 Marketing Guidebook* stated that there were 156,000 grocery stores in the U.S. in 1984, with just over 30,000 qualifying as supermarkets (sales of $2 million or more).

But numbers alone don't tell the whole story. The grocery industry is a rapidly changing one. It is affected by demographic shifts, food prices, consumer spending power, restaurant sales, and perhaps most importantly—changing consumer lifestyles and demands. There are several recent lifestyle changes that have been observed. Consumers are becoming more:

- Nutrition-conscious: They have improved their eating habits, consuming less red meat, and more fish, fruit, and vegetables.
- Informed: Today's shoppers are more intelligent. They read labels, checking for calories, salt content, and whether artificial coloring, flavoring, and/or preservatives have been added.
- Convenience-seeking: Many customers place a premium on fast service and buying food that is easy to prepare. Supermarkets can fulfill

more than just grocery needs. Customers are taking advantage of non-food products and services such as health and beauty aids, cut flowers, photo processing, and banking. Frozen and prepackaged meals are also increasing in popularity in our hurried society.

- Quality-minded: A large segment of the market is willing to pay a higher price for perceived quality products, such as Haagen-Dazs Ice Cream, fine wines, or gourmet cookies.
- Interested in ethnic foods: Many consumers want to prepare dishes at home that they have been eating in restaurants. Mexican and Oriental cooking are two notable examples.
- Interested in specialty departments: Bakeries, delicatessens, fresh fish, and produce sections are important to many shoppers.
- Variety-minded: Coke is not it, anymore. Consumers also want New and Classic Coke, Diet Coke, no-caffeine Coke, and so forth. Additionally, they want Pepsi products, bottled water, and a multitude of other beverage choices.

These forces have created a diverse mix of market segments with different needs and wants. To accomodate these more demanding customers, product merchandising and strategic marketing (including market segmentation) are becoming more critical to the supermarket chains' success.

The Evolution of the Supermarket: The Key Forces

The supermarket is continuing its evolution process, a half century after its origin. Mr. Jenkins identified three major innovations that revolutionized the grocery industry and led to the rise of the supermarket. These were self-service shopping, modern refrigeration equipment (including air conditioning), and the shopping cart. Recently, he added a fourth to this exclusive list—the development of computerized scanning technology. Not surprisingly, Publix was one of the first supermarket chains in the country to be entirely computerized for scanning.

Market Segmentation in the Grocery Industry

In James L. Brock's book, *A Forecast for the Grocery Retailing Industry in the 1980s*, he identifies the trend toward market segmentation as one of the key new developments in the industry. Grocery retailers are now identifying market segments by geographic and demographic variables, lifestyles, media exposure, price consciousness, desire for personal services and convenience, and other segmentation dimensions. In Brock's Delphi study of grocery industry experts, "being truly consumer-oriented" ranked first as a strategy for success, and "the need for better market segmentation and positioning" was mentioned as the fourth most important strategic issue of the 1980s. A recent trade journal assessment of the first fifty years of supermarkets concluded: "Food retailing is entering the age of professional management and professional marketing."

The Competitive Environment

Publix' major Florida competitor is Winn-Dixie Supermarkets, Inc. Winn-Dixie, a strong southeastern regional chain, is the fifth largest grocery company in the United States. According to *Progressive Grocer*, Winn-Dixie posted $7.3 billion in sales in 1984 through its 1,260 grocery stores. Unlike Publix, Winn-Dixie relies greatly on their own controlled brand labels, using more than ten different private labels on hundreds of their grocery and non-food products.

Other large supermarket competitors in the state include Albertson's and Kash 'N Karry. Other competition for the Florida retail food dollar comes primarily from wholesale distributors such as Super Valu Stores, Inc., Associated Grocers, and Affiliated of Florida. These companies sell to independent and small chain supermarkets, and grocery stores.

THE PUBLIX STRATEGY

Publix employees have been instrumental in its success. In fact, the company is where it is today because it is meeting its overall business objective—pleasing the customer.

The Publix Shopper

There is no one definition for the "Publix customer." The company recognizes that every geographic location has its own unique composition of potential customers, and merchandising and promotional tactics are tailored to these market segments. However, on a state-wide basis, a large share of the Publix shoppers are mature adults with middle to upper incomes, and a slightly above average education level. Given this "typical" customer profile, presently Publix is pursuing a younger, more upscale segment of the market.

Consumer Research

Unlike many large, consumer-oriented companies, Publix conducts relatively less formalized marketing research studies than their counterparts in other industries. This does not mean, however, that Publix is not on top of their market. They are. As strong believers in responding to the needs of the marketplace, the company's prime information gathering technique is "listening to the customer."

Locally, store management personnel are readily available to hear a customer's comments, criticisms, and suggestions. If a customer wants a product that is unavailable, the manager will make diligent efforts to order that product on a trial basis. At the store level, customer satisfaction is measured by sales, and sales per department. Additional consumer research is regularly conducted throughout the state. Methods used include strength-and-weakness research projects, parking-lot research, and focus groups. Also, VALS (Values and Lifestyles) profiles are considered. This Young and Rubicam service assists management in comparing and analyzing Areas of Dominant Influence (ADIs). This lifestyle information is used to "fine-tune" variables such as merchandise mixes or store hours (for example, differences between the Jacksonville and Fort Lauderdale markets can be determined).

Important marketing information is also generated through the computer scanners. This technology provides such valuable information as customer counts, sales-per-customer, sales effects based on various price levels, the impact of advertising and promotion on unit sales, and profiles of present customer bases by location or department. Furthermore, scanning data is extremely helpful in controlling inventories, merchandising, and improving customer service (expediting shoppers' checkout times). Since scanning technology is still in its relative infancy, it is likely that additional marketing applications will be found shortly.

Publix also uses sound research practices in selecting store sites. During the Publix expansion era, Mr. Jenkins and Mr. Blanton used to fly around Florida in a company-owned helicopter seeking growth areas for new store locations. Today, site selection techniques are more scientific. Mr. Schroter explains,

> "Store sites are selected by a multiplicity of factors. These would include census data, emerging growth patterns, highway and bridge construction and expansion, environmental and/or zoning regulations, personal observation and research by our real-estate department, market research

studies by staff, by media and by other resources, etc. Potential sites are then reviewed and evaluated against corporate requirements, which would include potential share-of-market, area demographics, psychographic customer profiles, and potential profitability of that location.''

The Publix Difference

Most people view grocery shopping as a chore. Publix has responded by creating an environment (both physical and emotional) whereby the shopping experience is more pleasurable. Publix stocks a complete assortment of nationally branded goods (350 to 400 private label brands have been introduced to compete with Winn-Dixie) and quality food and non-food products. Special departments such as the deli, bakery, meat, and produce are featured. However, for many people, it's the Publix ''atmosphere'' more than the grocery selection that induces them to shop there. The Publix difference is service. Employees are trained to appreciate the value of a customer. The company fosters their ''service plus'' mission in a variety of ways, including:

- In the Southeast Coast Division, bag-boys wheel shopping carts to customers' cars. When it rains, umbrellas are provided (company policy prohibits employees from accepting tips for these services).
- If a customer only wants three tomatoes or half a pound of ground beef, store personnel cheerfully comply with the request to break packages.
- S & H Green Stamps are provided as a value-added service to loyal shoppers, which allows them to obtain merchandise through the accumulation and redemption of stamp books. This bonus plan began as an experiment in the early 1950s. Based on its consumer acceptance, Publix continued the program and maintained grocery prices. This was possible due to the great sales volume the chain generates.
- Publix is very community-minded, and is a good corporate citizen. The company supports universities and schools on a rotating basis, as well as various charitable organizations and sports programs throughout the state.

Other strategic marketing areas that relate to the ''Publix Difference'' include pricing and promotion. Publix has a competitive pricing policy which considers what other grocery chains are charging, but they are not discounters, seeking to uphold the Publix image of quality and value. Publix divides the state into three divisions, each with special, competitive price zones which recognize cost-of-living and salary structure variations in setting grocery prices. Local pricing norms (competitive price strategies) are also acknowledged, and occasionally adjustments at the individual store level are necessary.

To reinforce the Publix image, customer-oriented advertising and promotional strategies are developed. As Mr. Schroter, the "brains" behind the corporate advertising department for many years, states:

> "The bottom line-judgment is always the question: Is it good for the customer, is it good for the employees, is it good for the company? Publix is perceived to be a "class" operation, hence, all advertising and promotional activity is disciplined to reflect this image . . . even to the choice of media and graphic techniques. It (such activities) must be in good taste."

In addition to using a mix of the major media (newspapers, television, radio, and other media), the company relies on another more unusual medium for promotion purposes. The Publix fleet of trucks (embellished with the Publix logo and slogan) provide hundreds of moving billboards throughout the state of Florida.

FUTURE PLANS

Despite its phenomenal success in Florida, Publix presently has no announced plans to branch outward to other states. One might wonder why the chain isn't seeking other market opportunities. The reason is that there are still many untapped areas and growth prospects within Florida (the market the company knows so well). Mr. A.J. Montgomery, Personnel Manager, Miami Division, points out:

> "The state of Florida is growing at such a rapid rate . . . The population that is going to be in Florida by the year 2000 dictates that we ought to have another 150 stores in Florida by that time."

Florida is presently the seventh largest state in population and is projected to be the fourth largest by 1990, according to the *U.S. Statistical Abstract*. As of July 1983, the state was home to almost 10.7 million people. With forecasted growth rates of 37% and 31% for the next two decades, Florida's population is expected to increase to 13.3 million and 17.4 million, respectively, by 1990 and the year 2000. Given this scenario, the Publix geographic segmentation strategy is a sound one—continue to build on what works—and Florida supermarkets have worked exceptionally well for the company.

Although some have characterized the company as being conservative (for example, for many years they remained closed on Sundays while their competitors were open for business), in actuality, they are an innovator. This pioneer spirit was proven by Mr. Jenkins in 1940 when he opened the first Publix Super Market, and even today, Publix looks ahead to the future. In addition to scanning, the company has taken a leadership role in developing cooperative banking relationships. This is a sound strategy since some industry observers have estimated that food retailers presently cash more checks than banks do. At the individual store level, Publix has implemented a network of automatic teller machines (ATMs) and is also instituting point-of-purchase electronic funds transfer (EFT) systems.

In a departure from tradition, the company recently opened its first Publix Liquor Store in Coral Springs. Publix executives also announced that a combination store, called the Publix Food and Drug Store, is also scheduled for introduction shortly. These may serve as models for the development of future stores.

PART FIVE

Segmentation Resources

APPENDIX A

Sources of Marketing Information

The following is a listing of references which are most appropriate for segmentation studies. Most of these sources are readily available for review at your local public or academic library. It is recommended that your company purchase those sources of information that are used on a regular basis (for example, key trade journals and industry directories). Also, this list is by no means complete, since research sources will vary considerably by industry and market. It does, however, represent an excellent general reference directory for the marketing professional. The appendix is organized into three parts: secondary sources, consumer demographics, and business demographics.

PART I. SECONDARY SOURCES

Trade Journals. One of the best sources for market information is trade journals. These industry-specific publications contain a wealth of information, and one or more trade journals typically exist for virtually every major market or industry. To locate trade journals, a variety of sources can be consulted. Some of these include *Ulrich's International Periodicals Directory, Standard Rate and Data Service - Business Publications Rates and Data, Bacon's Publicity Checker, Writer's Market,* and *IMS/Ayer Directory of Publications.*

Trade Journals (special issues). Three of the best sources of trade information that is published infrequently are:

- *Harfax Guide to Industry Special Issues*
- *Special Issues Index* by Greenwood Press
- Ulrich's Irregular Serials and Annuals

Business Indexes. Some of the major library indexes that can be used to access trade-related articles are:

Predicasts F&S Index: Many feel this is the best index for finding current information on U.S. companies and industries. It covers a wide range of business, industrial, and financial periodicals and also a few brokerage house reports.

Business Periodicals Index: A subject index to selected periodicals in the fields of accounting, advertising and public relations, automation, banking, communications, economics, finance and investments, insurance, labor, management, marketing, taxation, and other specific businesses, industries, and trades.

Wall Street Journal Index: An index to this national business newspaper which indexes articles as to corporate and general news. In addition to *The Wall Street Journal, Barron's Magazine* is also included.

New York Times Index: Provides good information about specific companies and industry profiles.

American Statistical Index: This is an index of statistical publications of the United States government.

Business Index and Magazine Index: These two computer-produced indexes provide an up-to-date listing of trade journal and consumer-oriented magazine articles which deal with a broad range of business topics.

Directories. Trade directories are one of the best sources for market and customer information. Literally hundreds of specialized directories are available, and they can be of tremendous value to companies seeking marketing information. Some of the most widely used directories include:

The Encyclopedia of Associations: This multi-volume directory provides a list of more than 20,000 national and international associations and professional or trade organizations. Trade associations are often one of the best sources for information about a particular industry.

National Trade and Professional Associations of the United States: Similar in concept to *The Encyclopedia of Associations*, this reference lists approximately 6,000 trade and professional associations and labor unions with national memberships.

Findex Directory of Market Research Reports, Studies, and Surveys: A publication from FIND/SVP, New York, this directory describes more than 11,000 U.S. and foreign reports arranged by industry and subject category from more than 450 research firms.

Thomas Register of American Manufacturers: A comprehensive nineteen-volume directory of American manufacturing firms. Included in this directory is company background information, product suppliers, and manufacturers' advertisements and catalog data. Thomas also has a three-volume *Grocery Register,* as well.

MacRAE's Blue Book: An annual industrial directory in print for more than ninety years, this five-volume publication includes a corporate and trade name index and product data and classifications for U.S. manufacturers.

State Industrial Directories: Almost all states publish industrial directories. For example, the Florida Chamber of Commerce publishes *The Directory of Florida Industries* which lists Florida companies by geographical area, industry, and Standard Industrial Classification (SIC) code. The MacRAE's series is also a good example of state industrial directories.

Standard and Poor's Register of Corporations, Directors, and Executives: Provides information on approximately 37,000 U.S. and Canadian corporations. Through analyzing SIC codes, the major firms in an industry can be easily identified. Standard and Poor's also publish other potentially useful directories such as Standard and Poor's Corporation Records.

Dun and Bradstreet's Million Dollar Directory: Similar to *Standard and Poor's Register,* with information about more than 47,000 U.S. companies with an indicated worth of $1 million or more. The sales data provided is helpful in analyzing competitors' market share. Note, Dun and Bradstreet also has other useful business references available.

The Directory of Directories: Don't know where to look? Consider this useful publication by Gale Research Company. *The Directory of Directories* is an annotated guide to business and industrial directories, professional and scientific rosters, and other lists and guides of all kinds.

Statistical Sources. There are a variety of useful statistical sources that provide descriptive information about markets. Some sources provide statistics only, such as *Predicasts Forecasts,* while others supplement statistical data with important narrative summaries such as the *U.S. Industrial Outlook.*

U.S. Industrial Outlook: This annual publication of the federal government contains information and projections for 350 industries (the 1985 issue). It is heavily illustrated with several special features, including industry reviews and forecasts, industry trends, and trade bibliographies.

Standard and Poor's Industry Surveys: A quarterly two-volume issue that examines industries and their environment, including trends and problems. In addition to frequent updates, the "Current Analysis," there is a "Basic Analysis" for an industry, with charts of up to ten years of statistical and financial data for the major companies in that industry.

Predicasts Forecasts: This reference gives short- and long-term statistical projections for U.S. basic economic indicators and products by SIC number. Much of this data is presented in the form of charts and tables.

Department of Commerce Publications: *The Business Conditions Digest* and *The Survey of Current Business* are two publications providing information on national economic statistics with some industry-specific data. Other Department of Commerce sources can be consulted as well. Also, many other government agencies provide valuable marketing or industry references. For example, the Small Business Administration offers more than 150 pamphlets and booklets which are nominally priced.

County Economic Data: There are a lot of locally generated government publications that can provide useful information about markets. A majority of these reports are published at the state level, with counties or cities often supplementing these efforts.

Computerized Data Bases. The latest entrant into the research "arena," on-line data bases are becoming more prevalent as a means of finding published information that is difficult to locate elsewhere. There are now dozens of potentially useful data bases for marketing applications. Some of the more important ones for researching markets include the Predicasts' series, ABI Inform, and Trade and Industry. Other on-line data bases should be checked according to specific market needs.

PART II: CONSUMER DEMOGRAPHICS

Census of Population.   Provides detailed characteristics of the population for counties, cities, and towns, including general social and economic characteristics. Separate "subject reports" series cover statistics on ethnic groups, migration, fertility, marital status, education, employment, occupation and industry, income, and low-income areas. This census is taken every ten years, on the year ending in zero (the next population census is 1990).

Census of Population and Housing.   These joint reports consist of a series of census tract reports for each MSA, reports on "General Population Trends for Metropolitan Areas," and a series giving "Employment Profiles of Selected Low-Income Areas." Census taken concurrently with Census of Population.

Statistical Abstract of the United States.   Also a Census Bureau publication, this annual reference is a summary of most of the statistical publications of the U.S. government. Besides being an abstract of the statistics collected and published by the federal government, this book also acts as a guide to those published sources. Each chart has a note indicating the original publication from which it was abstracted.

State Statistical Abstracts.   Many states have their own statistical abstracts which are filled with consumer demographic information. For example, the University of Florida's Bureau of Economic and Business Research publishes an annual *Florida Statistical Abstract*. It is comparable in breadth to the *Statistical Abstract of the United States,* however, since it only deals with the state of Florida, it tends to be much more detailed.

State and Metropolitan Area Data Book.   This government publication reports, via tables, charts, and maps, data on the U.S. MSAs. The largest part of this data book is arranged by city, and in that section each city is usually divided by suburbs, central city, and MSA. Includes business and government statistics as well as demographics.

Rand McNally Commercial Atlas and Marketing Guide.   This is an annual atlas of the United States and Canada. Besides being one of the largest books in print, this atlas includes traditional area maps, along with U.S. data on population, economics, communications, and transportation. Canadian statistics are also included.

Zip Code Sale Information Guide.   A two-volume publication consisting primarily of zip code maps of all cities with more than one zip code. The quality of maps varies significantly from place to place. The maps are arranged by state and then by city. Each zip code area indicates median family income and total households by use of a code. At the end of volume two, there are several tables: post offices by zip codes, economic characteristics for places of 50,000 population, and economic characteristics for urbanized areas.

Market Profile Analysis. This annual reference from Donnelley Marketing Information Services provides a wealth of demographic information reported on a census tract basis. It also includes some business statistics by zip code, financial (banking) data, construction activity information, and relevant census tract maps.

Survey of Buying Power. A two-part special issue from *Sales and Marketing Management* magazine, this is a valuable source for population estimates, age distributions, number of households, and retail sales information. The effective buying income index by area is a useful statistic for measuring market potential for various types of businesses.

Sourcebook of Demographics and Buying Power. This publication from CACI, Inc. is a reference to zip code demographics. Updated to include almost 35,000 zip code boundary changes since the 1980 census, this publication analyzes seventy-five demographic characteristics. Projections are also provided.

REZIDE: National Encyclopedia of Residential Zip Code Demography. This publication from Claritas uses the five-digit zip code as the basic information gathering unit. One hundred twenty-five demographic categories are provided. These include population, households, indicators of affluence, age, education, race, characteristics of housing units, characteristics of the work force, and other data.

Editor and Publisher Market Guide. This four-section annual reference provides data on U.S. and Canadian newspaper markets. Section 1 presents market ranking tables on population, income, and retail sales. Sections 2 and 3 provide facts and figures on U.S. and Canadian daily newspaper markets. Retail sales estimates for nine industries are offered in Section 4.

PART III. BUSINESS DEMOGRAPHICS

Business Census Reports. These consist of the following series of individualized reports: Census of Retail Trade, Census of Wholesale Trade, Census of Service Industries, Census of Manufacturers, and Census of Transportation. These reports provide statistics on different kinds of establishments, including the number of establishments, sales and employment size, and payroll, by designated geographic areas and SIC codes. The business censuses are taken every fifth year in years ending in a two or seven (e.g., 1987 or 1992). In addition to the basic data collected, a number of special subject reports are included detailing specific industries or market related facts.

County Business Patterns. A Census Bureau publication prepared on an individual state basis, this important reference provides data by SIC code and major industry group. Information provided includes number of establishments, number of employees, number of establishments by employment size, number of large establishments, and payroll for states and counties. Through this source, the industrial marketer can readily identify the number of prospects in a market, determine whether it is dominated by large or small firms, and estimate market share for a given industry and geographic area.

Sales and Marketing Management's "Survey of U.S. Industrial and Commercial Buying Power." An annual special issue appearing every April, this reference is a two-part guide to key market statistics about industrial-oriented establishments. Useful information in this publication includes the number of establishments nationwide with twenty or more employees (100 or more employees are considered large establishments), shipments/receipts by industry (SIC) and state (county), and the percentage of market concentration by large establishments. In addition to the basic survey, numerous other charts, tables, and articles for industrial marketers are provided.

Other sources. Business demographics are available from other sources in addition to the ones described above. Many state and local/county government agencies often can provide helpful business demographic information. Also, don't neglect the secondary and consumer sources discussed in Parts I and II of this appendix. For example, Donnelley's *Market Profile Analysis* and *The U.S. Industrial Outlook* are two of many other sources of information that contain some business demographics, even though that is not their primary purpose.

APPENDIX B

Companies Providing Market Segmentation Services

There are hundreds of full-service and specialized marketing research companies and consulting firms offering dozens of types of market segmentation services for all types of businesses and industries. This appendix lists the segmentation products and services provided by major companies in the field. Two major sources of information were used in compiling this reference; *American Demographic's* "Directory of Demographic Products and Services," and the American Marketing Association's *1985 Directory of Marketing Research Firms*. This latter source was used to conduct a letter writing campaign to nearly two dozen research firms (not listed in the *American Demographic's* directory) purporting that they specialize in market segmentation services. Information obtained from correspondence with these selected companies is provided.

This directory is divided into eight sections. This includes major and other census-based demographic companies, survey-based demographic companies, list-based demographic companies, demographic products, software for demographic analysis, demographic consultants, companies specializing in lifestyle analysis, and other companies specializing in market segmentation planning, analysis, and strategy. Many of these firms are well established, while others are relative newcomers quickly building a reputation. It is recommended that you carefully shop around before deciding which firm to use in your next segmentation project.

MAJOR CENSUS-BASED DEMOGRAPHIC COMPANIES

CACI

CACI's SUPERSITE system has 1980 census data, current-year estimates, and five-year forecasts for areas of any size or shape around a site. SUPERSITE is available on ten timesharing networks, on computer tape, or via the firm's SITELINE call-in service. The related SITE POTENTIAL reports estimate consumer demand for over 140 products and services for 16 retail store types plus commercial banks, savings and loans, and consumer finance companies. CACI also has SITE MAP, which displays demographic or customer data for any geographic area.

ACORN, A Classification of Residential Neighborhoods, is the company's cluster system, classifying all households in the United States into one of 44 market segments based on the demographic, socioeconomic, and housing characteristics of their neighborhood. The ACORN PLUS system allows additional segmentation based on over 400 demographic, socioeconomic, and housing characteristics from CACI's Demographic On-line Retrieval Information System (DORIS), which can also be used separately. Clients can use ACORN DIRECT, a cluster analysis of mailing lists, to increase the response rates of direct mail marketing efforts.

SITE PLAN analyzes customer addresses or an in-store survey combined with ACORN and SUPERSITE. ZIP DEMOGRAPHICS is historic, current, and projected demographics and sales potential for zip codes. The Buying Power Index combines the ACORN market segmentation system with product use data to estimate the consumer buying power of any area. CACI also sells products designed to produce stratified samples, and to process and tabulate large data files.

CACI's newest product is a condensed version of its demographic database on floppy disks for the IBM-PC and compatibles. The firm has selected 13 variables, such as household income, age distribution, and number of households, as well as its Purchasing Potential Index, for every zip code and census tract in the country. In addition to 1970–80 change, based on the census, the disks include current-year estimates and five-year projections.
1815 North Fort Myer Drive, Arlington, VA 22209; (800) 336–6600, ext. 2356, Dan Huck.

CLARITAS

PRIZM is Claritas's cluster analysis system. It assigns lifestyle classifications to census tracts, census block groups and enumeration districts, or zip codes based on demographic data and consumer buying patterns from several national surveys, including National Family Opinion, National Panel Diary, Arbitron, and Nielsen.

The PRIZM CrediTrend Service links customer addresses to PRIZM to give clients a better understanding of who their customers are. PRIZM Direct is a cluster analysis program for mailing lists. Other services provided by Claritas include computer mapping and graphics, census data processing, census updating, and statistical modeling. For microcomputers, Claritas sells census data and census updates on floppy disks along with software to analyze the data. Claritas also has a set of Affluent Market Services, which include a Neighborhood Rating report and an Affluent Market Namebank.
201 North Union Street, Alexandria, VA 22314; (703) 683–8300, Carrie Goodman • 206 Madison Avenue, New York, NY 10016; (212) 532–8200 • 401 Wilshire Boulevard, Santa Monica, CA 90401; (213) 394–6897 • 5 Revere Drive, Suite 200, Northbrook, Illinois 60062; (312) 272–4430.

DONNELLEY MARKETING INFORMATION SERVICES

Donnelley Marketing Information Services has a database called AmericanProfile that consists of census data, current-year estimates and five-year projections. The database produces site evaluation reports and market analyses for customer-specified geography. A related product, ZIPProfile, is designed for direct mailers, and includes a zip code boundary file for mapping demographic data.

Donnelley's cluster analysis product, ClusterPlus, is linked with VALS, Simmons Market Research Bureau, Arbitron Ratings, National Family Opinion, and other syndicated databases.

Market Potential has consumer expenditures for over 20 types of retail outlets, including current-year sales potential by detailed line item of merchandise. Graphic-Profile offers computer-generated maps of demographic and/or customer-supplied data. TargetScan allows clients to scan geography for a given set of demographic criteria.

All Donnelley products are available online or on a call-in basis. Data are available geometrically, geographically, by zip code, or on color-keyed maps. Donnelley's demographic data on floppy disks include 1980 census data, updates and projections, and clusters.
1351 Washington Boulevard, Stamford, CT 06902; (203) 965–5400, Stephen A.

Speier • 1301 West 22nd Street, Oak Brook, IL 60521; (312) 654–2000 • 1440 North Harbor Boulevard, Fullerton, CA 92635; (714) 879– 1600.

MARKET STATISTICS

Market Statistics specializes in sales and marketing analysis using demographic data. The Market Statistics Data Bank has annually updated county demographics, projections to the year 2003, and zip code demographics. Data can be arranged by metropolitan area, by television market, or by customer-specified sales territories. Data are available in printed reports or on computer tape.

Market Statistics creates custom buying power index programs to help firms measure their market potential and evaluate their sales performance and effectiveness. Market Statistics' zip code buying power indexes are designed to target direct marketing efficiently. The firm also offers sales/marketing territory and quota analysis. 633 Third Avenue, New York, NY 10017; (212) 986–4800, Ed Strauss.

NATIONAL DECISION SYSTEMS

National Decision Systems' Pop-Facts reports provide 1980 census demographics, current-year estimates, and five-year projections for any geographic area. The Consumer Expenditure Potential reports calculate potential sales for major retail categories in specific markets. Both products are available on-line or on a call-in basis.

NDS's new Infomark Laser PC System contains all of the above databases on a single mass storage optical disk accessed through a high-speed laser reader connected to an IBM-XT personal computer. Users can generate reports or maps on a standard printer for any geographic area. The disk is leased on an annual basis and is updated every year.

NDS's MIS Site Evaluation Model determines the demographic characteristics that have the greatest impact on a company's success, and examines potential sites for profitability. Site Search identifies promising sites by specific demographic character-

istics. Center Scan locates shopping centers that meet or surpass a client's criteria. NDS offers color mapping of demographic variables. Vision is NDS's clustering system.

NDS's product Business Facts database contains 7.5 million U.S. businesses, each geo-coded and listed by name, address, four-digit SIC code, and employment. The reports allow an analysis of an area's daytime population and provide information for businesses selling to other businesses. 539 Encinitas Boulevard, Encinitas, CA 92024; (619) 942–7000, Craig Curtner • 8618 Westwood Center Drive, Vienna, Virginia 22180; (703) 883–8900, George Moore.

NATIONAL PLANNING DATA CORPORATION

National Planning Data Corporation's Updates consist of current-year estimates and five-year projections of demographics for census tracts, zip codes, towns, counties, metropolitan areas, and states. They are available in printed reports, on computer tape, or on floppy disks. The firm also offers 1980 census demographics for census or zip code geography.

MAX is NPDC's on-line demographic data retrieval and analysis system and includes statistical tools such as multiple regression. MAX also generates color-coded maps and graphics. MAXlink is NPDC's software that links IBM-PCs to MAX. NPDC also has analysis and mapping software for the IBM-PC. The company sells floppy disks with census data, esti-

mates, projections, and mapping files for all geographic areas.

NPDC offers computer mapping services, as well as digitized boundary files. The firm processes census data on a custom basis. Its Yellow Pages Data System has data from more than 4,000 directories across the country.

NPDC has a series of 1980 census products for EEO/human resources professionals called LABOR FORCE ESSENTIALS and OCCUPATION PROFILES. The firm's proprietary database of current estimates and projections is called LABOR FORCE UPDATES. P. O. Box 610, Ithaca, NY 14851; (607) 273–8208, David Warren • Pittsburgh, (412) 471–6732 • Dallas, (214) 980–0198 • Los Angeles, (213) 557–0158.

URBAN DECISION SYSTEMS

Urban Decision Systems' ONSITE system provides 1980 census demographics, current estimates, and five-year projections for site evaluation and market research. ONSITE is available on-line and on a call-in basis. ONLINK downloads ONSITE data to microcomputers. UDS also sells ONSITE data on floppy disks.

ONSITE combines Claritas's PRIZM lifestyle cluster analysis and R.L. Polk's Vehicle Origin Survey market penetration reports. It includes color graphics and maps.

ONSITE's retail potential program provides estimates of consumer spending by merchandise line and type of store for a client's trade area. Reports include an estimate of supportable floor space by type of store. Using the MarketBase system, UDS matches ONSITE demographics with data from clients' customer files. UDS has integrated the database of SMG Marketing Group, Inc., publishers of the Hospital Marketing Atlas, with ONSITE. 2032 Armacost Avenue, Los Angeles, CA 90025; (213) 820–8931, Tom Siedzik • 180 Post Road East, Suite 10, Westport, CT 06880; (203) 226–8188, Andy Ancel.

OTHER CENSUS-BASED DEMOGRAPHIC COMPANIES

COMPUSEARCH

Compusearch offers on-line access to the full range of Canadian demographic data for use in site evaluation or market analysis. The firm's AreaSearch service locates markets with high concentrations of potential customers. TRADAREA evaluates sites, and SELECT MAIL is designed to improve response rates by supplying key demographic information by postal code area.

Compusearch produces Market Penetration Analyses by linking customer addresses with census data. The firm uses its Consumer Expenditure Reports to calculate a client's market share. Another service, Precision Prospect Analysis, profiles a client's customers and locates where a company's top prospects live. LIFESTYLES is the name of the firm's cluster system. Compusearch also produces maps and graphics and sells Canadian census data down to the six-digit postal code on floppy disks.

16 Madison Avenue, Toronto, Ontario M5R 2S1, Canada; (416) 967-5881, Michele Sexsmith.

CRITERION

DEMIS (Demographic Information System) is the name of Criterion's demographic database. It contains 1980 census data, geographic boundary files, estimates, and projections. Clients can merge their own data with DEMIS for analysis or mapping.

Criterion offers health administrators a patient origin/destination packet of maps and reports based on distance radii around a facility and zip code demographics. Related products include physician referral analysis and site location.

Criterion also offers microcomputer-based human resource analysis software, including STOPS for market analysis and CAAPS for affirmative action planning. A new product is PCMAP, software to create thematic maps on the IBM-PC. Criterion sells compatible coordinate files for states, counties, zip codes, census tracts, MCD/CCDs, and place centroids, along with demographic files for each of these geographic levels.

13140 Coit Road, Suite 318, Dallas, TX 75240; (214) 783-1818, Neil Felder.

DEMOGRAPHIC RESEARCH COMPANY

Demographic Research Company uses demographic data to predict direct response for large volume mailers. LIFT, List Indexing and Fine Tuning, is the name of its list segmentation program.

DRC also provides customized demographic analysis systems for consumer products companies, including market profiling and ranking, site evaluation and selection, trade area or dealer territory design, and media strategy analysis. The firm offers computer maps and graphics, and economic and market forecasting models. The firm's database is available on-line.

233 Wilshire Boulevard, Santa Monica, CA 90401; (213) 451-8583, Kathleen

Jones • 124 Chestnut Street, Philadelphia, PA 19106; (215) 922-5225, Raymond G. Young.

DUALABS

DUALabs specializes in custom processing of census data. It will produce extracts or special tabulations of the 1980 and 1970 censuses, and will combine census with client data. The firm supplies data on computer tape, floppy disk, microfiche, or paper.

1515 Wilson Boulevard, Arlington, VA 22209; 703/525-1480, David Petersen.

THE GLIMPSE CORPORATION

In a joint venture with the Chemical Bank, the Glimpse Corporation offers on-line access to a demographic database called STAR. STAR includes 1980 census data, demographic estimates, and projections. The firm offers demographic data on floppy disk, and will download data from computer tapes to floppy disks on a custom basis. It is also a vendor of CENDATA, the Census Bureau's on-line information service.

105A Oronoco Street, Alexandria, VA 22314; (703) 836-6800, Warren Glimpse.

MARKETING ECONOMICS INSTITUTE

MEI has a census-based database for U.S. counties and metropolitan areas, updated continuously. The firm makes five-year projections of population, households, income, and retail sales at the county level. MEI also has lifestyle information on car and appliance ownership, as well as demographic and economic data for Canadian counties and metropolitan areas. The firm provides data on computer cards or tape, and also publishes the most frequently requested data in its annual Marketing Economics Guide.

108 West 39th Street, New York, NY 10018; (212) 869-8260, Alfred Hong.

SURVEY-BASED DEMOGRAPHIC COMPANIES

ARBITRON RATINGS

Arbitron conducts diary surveys of television viewing and radio listening. Market reports measure station audiences by demographics for local areas by time period and program. Radio and Television AID (Arbitron Information on Demand) is an interactive computer-based system that allows subscribers to analyze any station's audience demographics.

TARGET AID categorizes viewers by lifestyle, purchasing habits, and economic status so that advertisers can choose the stations that deliver their target audience. It is based on Donnelley Marketing Information Service's ClusterPlus and Simmons Market Research Bureau's product profiles.
1350 Avenue of the Americas, New York, NY 10019; (212) 887-1300, Alison Conte.

MRCA INFORMATION SERVICES

MRCA has a national household Menu Census database. It contains detailed information on foods people eat at home and away from home, gathered in diaries kept by a nationally representative sample of households. Reports provide demographic information on over 900 in-home and 400 away-from-home foods and beverages, tabulated by meal characteristics (such as main meal or snack). In addition, special reports cover such topics as ethnic foods, dieters, geriatrics, and carried meals.

MRCA's on-line consumer packaged goods purchase database is called DYANA.

DYANAgrafs depict the demographic profile of a particular brand's buyers.

MRCA has a new product called FUNDS (Financial Usage and Needs Data Service), based on a panel of 2,400 nationally representative households that report their financial service transactions and preferences monthly. Half the panel has an annual income of at least $25,000; the other half earns at least $50,000.
2215 Sanders Road, Northbrook, IL 60062; (312) 480-9600, R.L. Schmidt.

MEDIAMARK RESEARCH

MRI has a database that measures magazine readership and product use by demographics. In addition to the national summary report, MRI tabulates data separately for ten large cities. It also has an Upper Deck report, which contains data on the affluent, and a Business-to-Business report, which contains the same information provided by people who purchase business-to-business items.

The MRI database is linked to SRI's VALS lifestyles typology, as well as to CACI's ACORN and Claritas's PRIZM. Subscribers can access the database on-line, or they can receive the data in print or on floppy disk.
341 Madison Avenue, New York, NY 10017; (212) 599-0444, Sylvia Cassel.

NATIONAL FAMILY OPINION

NFO maintains a database of over 300,000 panel households, classified by demographics and clustered by VALS, ACORN, or PRIZM type. NFO's clients commission surveys of the target population they want. Reports are delivered on computer tape or in bound volumes.

NFO's TRAC Division operates ongoing programs in several industries, including apparel, beverages, mail order, home furnishings, and home computers and video

games. In addition to tabular tracking reports, subscribers can purchase computer tapes or access the database on-line for special analytical tabulations.
P. O. Box 315, Toledo, OH 43654; (419) 666-8800, Richard F. Shay.

A.C. NIELSEN

A.C. Nielsen measures television audiences by demographics. In addition to its well-known Nielsen ratings, the firm does custom media research. Nielsen interviews households which are then cross-tabulated with their viewing habits. Or Nielsen can select samples of a particular type of household to measure target audiences. Nielsen audience estimates can be profiled by Donnelley's ClusterPlus.

Through its Cable On-Line Data Exchange, Nielsen offers zip code demographics on cable audiences. The firm also sells telephone samples.
Nielsen Plaza, Northbrook, IL 60062; (312) 498-6300, Ann Manning.

NPD RESEARCH, INC

NPD gathers purchasing data from two national panels of 6,500 families each, and one panel of 1,500 nonfamily households. Using current demographic estimates from National Planning Data Corporation, the firm weights the results to represent the U.S. population as a whole.

The panelists are classified by Claritas's PRIZM system and SRI's VALS lifestyle typology. In addition, NPD has developed its own classification system: the Nutritional Segmentation Service. This service is part of the firm's National Eating Trends database that relates consumer behavior to nutritional attitudes. Another ongoing NPD study is called Consumer Reports on Eating-out Share Trends (CREST).

NPD maintains market panels of 35,000 households in more than 40 separate local markets.

NPD's Home Testing Institute (HTI) is based on a panel of 200,000 households which have agreed to participate in research projects. Clients can specify the demographics they want for concept testing,

product testing, and attitude and usage tracking and studies.
900 West Shore Road, Port Washington, NY 11050; (516) 625-0700, Rita Turgeon.

THE PEOPLE PANEL

The People Panel has a panel of 15,000 nationally representative households, including singles, formerly marrieds, unmarrieds living together, men, and teens. The panel is used for custom research studies conducted by mail or telephone.
P. O. Box 431, Port Washington, NY 11050; (516) 944-7775, Sheldon Brooks.

SIMMONS MARKET RESEARCH BUREAU

Simmons publishes an annual comprehensive Study of Media and Markets. Thirteen volumes measure media audiences for newspapers, magazines, television, cable, radio, outdoor, and Yellow Pages, cross-classified by 27 demographic categories. Thirty of the volumes are devoted to consumption and purchasing data for over 800 product categories and 3,900 brands cross-tabulated by demographics and by media habits. Both the media and the product/brand usage data can be combined with other databases, such as VALS, PRIZM, and ClusterPlus.

The data are produced through personal interviews with a national probability sample of adults aged 18 and older in 19,000 households. In addition to the interview data, respondents fill out a questionnaire on product/brand usage to determine consumption and purchasing patterns, and keep a two-week diary of television viewing. Subscribers can receive printed reports, on-line access to the database, or data on floppy disks.

Simmons also studies demographic subgroups, such as teenagers. A new service called MatchUp matches names and addresses from a client's customer file against the names and addresses of the 38,000 Study of Media and Markets respondents.
219 East 42nd Street, New York, NY 10017; (212) 867-1414, Irene Ochs.

LIST-BASED DEMOGRAPHIC COMPANIES

METROMAIL

Metromail has a continuously updated national consumer file of 77 million households based on telephone lists, linked to census geography and matched with census information.

Metromail can select households by region, state, city, zip code, census neighborhood, and carrier route, even pinpointing specific streets and house numbers. Demographically, buyers can screen for more than 500 individual and neighborhood characteristics. Metromail can eliminate high probability nonresponse households from a client's mailing list using such factors as age, sex, income, and dwelling type. Other services include unique lists such as Catholic, Italian, Spanish, and Jewish surnames, affluent families, influential occupations, and new movers.

Metromail has a full range of census data, and will add demographic data to a client's files at the carrier route, census, or zip code level of geography. The company also offers MART—Market Analysis for Retail Trade—which analyzes store trading areas based on current customer characteristics.

Customized services include producing sample universes, trading area surveys, site location studies, testing procedures, and program evaluations. The data are available

See also Donnelley Marketing Information Services.

on-line, in printed reports, on maps, on labels, and in other formats.
901 West Bond Street, Lincoln, NE 68521; (402) 475-4591, Joanne Harms.

R.L. POLK

Polk's national consumer household file consists of 75 million households, developed by merging names and addresses from several sources, including auto registrations and telephone directories. This file is geocoded to the census tract or block group level to add census data and then aggregated to zip codes or postal carrier routes. Polk can geocode a client's mailing lists by matching them to the Polk list, which is updated quarterly. Companies can then target specific households for mailings.

Another Polk product is its Vehicle Origin Survey (VOS), which matches vehicle license plate numbers against Polk's national database to determine where customers live. In combination with Urban Decision Systems' demographic database, VOS clients receive information on market potential and trade area penetration, as well as analyses of their competitors.
6400 Monroe Boulevard, Taylor, MI 48180; (313) 292-3200, Don Waddell. • For Vehicle Origin Survey: R.L. Polk & Company, 431 Howard Street, Detroit, MI 48231; (313) 961-9470, Larry Crabtree.

SURVEY SAMPLING

This firm specializes in providing samples for telephone, mail, and door-to-door surveys for market researchers. Its database includes a regularly-updated file of all households listed in U.S. telephone directories, tied to 1980 census geography. In 35 states, the database is supplemented by auto registration lists to achieve coverage of more than 86 percent of the nation's households. The firm can provide targeted samples for reaching black, Hispanic, or high-income households anywhere in the country. The samples are available on-line, in printed reports, on call record sheets, on pressure sensitive labels, and on computer tape.
180 Post Road East, Westport, CT 06880; (203) 226-7558, Carol Goldman.

GEOGRAPHIC PRODUCTS

DATAMAP

Datamap specializes in computer-generated maps for small geographic areas. The firm produces maps of block groups, postal carrier routes, census tracts, zip codes, counties, or any other geographic area, accompanied by computer-generated overlays of color-coded demographic or client-supplied data such as product sales or store locations.

Datamap sells a complete microcomputer system, including both hardware and software. Clients who already have their own hardware can license Datamap's geographic databases. Datamap also sells census data on floppy disks compatible with any microcomputer with an RSX11M operating system.

6874 Washington Avenue South, Eden Prairie, MN 55344; (612) 941- 0900, Grant Warfield.

GEOGRAPHIC DATA TECHNOLOGY

Founded by a creator of the Census Bureau's DIME file, Geographic Data Technology specializes in digital map production. The firm sells boundary files for computer mapping of data, calculating area, and determining centroids for various levels of geography, including counties, census tracts, minor civil/census county divisions, block groups, and zip codes. GDT is one of the few producers of cartographic databases based on streets.

The firm also sells street network files for automated routing, and computerized address coding guides that are used to assign geographic coordinates to a given address. GDT geocodes address lists on a custom basis, or it will lease its database to clients interested in doing address-to-coordinate matching in-house.

GDT's newest product is a street network map of the entire United States in digital form on an optical disk.*

13 Dartmouth College Highway, Lyme, NH 03768; (603) 795-2183, Muriel Farrington.

* See Part I of this directory, American Demographics June 1985, for more on optical disks.

GEOGRAPHIC SYSTEMS, INC.

Geographic Systems produces computer maps for business analysis and sells software for in-house mapping as well. The firm's geographic files enable users to map geographic boundaries ranging from zip codes and census tracts to metropolitan statistical areas (MSAs), states, and other marketing areas. It also has a cartographic file of the U.S. highway network. Clients can plot census or other data on the maps and use the firm's modeling packages for sales territory realignment, media targeting, and site location.

204 Andover Street, Andover, MA 01810; (617) 470-3760, Spencer Joyner.

GIBBS & HILL

Gibbs & Hill offers a variety of computer maps, including shaded, contour, and point symbol. The firm digitizes client-supplied and other data, incorporating them in a mapping database. The database allows the client to merge selected maps and to create three-dimensional perspectives and cross-sectional displays.

Geographic Information Services, 11 Penn Plaza, New York, NY 10001; (212) 760-8425.

RAND MCNALLY-INFOMAP

RANDATA is an electronic database that combines geographic information with annually revised demographic and economic statistics. It links all populated places to their zip, MSA, county, and state codes, and towns with over 1,000 inhabitants to ADI and DMA codes. The database includes Ranally Trading Areas covering the entire United States, and Ranally Metro Areas, which resemble the government-defined MSAs except that they cross county lines. RANDATA boundary files include digitized files for census tracts, zip codes, minor civil divisions, and counties, and they can be bought for MSAs, states, or the entire country. Both the geodata files and geoboundary files are available on floppy disk and computer tape.

Rand McNally-Infomap produces thematic maps incorporating client-supplied and public data by zip code, census tract, minor civil division, county, and state. THEMAP, the firm's computer mapping service, will map client-defined areas such as sales territories, school districts, broadcast areas, or trade circles. Rand McNally-Infomap also sells STATMAP, a marketing and demographic mapping package formerly owned by Ganesa Group International.

8255 North Central Park Avenue, Skokie, IL 60076; (312) 673-9100, Michael Kelly.

SAMMAMISH DATA SYSTEMS

Sammamish Data Systems was the first to make census data available for microcomputers. Its Census Data System is an integrated package of software and a subset of data from the census information that the Bureau released on computer tapes. The floppy disks are for states, but extracts for single counties or groups of counties are available.

The Desktop Information Display System (DIDS) allows users to prepare full-color thematic maps for zip codes, census tracts, and counties on a microcomputer. To go with DIDS, the firm sells geographic coordinate boundary files for census tracts, zip codes, counties, and states.

P.O. Box 70382, Bellevue, WA 98007; (206) 644-2442, Richard Schweitzer.

URBAN SCIENCE APPLICATIONS

Urban Science Applications specializes in using computer graphics to analyze markets. It merges client-supplied data with other databases such as those from the census and automobile registrations. It offers site location analysis, buyer preference analysis, and other market research maps and charts. Clients can order custom reports or lease the hardware and software for their own use.

200 Renaissance Center, Suite 1230, Detroit, MI 48243; (313) 259-6933, Carl Hendrickson.

WESTERN ECONOMIC RESEARCH

Western Economic Research specializes in preparing marketing maps and reports for planners and administrators in California and the western states. Its prepackaged products offer 1980 census data at the census tract and zip code levels.

15910 Ventura Boulevard, Suite A-8, Encino, CA 91436; (818) 981- 9762, C. Michael Long.

These firms also offer geographic products: CACI, Claritas, Compusearch, Criterion, Demographic Research Company, Donnelley Marketing Information Systems, The Glimpse Corporation, National Decision Systems, and National Planning Data Corporation (Part I); and Comarc, Compucon, Election Data Services, Financial Marketing Corporation, Horizon Marketing Systems, Instant Recall, Modeling Systems, National Planning Association, Planning Data Systems, Strategic Locations Planning, and Urban Data Processing (Part II).

SOFTWARE FOR DEMOGRAPHIC ANALYSIS

These firms also sell software: Claritas and Criterion (Part 1); Biddle & Associates, Geographic Systems Incorporated, Horizon Marketing Systems, LAM Consulting, Mathematica Policy Research, Personnel Research Incorporated, Sammamish Data Systems, and Wharton Econometric Forecasting Associates

COMARC SYSTEMS

Comarc has developed a series of software products that analyze geographically-based data. GDMS (Geographic Data Management System) can serve as a stand-alone software product, or as the data management system for all other software products. It digitizes and encodes multiple layers of geography that a client can fill with tabular data. The package can take financial deposits by zip code and income by census for example, and create polygons with certain characteristics.

Comarc has a Financial Services Package Product, which encodes a financial institution's location and performance information, and combines it with census data, financial data, and geography—roads and features, census tracts, and zip codes. Comarc helps users install the hardware and software, and trains the client's staff to produce analytical maps and reports.

150 Executive Park Boulevard, San Francisco, CA 94134; (800) 227-3808, Marci Belcher.

COMPUSULTING ASSOCIATES

Compusulting Associates sells software for analyzing 1980 census data on microcomputers. It will also download the data from the Census Bureau's computer tapes to floppy disks. Clients can retrieve the demographics for a census tract or block group, and redefine that geography to make it more relevant to their business. Clients can retrieve data in circles of a given radius around a point, or scan to find the pieces of geography that match a demographic profile.

P.O. Box 418, Centerport, NY 11721; (516) 261-0488, Ron Friedmann.

INSTANT RECALL

Instant Recall sells an integrated microcomputer system called USA DISPLAY that runs on the IBM-PC and some compatibles. It is a database in spreadsheet format, and also does simple graphics and mapping. The database comes from the *1983 County and City Data Book*, and consists of 226 items for the states and the District of Columbia, including population, age, vital statistics, households, and income. Users can compute new data items and feed them back into the database. The system will be updated each time the *County and City Data Book* is updated. The firm plans to offer an expanded database of over 2,000 variables for hard disks this year.

P.O. Box 30134, Bethesda, MD 20814; (301) 530-8098, David Shaw.

MODELING SYSTEMS

Modeling Systems applies mathematical models to problems involving spatial distributions of people, firms, or activities. Its model TARGET analyzes and designs sales territories by dividing zip code level data into sales areas. TARGET can also be used to design distribution networks and refine route schedules. Modeling Systems will sell its software and the necessary hardware to clients who want in-house systems.

1718 Peachtree Street, NW, Atlanta, GA 30309; (404) 876-9977, Geoffrey N. Berlin.

PLANNING DATA SYSTEMS

Planning Data Systems specializes in map digitizing, address matching, and census data processing. Planning Data has created a mapping software package for microcomputers called MULTIMAP. The program produces maps using standard boundaries and census data.

1616 Walnut Street, Suite 2103, Philadelphia, PA 19103; (215) 732-1300, Barry Cohen.

RESOURCE SOFTWARE

Census-80 is a 1980 census reporting system for microcomputers. Resource Software downloads data from the 1980 census computer tapes onto floppy disks, and provides clients with the software to generate reports from them. For clients who have computer facilities, the firm will provide the software programs so that clients can download data to floppy disks themselves.

125 North Main Street, Eaton Rapids, MI 48827; (517) 663-7139, Stephen E Tilmann.

STRATEGIC LOCATIONS PLANNING

Strategic Locations Planning offers ATLAS, an interactive menu-driven software package for microcomputers that generates maps and displays data for states, counties, congressional districts, ADIs, DMAs, zip codes, or census tracts. Users can also create their own boundaries. The firm offers geographic boundary and data files, including current demographic estimates and five-year projections produced by National Planning Data Corporation and Market Statistics. It will digitize client-provided maps, and download demographic data onto floppy disks.

A new product is MicroPACE, a site evaluation program for banks and savings and loans that runs on IBM-PCs and compatibles. SLP sells the data for this program by metropolitan area.

4030 Moorpark Avenue, Suite 123, San Jose, CA 95117; (408) 985-7400, Thomas Cook.

DEMOGRAPHIC CONSULTANTS

ANALYSIS AND FORECASTING

Analysis and Forecasting sells customized demographic data, analyses of recent trends, and demographic forecasts for local, state, and regional areas within the United States. It specializes in developing community profiles using census data, and in analyzing and projecting trends in households and housing. Its data can be integrated with client-supplied data.
P.O. Box 415, Cambridge, MA 02138; (617) 491-8171, George Masnick.

APPLIED DEMOGRAPHIC RESEARCH GROUP

The Applied Demographic Research Group specializes in helping companies expand into the nation's middle-sized and smaller

markets. It combines census and client-supplied data and creates statistical models that rank potential markets or evaluate performance in existing markets.
642 South Evergreen Avenue, Arlington Heights, IL 60005; (312) 253-7706, Kenneth M. Johnson.

BASELINE DATA CORPORATION

Formed by a group of former federal statistical experts, Baseline Data Corporation offers customized demographic studies for clients who need more than standard reports. It analyzes client data, and correlates them with socioeconomic and demographic data.
1522 K Street, NW, Suite 1112, Washington, DC 20005; 202/682- 1350, George E. Hall.

BRACHMAN ASSOCIATES

Founded by Eastman Kodak's former decision support systems' director for worldwide market intelligence, Brachman Associates is a new consulting firm specializing in integrating business planning, information systems planning, and organization development. The firm helps clients use demographic and competitive intelligence information, along with market research to gain a strategic advantage for market planning.
29 Sumner Glen Drive, Penfield, NY 14526; (716) 377-1479, Fred Brachman.

DUAL-COMM

DUAL-Comm processes census data and offers related consulting services. The firm projects client-specified populations. Through the EEO DATA SYSTEM, DUAL-Comm provides data and technical advice for affirmative action and human resource planning.
Suite 1250, 1015 15th Street, NW, Washington, DC 20005; (202) 789-8695, John Beresford.

FLORIDA APPLIED DEMOGRAPHICS

A group of academic demographers at Florida Applied Demographics provide a full range of demographic consulting at the local, state, and national levels. The firm specializes in population estimates and projections, socioeconomic projections, analytical population studies, and small-scale demographic surveys.
P.O. Box 20071, Tallahassee, FL 32316; (904) 681-8119, David F. Sly.

HAGAN ASSOCIATES

Staffed by former government statistical professionals, Hagan Associates offers a full range of statistical consulting, from assessment of a client's data needs through data acquisition and analysis. For business clients, the firm provides information and analytic services for making decisions regarding policy, programs, marketing, advertising, forecasting, expansion, and site location. It also helps clients who are dealing with the federal government in preparing plans and grant applications or meeting the requirements of regulatory agencies.
3703 Riverwood Court, Alexandria, VA 22309; (703) 780-7569, Robert L. Hagan.

LAM CONSULTING

LAM provides consulting in research data management. Its services include developing market profiles using census data, digital mapping, and custom design and use of data management software. Areas in which the firm has specialized include education, communication, medicine, and politics.
220 Albert Street, Suite 211, East Lansing, MI 48823; (517) 337- 7750, Jacquard W. Guenon.

MANAGEMENT HORIZONS

Management Horizons primarily serves retailers, wholesalers, and consumer goods manufacturers with sophisticated site selection strategies, based on research into the target market population. It helps com-

panies develop marketing strategies, including site location, repositioning, and market diversification.
450 West Wilson Bridge Road, Columbus, OH 43085; (614) 846–9555, Terri A. Barnett.

MATHEMATICA POLICY RESEARCH

MPR offers a wide range of consulting services based on the use of census and other data: product design, market segmentation, pricing strategies, demand projections, forecasting, surveys, and customer information systems.

MPR supplies 1980 census data for states, counties, and cities on floppy disk, and sells statistical analysis and tabulation software for analyzing and generating reports on microcomputers. MPR also provides clients with information from large databases, such as the Current Population Survey, on computer tapes, in tables, or in reports.
600 Maryland Avenue, SW, Suite 550, Washington, DC 20024; (202) 484–9220, Myles Maxfield.

POPULATION RESEARCH SERVICE

A new firm, Population Research Service specializes in providing updated population estimates for states, cities with populations greater than 200,000, and metropolitan areas with populations greater than 500,000. The firm derives its estimates from a model based on census data and updated housing information. Reports are available quarterly, with an annual report in the fall. The firm produces reports for any census-designated location that has new housing data available.
P.O. Box 181032, Austin, TX 78718; (512) 837–0135, Bryan Lambeth.

SALES EVALUATION ASSOCIATES

Sales Evaluation Associates, recently established by the longtime vice-president for marketing of Market Statistics, specializes in measuring sales potential and objectively evaluating sales performance. It works in such sales management areas as sales projections, quota/goal setting, sales territory design, and distribution analysis.
14 East 4th Street, Suite 826, New York, NY 10012; (212) 228– 5887, David Glazer.

STRATEGY RESEARCH CORPORATION

Specializing in conducting Hispanic survey research and focus groups, Strategy Research does media, real estate, traffic and transportation, and financial institution research. It also produces intercensal demographic profiles of the Hispanic market.
100 NW 37th Avenue, Miami, FL 33125; (305) 649–5400.

TRI-S ASSOCIATES

Tri-S Associates prepares population projections, conducts special census counts, and provides demographic data for legal briefs. It also conducts consumer surveys and helps clients evaluate sites, target markets, and make affirmative action plans.
206 West Mississippi Avenue, P.O. Box 130, Ruston, LA 71270; (318) 255–6710, Wayne Hatcher, Jr.

WELCH ASSOCIATES

Welch Associates provides economic and demographic consulting for business and the legal profession. Its computer library has all the national demographic databases, including the censuses since 1940, the Current Population Survey, the National Longitudinal Survey, the Panel Survey on Income Dynamics, and the Equal Employment Opportunity Commission database. The firm helps clients use their proprietary data alone, or in conjunction with these public databases. It helps clients develop data sets and downloads them to microcomputers. The databases can be used on-line.
10801 National Boulevard, Third Floor, Los Angeles, CA 90064; (213) 470–4466, Michael Ward.

LIFESTYLE ANALYSIS

JUDITH LANGER ASSOCIATES

Judith Langer Associates specializes in qualitative research, using focus groups, in-depth interviews, and lifestyle studies targeting specific demographic segments.

Recent reports have focused on older mothers, the mature market, and single male consumers.
133 East 58th Street, 2nd Floor, New York, NY 10022; (212) 688– 6066, Judith Langer.

SRI INTERNATIONAL

SRI's VALS (Values and Lifestyles) is a typology that categorizes Americans by their attitudes, needs, wants, and beliefs. It segments the population into nine VALS types. Subscribers get reports on changes in society and the marketplace, both in general and for particular industries. Simmons Market Research Bureau, Inc., Mediamark Research, Inc., National Family Opinion, and National Panel Diary all have joint ventures with SRI incorporating the VALS typology into their consumer databases.
333 Ravenswood Avenue, Menlo Park, CA 94025; (415) 859–3882, Jane O'Connor.

YANKELOVICH CLANCY SHULMAN

Yankelovich's product Monitor is based on an annual survey of approximately 2,500 adults. Its purpose is to track changes in social values that can affect consumer marketing. In addition to a written report and in-house presentation, survey sponsors receive year-long consulting from Yankelovich. The database includes a wide range of demographic variables.
8 Wright Street, Westport, CT 06880 (203) 227-2700

These firms also provide lifestyle analysis: CACI, Claritas, Donnelley Marketing Information Systems, and National Decision Systems

OTHER MARKET SEGMENTATION SPECIALISTS

Company/Contact   Areas of Expertise

Applied Research Techniques, Inc.   Product attribute segmenta-
1200 Route 46, West   tion, attitude segmentation,
Parsippany, NJ 07054   flavor segmentation, psycho-
  Art Boudin, President   graphics, perceived value and
  (201) 263-0880   utility segmentation and indus-
                                         trial segmentation.

The Burke Institute   Market structure analysis,
800 Broadway   trade-off and conjoint analy-
Cincinnati, OH 45202   sis, and custom projects.
  (513) 961-8000

Demby and Associates   Psychographics.
50 East 42nd Street
New York, NY 10017
  Emanuel H. Demby
  (212) 692-9220

Dun's Marketing Services   Dun's Market Segmentation
Three Century Drive   Service.
Parsippany, NJ 07054
  (201) 455-0900

Pro-Mark Services   Demographic consultation and
5830 Red Road, Suite 100   studies; product usage analy-
Miami, FL 33143   ses; and lifestyle, benefit,
  Art Weinstein   perceptual, and image-concept
  Director of Marketing   segmentation studies.
  (305) 347-5172

Research In Perspective, Inc.
15 East 26th Street
New York, NY 10010
　Richard M. Giller, Exec. VP
　(212) 685-8980

Perceptual segmentation.

Sophisticated Data Research, Inc.
2251 Perimeter Park Drive
Atlanta, GA 30341
　Gary M. Mullet, Director
　Statistical Services
　(404) 451-5100

Segmentation software and consulting for most multi-variate procedures including: discriminant, factor, and cluster analysis, and perceptual mapping.

Sorkin-Enenstein Research Service, Inc.
SERS
500 North Dearborn Street
Chicago, IL 60610
　Lois Steinberg, Client Services Mgr.
　(312) 828-0702

Consumer market segmentation, lifestyle research, and statistical consultation. SERS also has published a number of market segmentation research papers (call or write for further details).

APPENDIX C

Selected Readings On
Market Segmentation

Books

Haley, Russell I. *Developing Effective Communications Strategy: A Benefit Segmentation Approach.* New York: Wiley, 1985.

Bonoma, Thomas V. and Shapiro, Benson P. *Segmenting the Industrial Market.* Lexington, MA: Lexington Books, 1983.

Scotton, Donald W. and Zallocco, Ronald L., editors. *Readings in Market Segmentation.* Chicago: American Marketing Association, 1980.

Myers, James H. and Tauber, Edward. *Market Structure Analysis.* Chicago: American Marketing Association, 1977.

Michman, Ronald D.; Gable, Myron; Gross, Walter. *Market Segmentation: A Selected and Annotated Bibliography.* Chicago: American Marketing Association, 1977.

Wells, William D., editor. *Lifestyle and Psychographics.* Chicago: American Marketing Association, 1974.

Sheth, Jagdish N., editor. *Models of Buyer Behavior: Conceptual, Quantitative, and Empirical.* New York: Harper and Row, 1974.

Engel, James F.; Fiorillo, Henry F.; Cayley, Murray A.; editors. *Market Segmentation: Concepts and Applications.* New York: Holt, Rinehart and Winston, Inc. 1972.

Frank, Ronald E.; Massey, William F.; Wind, Yoram. *Market Segmentation.* Englewood Cliffs, NJ: Prentice-Hall, 1972.

Recent Articles

Weinstein, Art and Nesbit, Marvin. "How to Size Up Your Customers." *American Demographics,* July 1986, pp. 34-37.

Weinstein, Art. "Ten-Point Program Customizes Segmentation Analysis." *Marketing News,* May 23, 1986, p. 22.

Townsend, Bickley. "Psychographic Glitter and Gold." *American Demographics,* November 1985, pp. 23-29.

Rosenfeld, Judith. "Segmentation Theory in Practice." *Marketing Communications,* October, 1985, pp. 84-86.

Flint, Jerry. "Plain Vanilla Just Won't Do." *Forbes,* October 21, 1985, pp. 146-147, 150.

Moore, Thomas. "Different Folks, Different Strokes." *Fortune,* September 16, 1985, pp. 65, 68.

Demby, Emanuel. "When Should You Segment?" *Marketing News,* September 13, 1985, pp. 48, 55.

Francese, Peter K. "How to Manage Consumer Information." *American Demographics,* August 1985, pp. 23-25.

Zeithaml, Valarie A. "The New Demographics and Market Fragmentation." *Journal of Marketing,* Summer 1985, pp. 64-75.

McDonald, Frank P. "Whither the New Segmentation Systems?" *Marketing and Media Decisions,* May 1985, pp. 94, 96.

Russell, Cheryl. "A High Yield Investment." *American Demographics,* March 1985, p. 7.

Plummer, Joseph T. "How Personality Makes a Difference." *Journal of Advertising Research,* December 1984/January 1985, pp. 27-31.

Kinal, Destiny. "Dip Into Several Segmentation Schemes to Paint Accurate Picture of Marketplace." *Marketing News,* September 14, 1984, p. 32.

Lewis, Ray. "Targeting Through Direct Marketing." *Marketing Communications,* October 1984, pp. 19-26.

Nelton, Sharon. "Adapting to a New Era in Marketing Strategy." *Nation's Business,* August 1984, pp. 18-23.

Gardner, Fred. "Can Geodemographics Simplify Media Planning?" *Marketing and Media Decisions,* August 1984, pp. 66-68, 79-82.

Orrin, Benn. "A Segmentation Approach to the Market." *Marketing and Media Decisions,* May 1984, pp. 134, 136.

Haley, Russell I. "Benefit Segments: Backwards and Forwards." *Journal of Advertising Research*, February/March 1984, pp. 19-25.

Lehmkuhl, David C. "Marketing: Segmenting Not Marketing." *Marketing and Media Decisions*, March 1984, pp. 88-91.

Jereski, Laura K. "Do You Know Your Consumers." *Marketing and Media Decisions*, February 1984, pp. 76-78, 142, 144.

Winter, Frederick W. "Market Segmentation: A Tactical Approach." *Business Horizons*, January/February 1984, pp. 57-63.

Jaffe, Bernard. "Use Perceptual Segmentation Research to See Brands through Eyes of the Consumer." *Marketing News*, September 17, 1982, Section 2, p. 4.

Recent Articles (Industrial Markets)

Doyle, Peter and Saunders, John. "Market Segmentation and Positioning in Specialized Industrial Markets." *Journal of Marketing*, Spring 1985, pp. 24-32.

Belth, Ira. "The SIC Code Needs Therapy." *Business Marketing*, August 1984, pp. 50-53.

Shapiro, Benson P. and Bonoma, Thomas V. "How to Segment Industrial Markets." *Harvard Business Review*, May/June 1984, pp. 104-110.

Church, Nancy J. and McTavish, Ronald. "Segment Buyers' 'Sophistication' to Reach Industrial Markets Efficiently." *Marketing News*, September 16, 1984, Section 1, p. 8.

Maloch, David T. "Market Segmentation Differs Significantly in the Industrial Field." *Marketing News*, December 10, 1982, p. 10.

Classic Articles

Wind, Yoram. "Issues and Advances in Segmentation Research." *Journal of Marketing Research*, August 1978, pp. 317-337.

Wells, William D. and Tigert, Douglas J. "Activities, Interests, and Opinions." *Journal of Advertising Research*, #11, 1971, pp. 27-35.

Haley, Russell I. "Benefit Segmentation: A Decision-Oriented Research Tool." *Journal of Marketing*, July 1968, pp. 30-35.

Yankelovich, Daniel. "New Criteria for Market Segmentation." *Harvard Business Review*, March/April 1964, pp. 83-90.

Smith, Wendell R. "Product Differentiation and Market Segmentation as Alternative Marketing Strategies." *Journal of Marketing*, July 1956, pp. 3-8.

Subject Index

School Sense
How to Help Your Child
Succeed in Elementary School